United Kingdom Governance

United Kingdom Governance

Edited by

Robert Pyper

and

Lynton Robins

First Published in Great Britain 2000 by
MACMILLAN PRESS LTD
Houndmills, Basingstoke, Hampshire RG21 6XS and London
Companies and representatives throughout the world

A catalogue record for this book is available from the British
Library

ISBN: 0–333–736044 (paperback)
0–333–736036 (handback)

 First published in the United States of America 2000 by
ST. MARTIN'S PRESS, LLC.,
Scholarly and Reference Division,
175 Fifth Avenue,
New York, N.Y. 10010

ISBN: 0–312–23187–3

Library of Congress Cataloging-in-Publication Data

United Kingdom governance / edited by Robert Pyper and
Lynton Robins.
p.   cm.
Includes bibliographical references and index.
ISBN 0–312–23187–3 (cloth)
I. Great Britain–Politics and government–20th century.
I. Pyper, Robert.   II. Robins, L. J. (Lynton J.)
JN231 U55 2000
320.941'09'049–dc21   99–056734

Selection, editional matter. Introduction and Conclusion © Robert Pyper and Lynton
Robins 2000
Individual chapters (in order) © Peter Barberis Kevin Theakston; Tony
Butcher; Philip Norton; Michael Rush; Richard Kelly; Bill Jones; Neill
Nugent; Allan McConnell; David Wilson; Clive Gray 2000

This book is printed on paper suitable for recycling and made from fully managed and
sustained forest sources.

10   9   8   7   6   5   4   3   2   1
09   08   07   06   05   04   03   02   01   00

Printed in Hong Kong

Contents

List of Tables and Figures

Tables

Figures

Abbreviations

AMS	Additional Member System
ASLEF	Associated Society of Locomotive Engineers and Firemen
AUEW	Amalgamated Union of Engineering Workers
C&AG	Comptroller and Auditor General
CAP	Common Agricultural Policy
CCT	Compulsory Competitive Tendering
CLP	Constituency Labour Party
CND	Campaign for Nuclear Disarmament
COSLA	Convention of Scottish Local Authorities
CSA	Child Support Agency
CSR	Comprehensive Spending Review
DETR	Department of the Environment, Transport and the Regions
DHA	District Health Authority
DoE	Department of the Environment
DTI	Department of Trade and Industry
DUP	Democratic Unionist Party
EC	European Community
ECHR	European Convention on Human Rights
ECJ	European Court of Justice
EMU	European Monetary Union
EQ(O)	European Questions (Officials) Committee
EQ(O)L	European Questions (Officials) Committee – Legal Questions
EQ(O)*	European Questions (Officials) Committee – Senior Officials
ERDF	European Regional Development Fund
ERM	European Exchange Rate Mechanism
EU	European Union
EUD(E)	European Union Department (External)
EUD(I)	European Union Department (Internal)
FCO	Foreign and Commonwealth Office
FDA	First Division Association
FMI	Financial Management Initiative

GDP	Gross Domestic Product
GIS	Government Information Service
HAT	Housing Action Trust
IEA	Institute of Economic Affairs
IGC	Intergovernmental Conference
IRA	Irish Republican Army
IRO	Integrated Regional Office
JCC	Joint Consultative Committee
LEA	Local Education Authority
LGA	Local Government Association
MEP	Member of the European Parliament
MSP	Member of the Scottish Parliament
NAO	National Audit Office
NATO	North Atlantic Treaty Organisation
NEC	National Executive Committee of the Labour Party
NHS	National Health Service
NPM	New Public Management
Offer	Office of Electricity Regulation
Ofgas	Office of Gas Supply
Oflot	Office of the Lottery Regulator
Ofsted	Office for Standards in Education
Offtel	Office of Telecommunications
Ofwat	Office of Water Services
OMOV	One Member, One Vote
OPRAF	Office of Passenger Rail Franchising
OPS	Office of Public Service
ORR	Office of the Rail Regulator
PAC	Public Accounts Committee
PAYE	Pay-As-You-Earn
PESC	Public Expenditure Survey Committee
PFI	Private Finance Initiative
PLP	Parliamentary Labour Party
PMQs	Prime Minister's Questions
PPS	Principal Private Secretary
PRO	Public Record Office
PS	Press Secretary
RDA	Regional Development Agency
RUC	Royal Ulster Constabulary
SDLP	Social Democratic and Labour Party
SEA	Single European Act

SEM	Single European Market
SNP	Scottish National Party
SSC	Special Standing Committee
TCSC	Treasury and Civil Service Committee
TECs	Training and Enterprise Councils
TEU	Treaty on European Union (Maastricht Treaty)
UKREP	United Kingdom Permanent Representation to the European Community
UNESCO	United Nations Educational, Scientific and Cultural Organisation
UUP	Ulster Unionist Party

Notes on the Contributors

Peter Barberis is Professor of Politics at the Manchester Metropolitan University. He is the author of *The Elite of the Elite: Permanent Secretaries in the British Higher Civil Service* and, with Timothy May, of *Government, Industry and Political Economy*. In addition, he has edited two volumes on the civil service and is the editor and co-author of *The Encyclopedia of Twentieth Century British and Irish Political Organisations*.

Tony Butcher is Senior Lecturer in Government in the Department of Social Policy and Politics at Goldsmiths College, University of London. He has published extensively on British public administration and on the civil service. He is co-author (with Gavin Drewry) of *The Civil Service Today* and author of *Delivering Welfare: The Governance of the Social Services in the 1990s*.

Clive Gray is Principal Lecturer in Politics and Public Administration, De Montfort University. His publications include *Government Beyond the Centre*.

Bill Jones is Research Fellow in the Department of Government at the University of Manchester. He is author and co-author of numerous books including *Politics UK* and *British Politics Today*.

Richard Kelly teaches Politics at the Manchester Grammar School and the University of Manchester. He is author of *Conservative Party Conferences*, co-author of *British Political Parties Today*, co-editor of *Modern British Statesmen* and editor of *Changing Party Policy in Britain*.

Allan McConnell is Senior Lecturer in Public Administration at Glasgow Caledonian University. He is author of *State Policy Formation and the Origins of the Poll Tax* and *The Politics and Policy of Local Taxation in Britain* as well as numerous articles on areas such as local taxation, Scottish affairs, party funding, accountability and House of Commons select committees. He is currently working (with Robert Pyper) on a book entitled *The Westminster Parliament* to be published by Macmillan.

Lord Norton of Louth is Professor of Government, and Director of the Centre for Legislative Studies, at the University of Hull. He is author, co-author or editor of 24 books, including *The British Polity*, *The Constitution in Flux*, *Does Parliament Matter?*, *Back from Westminster*, *The Conservative Party*, and *Legislatures*. He is President of the Politics Association and editor of *The Journal of Legislative Studies*. He was elevated to the peerage in 1998 and is a member of the sub-committee of the House of Lords European Communities Committee dealing with law and institutions.

Neill Nugent is Professor of Politics and Jean Monnet Professor of European Integration at Manchester Metropolitan University. Amongst his recent publications are *The Government and Politics of the European Union; Developments in the European Union*, (co-editor) and *At the Heart of the Union: Studies of the European Commission* (editor).

Robert Pyper is Reader in Public Administration at Glasgow Caledonian University. He is the author of *The Evolving Civil Service* and *The British Civil Service*, editor of *Aspects of Accountability in the British System of Government* and joint editor of *Britain's Changing Party System* and *Governing the UK in the 1990s*. His articles on aspects of UK government have been published in a wide range of journals.

Lynton Robins is co-ordinator for Public Administration at De Montfort University, Leicester. He is co-author and co-editor of *Contemporary British Politics*, *Public Policy in Britain*, *Britain's Changing Party System*, *Governing the UK in the 1990s*, *Half a Century of British Politics*, *British Politics since the War* and *Serving the State*.

Michael Rush is Professor of Politics at the University of Exeter. He is the author of *The Selection of Parliamentary Candidates, Parliament and the Public, Parliamentary Government in Britain* and *The Cabinet and Policy-Making*, co-author of *The MP and His*

Information and *British Government Since 1945: Changes in Perspective*, co-editor of *The House of Commons: Services and Facilities*, and editor of *Parliament and Pressure Politics*. He is also author of two textbooks on political sociology and is currently working on a book on the role of the Member of Parliament.

Kevin Theakston is Professor of Government at the University of Leeds. He is the author of *Junior Ministers in British Government*, *The Labour Party and Whitehall*, *The Civil Service Since 1945*, and *Leadership in Whitehall*.

David Wilson is Professor of Public Administration and Head of the Department of Public Policy, De Montfort University, Leicester. He is author of *Power and Party Bureaucracy in Britain* and co-author of *Public Administration in Britain Today*, *Local Government in the United Kingdom*, and *Patterns of Local Political Leadership*.

Preface

This book was designed as a successor volume to our earlier edited collection, *Governing the UK in the 1990s*. We have retained the same broad textual structure, while changing the titles and emphases of some chapters. As part of the text's evolution, the opportunity has been taken to introduce some new contributors. Although all of the contributors were offered considerable scope to develop their own themes and perspectives, each chapter contains a brief analysis of the legacy of 18 years of Conservative Government, a central focus on the Labour Government's agenda and impact and an incorporation of developments within the relevant academic literature and debates.

Once again, we owe a debt of gratitude to Steven Kennedy and Cecily Wilson at the publishers. Steven played a major part in shaping the content of the book, and his characteristic combination of patience and prodding ensured that the deadlines were met (more or less!) Cecily's gentle reminders served to keep the project on course.

Our contributing authors deserve special thanks for meeting our thematic requirements, cooperating with our requests and delivering their work on time. Naturally, we assume full responsibility for any weaknesses or failings in the final text.

ROBERT PYPER
LYNTON ROBINS

This book is dedicated to **Bill Coxall**, (1937–99)

The publishers and editors would like to thank *The Economist* for permission to use material contained in Chapter 7.

Introduction

ROBERT PYPER AND LYNTON ROBINS

This book examines the impact of New Labour on changing patterns of governmental and political activity within three broad areas: the central executive; Parliament and the political parties; and the political world beyond Whitehall and Westminster. Eighteen years under a Conservative regime had seen many of the corporatist arrangements set up by previous governments dismantled and replaced by a variety of new arrangements which were either modelled on or involved the free market, or reshaped by management practices imported from the private sector. Necessarily for a successful transformation, the Thatcher 'project' also concerned cultural engineering in which definitions of concepts such as 'service', 'need', 'accountability', and indeed, 'citizen' became based more in the realm of the economic than the social or political. How far has Labour accepted these Conservative agendas for reform? To what extent has Labour moved forward defining its own, new set of definitions which result in further restructuring of the public and quasi-public sector?

Numerous political commentators announced the emergence of a one-party dominant state in Britain following the fourth Conservative election victory in 1992. It appeared that an electorate willing to tell pollsters prior to the general election that it intended to vote in a Labour government suffered last minute doubts and swung back to support the Conservatives. At the time it seemed that if Labour could not win under the favourable circumstances prevailing in 1992, then pessimistic political scientists were correct in their diagnosis and that Labour was indeed a party in terminal decline. The one-party state thesis went beyond electoral statistics. For not only was the electorate seemingly loyal to Conservatism, resulting in the Conservative domination of Parliament, but the values of radical

Conservatism appeared now to form the civil service orthodoxy, to dominate quasi-government, health care, education as well as much of local government.

What was unpredictable in 1992 was how quickly John Major's Conservative government would display the symptoms of a tired and accident-prone administration, exhausted by internal party divisions and increasing unpopularity as it drifted from one policy crisis to another. A litany of policy disasters marked what were to be the final years of Conservative government, in what had been described as 'the Conservative century' (Seldon and Ball, 1994), which embraced external relations in the arms to Iraq and Pergau Dam affairs to the primarily domestic scandals of BSE and increasing corruption at both national and local levels. Conservative ex-Chancellor Norman Lamont's understated observation was that the Conservatives now gave 'the impression of being in office but not in power'.

Labour did not rely solely on growing public hostility to the Conservatives for electoral advantage, but continued with the modernisation of the party inaugurated by Neil Kinnock, continued by John Smith and accelerated by Tony Blair. The result was the transformation of Labour into a less federal, more centralised and less ideological party in traditional terms. Symbolic of change which was taking place throughout much of the party was Tony Blair's victory in replacing 'socialist' Clause IV with Labour's acceptance of 'the enterprise of the market and rigour of competition'. A reformulation of social democratic values focused on communitarianism and stakeholding, ideas which were to become central in the development of Labour's version of the 'third way' once in office.

Critics of the third way, such as Stuart Hall, dismissed it as an unrealistic philosophy which was both vague and contradictory as well as based on the defeatist acceptance of the global economic environment as one in which Labour could no longer wield domestic control (Hall, 1998). Many of its contradictions, it was argued, resulted from the catch-all basis of the third way which tried to please all factions by taking the politics out of politics (cited as an example was Labour's policy of banning tobacco sponsorship of sport, but with the exception of Formula One motor racing). Critics argued that Labour's newly promised structures and processes for governing would not empower ordinary people any more than did the market-based systems introduced by Thatcher and Major. In short, Labour's third way was condemned as a betrayal of social democratic values representing nothing more than thinly disguised populism and authoritarianism.

Others were less critical of early formulations of the third way. Andrew Heywood, for example, has argued that structural changes were of secondary importance to New Labour. Of central importance to the success of the third way, as with Thatcherism, was cultural engineering (Heywood, 1998). What Blair was primarily concerned about in his 'project' was changing attitudes towards family responsibilities, education, work, etc. Once attitudes had changed, then any necessary structural adjustments would follow.

A parliamentary landslide carried Labour into office in 1997, with Blair leading a party which had a majority greater than the total number of seats won by the Conservatives. The scope of Labour's victory resulted in large part from it being a catch-all party, strong on voter-friendly programme generalities but offering little regarding risky policy specifics.

What forms of government did Labour inherit from the Conservatives? The pattern of change since Labour was last in government in 1979 was immense in scope although uneven in depth depending on sector. Then Labour governed principally through the big bureaucracies established to administer the welfare state, local government and nationalised industries. Debates of the day focused on the wisdom of creating 'super departments', the optimal degree of state intervention, corporatist arrangements regarding incomes policies, with perhaps one issue surviving from the 1970s to the 1990s being how to curb Treasury influence. Under Blair, Labour inherited a public administration in which most of the large bureaucracies had disappeared from the public sector, been eroded, or been transformed into alternative structures.

The Thatcher governments were ideologically opposed to 'big government' which the welfare state and nationalised industries represented. Most Thatcherites as well as many traditional Conservatives perceived the public sector as inefficient, since it was protected from the rigours of the market place; over manned, since previous governments used it as an instrument of employment policy; and parasitic, since it thrived on resources which would better have been diverted to the private sector where they would have been used more effectively. In addition it was argued that big government had detrimental effects on wider society, creating a culture of dependence, restricting consumer choice as well as worsening the very problems the bureaucracies were established to solve (see Duncan and Hudson, 1995).

New patterns of government in which the state played a smaller role were developed during the Thatcher–Major regime. There was much remodelling, as in education, based on the premise that the existing service was shaped by producer interests rather than consumer needs. Within the civil service the traditional structure was replaced in large part by agencies which were given greater commercial freedom. In health care, the purchaser-provider function became the basis of contractual relationships which shaped delivery to the doctor and so to the patient. Complex contracts characterised many new partnership arrangements, such as the Private Finance Initiative. Many traditional areas of state and municipal activity were privatised, and those which were not were subject to private sector management processes in order to improve their performance. In short, a mosaic of new bodies – from privatised, semi- or part-privatised, partnership, agency, quango, trust and governing – emerged alongside what remained of the unreconstructed structures but which nevertheless were involved in contracting out, market testing and meeting Charter standards.

Many academics referred to these changes, in sum or in part, as representing a movement from government to governance. It has not been a straightforward and uni-directional process. Rhodes commented that

> British government has adopted a strategy of 'more control over less'. It privatized the utilities. It contracted out services to the private sector. It introduced quasi-markets through purchaser-provider splits when services could not be privatized. It bypassed local authorities for special-purpose bodies. It removed operational management from central departments and vested it in separate agencies. Central departments rarely delivered services themselves; they were non-executant. Government policy then fragmented service delivery systems. It compensated for its loss of hands-on controls by reinforcing its controls over resources. Decentralizing service delivery has gone with centralizing financial control. Such hands-off controls may not provide enough leverage for the centre to steer the networks. As networks multiply, so do doubts about the centre's capacity to steer. (Rhodes, 1997, p. 16)

The contradiction whereby fragmentation of the public sector coexisted alongside greater centralisation of government characterised much of governance. In some ways it was a reflection several mirrors along of the contradiction within Thatcherism whereby a stronger state was required in order to establish a more vigorous free market. Simon Jenkins referred to Margaret Thatcher's 'nationalised state' as one in which stricter budgetary controls from the centre were imposed on sectors such as the police, the health service and universities. Yet, in terms of spending as a percentage of GDP, the state remained as strong as ever (Jenkins, 1995). But was political direction from the centre no more than indirect and compromised control through budget allocations? Thus a crude generalisation concerning changing patterns becomes subject to debate: whilst functions performed by traditional government structures may be characterised more by command from the centre, those performed through governance were the result of bargaining and negotiation.

In short, Labour returned to office after eighteen years to find that control of policy falling to autonomous and near-autonomous bodies now lay predominantly in the area of financial control. The most that could be done was to audit how public money was spent and what was got in return for it through over 500 public service agreements with the Treasury. Where the chain of accountability was once visible in linking the public via ministers to Parliament, there was now confusion and dispute regarding 'policy' and 'operational' responsibilities and the role of Parliament. Where Europe impinged marginally on Harold Wilson and Jim Callaghan's Labour government, EU concerns dominate much of the business of many of the departments under Tony Blair's Labour government. Finally, where there was a discernible public service ethos which survived events such as the 'winter of discontent' to influence the culture of many state workers there then developed a more business-like culture which put a lower value on collegiality, a greater value on income disparity, and which has become associated with greater risks of corruption.

The Central Executive

As we have noted, political commentators have had mixed views on the substance of the Blair 'project', some dismissing its third way philosophy as vacuous and its 'Cool Britannia' imagery as media hype. Others have been more sympathetic, noting that the modernising process has already transformed the Labour Party and party system, that entrenched dependency amongst the poor and unemployed has been confronted by Labour ministers who have promised new opportunities for social advancement and, as these commentators anticipated, Blair's project has also included reforming the machinery of central government. However, whether Blair's reforms were simply an extension of existing trends, an adaptation of previous arrangements, or a novel innovation is an issue which is examined in the chapters contributed by Peter Barberis, Kevin Theakston and Tony Butcher.

The arrival of the Labour government in 1997 was accompanied by more political advisers being brought into government than under previous governments, many of them to serve on numerous new task forces and advisory bodies. Introducing political strategists and aides, some of whom flitted between the worlds of lobbying, the media and party politics, as well as establishing new quango-like bodies on which sympathetic outsiders served, led, in part, to accusations of 'cronyism' by the Opposition. Labour's defence was that eighteen years of uninterrupted Conservative government had reduced much of the civil service to a weak and demoralised condition. Fresher minds were needed to undertake the massive task of reviewing policies and this necessarily involved tapping talent from outside the service. At the same time, it was argued, many of the social problems to be tackled were spread across the responsibility of more than one department and the thinking of 'outsiders' was less likely to be constrained by departmentalism than the mindsets of civil servants.

Some political commentators were surprised that a new Prime Minister's Department was not established, particularly since it was known that some of Blair's closest advisers supported this idea. There were, however, changes inside Number Ten which resulted in strengthening the position of Blair as head of government. Measures resulting in increased control should bring greater coordination, saving Blair from the 'battle of the memos' endured by his predecessor inside Number Ten. A reinvention, the so-called Cabinet 'enforcer', promised to strengthen the Prime Minister's position in the policy process. However, previous attempts at this task by others do not hold out much promise of success and it will be interesting to monitor whether its first incumbents, Jack Cunningham and Mo Mowlam, have the additional resources necessary for a greater impact on policy direction and coordination.

In Chapter 1 Peter Barberis explores crucial aspects of the debate in British politics about prime ministerial government. Traditionally this debate posed one system against an alternative, but this over-simplification ignores other, more complex models which connect the executive to a wider set of policy networks. In Chapter 2, Kevin Theakston assesses where the balance is struck between ministers' policy aspirations and civil servants' advice on what they assess is realistically operational. The influx of advisers and spin doctors into government probably does represent a new form of politicisation, but those who claim it marks the 'Americanisation' of government exaggerate the significance of Labour's contribution to what is a long-term trend in government. Tony Butcher measures the Labour government's response to the changes in civil service structure and management, many of which it had criticised during the years of opposition. Labour is keen on reforms which promise better government and has been converted to Conservative wisdom of breaking up traditional bureaucracies as well as encouraging greater private sector involvement in delivering services. Even the Citizen's Charter, once derided by Labour, has been retained and relaunched. If Labour makes a distinctive contribution, then it is likely to be in areas where IT will bring radical change to communication and service delivery.

Parliament and Parties

A number of difficulties resulted from the parliamentary arithmetic following the 1997 general election. It appeared that there were far more Labour MPs than the new government required for a comfortable majority. It seemed reasonable to argue that once many of Labour's backbenchers saw that neither their talents nor their vote was needed, they would become troublesome. The same parliamentary arithmetic meant that the Conservatives might be too few in numbers to mount effective opposition. This carried the dangers of poorer scrutiny of government by the Commons and, following the removal of hereditary peers' right to vote, weaker scrutiny by their lordships.

Some of these early anxieties have not materialised to the extent feared by those who expressed them. Despite their ambitions being frustrated, Labour backbenchers have remained surprisingly disciplined. The temptation to stand out from the crowd by winning a reputation for being single-minded and rebellious has generally been resisted. A higher level of Labour dissent is anticipated however, particularly if public support declines and the most marginally-elected Labour MPs fear defeat in the approaching general election. At the same time fears of Conservative underperformance in opposition were exaggerated; indeed, the Conservatives have caused considerable parliamentary discomfort for the Labour front bench despite their depleted numbers and continuing internal problems.

The intake of 120 women MPs led to speculation by some commentators that the conduct of the new House would change in nature resulting from the 'feminisation' of party politics. Although it can be argued that the texture of party politics inside the Commons has changed, there is no evidence that such change results from the increased female presence. Although it can be overstated, 'tribalism' has declined to some extent because of closer relations between senior Labour and Liberal Democrat MPs. The Liberal Democrats' political strategy of 'equidistance' was reappraised and discarded in favour of 'constructive opposition', which included participation in a sub-committee of the Cabinet concerned primarily with constitutional matters.

Philip Norton recognises that a number of constitutional changes, including those in which Liberal Democrats have collaborated, pose problems for the House of Commons. If it is to survive as more than a marginalised legislature, it will have to perform its more limited future role with greater effect. In Chapter 4 he considers recent proposals for the modernisation of the Commons. Michael Rush develops this theme in Chapter 5, examining the means by which parliamentary scrutiny is, or is not, discharged. The House of Lords is generally recognised as being particularly effective in scrutinising delegated legislation which emanates from the EU, a judgement which has to be suspended until the final details of the reformed upper chamber become known.

Richard Kelly explores the question of whether political parties are of declining importance in the processes of contemporary government. Chapter 6 contains an analysis of the changing power structures of the two main parties which result from recent modernisation. Both have loosened ties with their traditional backers, both exhibit an elitism resonant of the McKenzie thesis since both consult their respective grass roots routinely in ways which restrict authentic participation. New and intriguing political realities are taking shape: Labour seems on the verge of existing without the labour movement whilst the Conservatives cope with the problems of defeat at the very time when the tenets of radical Conservatism have triumphed over those of corporatism, collectivism and social democracy.

Beyond Whitehall and Westminster

The Labour government's honeymoon with the electorate was a remarkably lengthy one. Despite a number of political difficulties, some of which resulted in ministerial resignations, the Government entered 1999 with MORI giving Labour a substantial 32 per cent lead over the Conservatives (*The Times*, 28 January 1999). The final section of this book examines four arenas where public and government interact, albeit in differing ways.

The lessons Labour learnt in opposition about good media relations being crucial for victory were carried into office as part and parcel of delivering good government. Was Labour's expertise in media management used, however, to obscure its shortcomings and inexperience once in office? In Chapter 1 Peter Barberis has already questioned whether inexperience of holding office was necessarily a handicap for the new Labour team, a question which is justified given the disasters presided over by Major's 'experienced' government. In Chapter 7 Bill Jones analyses the impact of Labour's professional spin doctors on the party's emerging image as 'fit to govern' and the new relationships established with media professionals.

Political communication became central to the emergence of New Labour. A highly visible measure of success was the swing towards Labour by the traditional Tory press during the 1997 general election campaign, including the politically significant early conversion in March headlined by 'The Sun backs Blair'. It has been estimated that at the time of the election 37 per cent of newspaper readers were purchasing pro-Conservative papers while 63 per cent were buying pro-Labour papers (Seymour-Ure, 1997). The realignment of traditional Fleet Street sympathies was part of a process which predated the general election by several years. As early as 1995 Labour's commanding lead in the opinion polls was being reflected in newspaper readership with, for example, only 37 per cent of *Times* readers supporting the Conservatives compared with 64 per cent in 1992, and the fall in Conservative support amongst *Telegraph* readers being from 72 to 52 per cent during the same period. Neither of these papers gave explicit support to Labour but, with large percentages of their readerships now supporting Labour, their respective editors were put in a difficult position and responded by moderating both their support for the Conservatives and their opposition to Labour, so as not to offend their realigned readers.

The importance to Labour of managing good media relations has projected the party's media advisers into the public realm, so much so that serious political commentators have speculated on their media-evaluations as a deciding factor on the direction of much government policy (see Michael White and Ewen MacAskill in *The Guardian*, 26 January 1999). Bill Jones explores the frenetic world of Labour's spin doctors which by early 1999 had claimed three high-profile casualties.

New Labour has received a better press than the EU seems ever likely of enjoying. The EU has customarily been portrayed as excessively bureaucratic, eager to meddle in areas where it is not welcomed. British people have been informed, frequently misinformed, about 'Brussels bans' on ice cream, sausages, King Edward potatoes or some other cherished fare. Waste and inefficiency have formed part of the EU's image, but more recently corruption has been added as an additional elaboration. Under Margaret Thatcher's premiership Europe provoked fears of creeping socialism and federalism, which still find a place in much Conservative thinking about Britain's role in the EU. In Chapter 8 Neill Nugent analyses changing Conservative attitudes towards the EU which marked its conversion from being a broadly pro-European party to one which represented Euro-scepticism amongst the electorate.

Labour has also experienced a radical change of position on European policy. From being hostile to continued membership of the European Community in the early 1980s, Labour became increasingly committed to Britain in Europe during the 1990s and has conveyed the impression to many political commentators that it will recommend entry to the euro sooner rather than later. Neill Nugent explores the changing patterns of EU governance as it affects Labour's ambitions regarding UK governance.

New vertical patterns of governance seem likely to emerge resulting from the related processes of deeper European integration and
regional devolution. New alliances, coalitions, partnerships and
other arrangements involving the various institutions of the EU,
the institutions of devolved government including the Regional
Development Agencies, local authorities and already existing
multi-agency arrangements will characterise the pattern of modern
governance. The interconnectedness of governance beyond the centre was illustrated by the announcement that the elected assemblies
in Wales and Northern Ireland along with the Scottish Parliament
were soon to open offices in Brussels (*Financial Times*, 22 January
1999). They will be joining 160 regional representatives networking
alongside those pursuing local government interests for information
on relevant developments which is gathered early enough to facilitate preparation and action, as well as their central task of lobbying
for resources. Allan McConnell examines in Chapter 9 the domestic
impact of regional aspirations on patterns of governance.

The political situation within the component parts of the UK had
been becoming increasingly unsatisfactory as Conservative dominance of the 'core' was contrasted with Conservative decline in the
'periphery'. Emerging patterns of governance appeared to exarcerb-
ate the situation with public suspicions that defeated Conservative
representatives on local councils were being replaced by numerous
quangocrats appointed because of their Conservative sympathies.
Allan McConnell recounts how the Conservatives' response to these
mounting frustrations was seen as too little, too late. Electoral
punishment saw the 1997 general election delivering half of the
'Doomsday scenario', with not a single Conservative MP returned
by either the Welsh or Scottish electorates. He continues to examine
the new structures of territorial governance which are emerging in
Scotland, Wales and Northern Ireland, noting some inbuilt political
tensions, particularly between the Scottish Parliament and Westminster. What, now, is the nature of the United Kingdom? In his
conclusion McConnell considers the extent to which Britain can be
described still as a unitary rather than a federal state.

In the context of local governance David Wilson examines how
old patterns continue to exist alongside the frequently more publicised new patterns. In Chapter 10 he notes that the world of local
government has been seen as a laboratory for new forms of service
delivery which fit in with the new 'enabling' mission. His advice,

however, is that heavy generalisation about contemporary developments should be treated with caution since there is much variation
between local authorities. At the same time there is a tendency to
concentrate academic attention on the novel and thereby underestimate how far local authorities have remained in their traditional
role of 'providers'.

Although it was a minister in a previous Labour government who
informed local councillors and officers that their 'party was over',
many political commentators expected that the new Labour administration would restore local government as far as possible to its
former importance. In many ways this has been the case, with
Labour keen on further local government reforms – but not on
counter-revolution – which will reconnect local people with local
decision-makers. David Wilson reviews the various experiments
which have been promoted to make these connections, including
the elected mayor and assembly for London. He considers some of
the barriers to successful innovation, including the 'democratic
deficit' in British local government which is particularly evident
when European comparisons are drawn, as well as the not unrelated
problem of chronic apathy on the part of many local electors.

Clive Gray concludes this section with an exploration of numerous facets of the 'hollow state' concept. How far have processes
such as privatisation, the development of quasi-autonomous agencies of governance, along with an increasing EU policy role, resulted
in a loss of control by central government over the public sector? Or,
alternatively, is the portrayal of a weakened state an illusion which
has resulted from a modest reorganisation which simply drew a
sharper division between the policy-making and policy-implementa-
tion processes? Or, finally, has there been a reconstruction of the
state in which power and control has been retained, albeit relocated?

Within the wider discussion contained in Chapter 11, Clive Gray
considers the implications of imposing an essentially economic con-
ception on the public sector and its citizens. Whichever interpretation of the 'hollow state' is seen as most useful in explaining recent
changes, it is important to clarify which private sector model is
driving public sector reforms. Gray suspects that public sector
reforms have been based on a crusading vision of private enterprise
which bears little resemblance to the customer responsiveness of
Virgin trains, private pension providers or beleaguered Marks and
Spencer. The guiding operational ideology – new public manage-

ment – risks similar distortion from the actual practices of the private sector. In an attack on the BBC Brian Appleyard identified NPM as the new Stalinism which 'nobody within the state or organisation believes yet to which everybody is blackmailed into paying lip service' (*The Sunday Times*, 24 January 1999). Whilst not disagreeing with Appleyard, Gray believes that the passage of time will see under Labour the promotion to high positions of younger managers more likely to be true believers in NPM.

References

Duncan, A. and Hudson, D. (1995) *Saturn's Children: How the State Devours Liberty, Prosperity and Virtue* (London: Sinclair-Stevenson).

Hall, S. (1998) 'The great moving nowhere show', *Marxism Today*, November–December, pp. 9–14.

Heywood, A. (1998) 'It's the culture, stupid – deconstructing the Blair project', *Talking Politics*, 11(1), pp. 42–6.

Jenkins, S. (1995) *Accountable to None: The Tory Nationalization of Britain* (London: Hamish Hamilton).

Rhodes, R. A. W. (1997) *Understanding Governance: Policy Networks, Governance, Reflexivity and Accountability* (Buckingham: Open University Press).

Seldon, A. and Ball, S. (eds) (1994) *Conservative Century: The Conservative Party Since 1900* (Oxford: Oxford University Press).

Seymour-Ure, C. (1997) 'Editorial opinion in the national press', *Parliamentary Affairs*, 50(4), pp. 586–608.

1

Prime Minister and Cabinet

PETER BARBERIS

This chapter could almost be subtitled 'ancient and modern'. For it maintains acquaintanceship with an old debate: whether Britain has prime ministerial or Cabinet government – that is to say whether the Prime Minister has the whip hand or whether the Cabinet is the effective frame of reference, providing a collective counterweight. Usually the focus is upon the relative capacities of the premier and of the Cabinet to make, shape or influence decisions; at other times there is a more specific emphasis upon the ability of the Prime Minister to retain the confidence of the rest of the Cabinet and, ultimately, to keep his or her position in 10 Downing Street. There is an assumption – by no means universally accepted – that the Prime Minister and Cabinet are locked into a competitive relationship, institutionally and perhaps personally. Such, in brief terms, is the substance of the prime ministerial – Cabinet government debate. As Hennessy (1995, p. 98) says, this particular debate may be on a Zimmer frame – but a Zimmer frame that remains warm. Since Crossman (1963) there have been periodic reassertions about the alleged reality of prime ministerial government. Such pronouncements were legion during the 1980s under the premiership of Margaret Thatcher. More recently, the government of Tony Blair has been characterised as highly personalised, even presidential, in style as Downing Street tries to control more and more of the levers of power. Media observers are intrigued not to say obsessed with the exercise of personal power. Academics, too, continue to find reward in such pursuits, while acknowledging the limitations involved (Giddings, 1995; Thomas, 1998).

The first section of this chapter examines the office of Prime Minister and some of the office-holders. There then follows a reppraisal of the arguments and counter-arguments attending the debate about prime ministerial power. One of the observations to emerge from this discussion is that there needs to be a broader and more inclusive focus which betrays something of the 'synoptic reality' at the heart of British government. The third and final section therefore adopts the perspective of the Cabinet *system*, featuring the related concepts of a core executive and policy networks. Finally, there will be a few concluding remarks.

Prime Minister: The Office and Office-Holders

Neither the office of Prime Minister nor the Cabinet as an institution are products of legislation. Nor are their functions or powers specified by statute – or indeed by any other formal document which has, or may have, the force of law. This observation reflects two characteristics of the British system: first, that there is no comphrensive, unified written constitution; second, that it is a parliamentary not a presidential system. Elementary as these points are, they both bear further brief consideration.

Convention implies that the British system is the product of day-to-day working practices, refashioned to meet specific needs as they arise. This malleability further implies that old 'rules' (practices) may be abandoned or quickly discarded and new ones invented almost 'on the hoof' – thought not quite. For convention also implies a respect for tradition. Thus the Prime Minister must, nowadays, be a member of the House of Commons. The last peer to occupy 10 Downing Street was Lord Salisbury in 1902. He was also, incidentally, the last incumbent *not* simultaneously to have been First Lord of the Treasury. When in 1963 Lord Home took the premiership he was obliged to renounce his peerage and seek a constituency for election to the House of Commons – which he duly did, returning as Sir Alec Douglas-Home. Apart from the Lord Chancellor (a peer), other Cabinet ministers can technically be drawn from either chamber though, again, the more important ones usually (not always) sit in the Commons. The cardinal principle is that there must be someone, if only a junior minister, who can answer directly to the Commons for the work of each main central government department.

The last point connects with the second characteristic of the British system: that it is a parliamentary not a presidential one. In Britain the Prime Minister and other Cabinet ministers stand not only at the apex of the executive branch of state but are also individual members of the legislature. Voters in Britain elect some 650 MPs – at present one for each geographical constituency. Approximately 110 people are in the government, of whom 20–24 constitute the Cabinet. Parliament is the law-making body whose formal approval the Prime Minister and Cabinet must obtain, notwithstanding the increasing precedence given to EU legislation. In fact Britain has a particular type of parliamentary system. It is one in which formal authority is relatively centralised: local and other forms of sub-national and quasi-governmental institution operate and indeed owe their existence to Parliament. In practice, one party tends to command a clear majority within the House of Commons so that Parliament generally (not always) approves government proposals. As King (1991, p. 43) says: 'The British system of government contains checks and balances... but it contains fewer checks and balances than can be found in almost any other country calling itself a democracy'. Occasionally Parliament bears its teeth. It can sometimes bite deeply, especially where the government has only a small majority or indeed no overall majority at all – as for example with Callaghan's Labour government (1976–79) or during the last couple of years (1995–97) of John Major's premiership. Conversely, governments which enjoy large or comfortable majorities normally do, but occasionally do not, get their way with Parliament – or, to be more precise, with their own backbenchers. Yet even the seemingly unassailable Margaret Thatcher was usually careful to listen and sometimes to adjust to the signals of her colleagues and party supporters. Her failure to do so, especially over the poll tax and over Europe, was a major factor in her demise in November 1990.

Thatcher was defeated not by the electorate but by the parliamentary Conservative Party. Her downfall was the clearest instance since May 1940 of Parliament driving a Prime Minister from office. On that earlier occasion it was a cross-party consensus which determined that Winston Churchill should replace Neville Chamberlain, having regard to the latter's perceived inadequacies in time of war. Four post-war premiers have resigned from office. Two of them departed under cover of illness, though amidst mounting unpopularity – Anthony Eden in 1957 and his successor, Harold Macmillan, in 1963. The other two retired – Churchill in 1955, Harold Wilson in 1976. Of the four, probaly only Eden was under compelling pressure to resign.

These examples are further testimony to the permeability of the British system. While tenure of the US presidency is for a fixed period, that of the UK premiership is unspecified. Margaret Thatcher's $11\frac{1}{2}$ years in Downing Street (1979–90) is the longest spell since 1945, indeed of the twentieth century. Sir Alec Douglas-Home's (October 1963–October 1964) is the briefest post-war premiership, Andrew Bonar Law's seven-month tenure (1922–23) being the shortest of the century, truncated as it was by serious illness. It is normally taken for granted that the Prime Minister is the leader of the largest party in Parliament. Yet even here there have been exceptions. David Lloyd George, a Liberal, headed the wartime coalition from December 1916 and remained in Downing Street as Prime Minister until 1922, though most of the ministers in his Cabinet were Conservatives. He did not even become the sole and undisputed leader of his own party until 1926, by which time the Liberals were a spent force. In 1924 Ramsay MacDonald formed the first Labour government. Not only was it a minority government, Labour was not even the largest party in Parliament. And although Churchill became Prime Minister in May 1940 he did not become leader of the Conservative Party until later that year when terminal illness forced Neville Chamerlain to stand down. More recently, in 1995 John Major tried to shock his troops into obedience by resigning the Conservative leadership while retaining the premiership. He won the ensuing party leaderhsip election, though had he not done so he would have been obliged to relinquish his position in Downing Street.

It may rightly be said that these illustrations are anomalies or exceptions which prove the rule about incumbents of Downing Street. They are mostly old examples at that. Still, echoes from the past could resonate at the centre of the British system – if only as an expedient to square awkward circles – if the Blair government were to pursue a radical line on constitutional change (see below, Conclusions). At any rate it is worth emphasising the duality of roles involved in being party leader as well as Prime Minister. Effective leadership of a party is different from and requires attributes other than those necessary for the executive conduct of government, to say nothing of the additional workload. Since whoever is party leader becomes Prime Minister and since the leader is chosen by the party to suit the party it may seem almost as if the incumbency of Downing Street is a secondary, hit-or-miss affair. In fact the constitutional overlapping of the executive and legislature means that the political skills of party management are inherent to the day-to-day conduct of government. The two roles are complementary. Moreover, when major parties choose their leaders they have at least half an eye on the perceived suitability of candidates for Downing Street, even when the party is in opposition. Where these considerations yield undue favour to internal party manoeuvrings then electoral reversal is the likely outcome. Such may be said about Michael Foot's advance to the Labour leadership in 1980, though few would hold him solely or even mainly responsible for the severity of his party's defeat in the General Election of 1983.

It has been said that high office in Britain is dominated nowadays by the career politician – an observation that applies to other Cabinet ministers as well as to Prime Ministers (King, 1981; Riddell, 1993). There are occasional exceptions – such as Glenda Jackson who, upon becoming a government (though not Cabinet) minister in 1997 after five years as an MP, was still better known to most citizens from her former career as a film star. It is unlikely, though, that anyone would enter 10 Downing Street with the credentials of a Jimmy Carter or a Ronald Reagan, presidents of the USA from 1977–81 and 1981–89 respectively. Neither Carter nor Reagan had spent even the majority of their careers holding political office. In Britain, Tony Blair is the only premier this century not to have had previous experience as a Cabinet minister, a consequence both of his being the century's youngest Prime Minister and of his party's sustained period in opposition prior to its spectacular victory in May 1997. In fact, even Blair had already spent fourteen years in Parliament. He was associated in the public mind with no career other than politics. All other post-war premiers had already served time in Cabinet. In some cases, incumbents have entered Number Ten having already held one or more of the other high offices of state, especially where they have taken over with their party already in government rather than as the result of a general election. Table 1.1 provides a summary of post-holders since 1940.

Mention has already been made of the Prime Minister's dual roles as head of the government and as party leader. There is a third role

TABLE 1.1 *British Prime Ministers, 1940–99*

Premiership	Age on appointment	Previous high office (see key)	Previous experience (years to nearest whole year)	
			Cabinet Minister	MP
Churchill (Coalition) 1940–45	65	b,d	18	38
Attlee (Lab.) 1945–51	62	–	5	23
Churchill (Cons.) 1951–55	76	a,b,d	23	49
*Eden (Cons.) 1955–57	57	c	12	32
*Macmillan (Cons.) 1957–63	62	b,c	5	30
*Douglas-Home (Cons.) 1963–64	60	c	8	15 (+12 in Lords)
Wilson (Lab.) 1964–70	48	–	4	19
Heath (Cons.) 1970–74	53	–	5	20
Wilson (Lab.) 1974–76	57	a	9	29
* Callaghan (Lab.) 1976–79	64	b,c,d	8	31
Thatcher (Cons.) 1979–90	53	–	4	20
* Major (Cons.) 1990–97	47	b,c	3	11
Blair (Lab.) 1997–	43	–	–	14

* Became Prime Minister while party was in office
Key to high offices: a = Prime Minister
　　　　　　　　b = Chancellor of the Exchequer
　　　　　　　　c = Foreign Secretary
　　　　　　　　d = Home Secretary

– that of national leader. Of course, the monarch is the formal head of state and discharges many of the ceremonial functions. But it is the Prime Minister who represents the country at gatherings of other heads of state where important decisions are taken, or where the foundations are being laid for the taking of important decisions. It all means that many of the day-to-day functions of any premiership are predetermined. There are quite a number of specific functions which will have to be performed by any Prime Minister, some of which are discussed in the next section. To some extent the emphasis given depends upon the inclination of the incumbent and upon the prevailing circumstances. Beyond that, commentators tend to differ. Robert Blake (1975, p. 67), for example, concludes that 'the study of an office such as this depends very largely on the study of individuals'. In other words, the office of Prime Minister is largely what incumbents have made it – or at any rate there is a good deal of latitude. Others have tried to identify broader contingencies which seemingly offer little scope for variation between one premiership and the next. Thus Richard Rose (1991a, p. 9) has written that 'differences between national political institutions create more variation in the office of prime minister than do differences of personality and circumstances'. Perhaps both are valid in their own ways, one the political historian, the other a comparative political scientist. Simply by looking down the telescope from the other end, it is possible to get a different image of the same reality. Either way, there is one question which continues to exercise many observers: whether Britain really has prime ministerial government.

Prime Ministerial Government: A Reappraisal

The assertion that Britain has prime ministerial government rests on the belief that, whatever may be the formalities or constitutional niceties, the Prime Minister (whoever he or she may be) enjoys a position of growing supremacy over the rest of the Cabinet, hence over the rest of the government, Parliament and the party outside Parliament. In different ways such views have been expressed by many down the years (Benn, 1981; Brazier, 1991; Foley, 1993). By contrast others, with varying degrees of circumspection, have emphasised the (continuing) reality of Cabinet government (Jones, 1985b; Hennessy, 1986; James, 1999). The Prime Minister may be the most powerful individual; but others have their own power bases and, should a number of departmental ministers coalesce, then the premier can find it tough going and may have to give ground.

The factors typically adduced to support the prime ministerial government thesis are fairly familiar and can be easily itemised. The Prime Minister

- appoints (and may dismiss) ministers to all Cabinet and other government portfolios;
- determines the constitution and membership of Cabinet committees;
- determines the agenda and vets the official record of Cabinet meetings;
- approves the filling of all senior positions within the civil service, for which he or she is also the chief minister;
- is the political chief of the security services;
- has a uniquely panoramic view of all aspects of government and is able to transcend the departmental brief;
- represents the nation at important meetings of heads of state;
- commands and may turn to advantage increasing media attention;
- is supported by a formidable corps of assistants through which the levers of power within Whitehall may be mobilised; and
- in effect, makes the decision to dissolve Parliament.

Brief comment may be made about each in turn of these points – enough to show that, while substantial, many of them are less compelling than at first they appear.

The appointment and dismissal of ministers is one of the most explicit forms of patronage at the Prime Minister's disposal. Many a promising career has been frozen in bud, never coming to full flower because the aspirant has displeased the Prime Minister or else Downing Street has received 'unfavourable reports'. Yet at any moment most of the viable candidates for Cabinet membership and indeed most of the available portfolios will be virtually self-selecting. The passage of time will give the Prime Minister greater latitude, certainly in the allocation and reallocation of individual ministers to particular portfolios. Reshuffles can and have been used to strengthen a premier's grip, though their very necessity suggests a prior position in which strength was felt to be lacking. Periodic reshuffles may or may not be conducive to good government: some have been critical of the frequency of turnover (Rose, 1991b), others more sanguine (Alderman, 1995). But reshuffles can look like an act of desperation and an undermining of the Prime Minister's position if conducted during a sticky period – as was discovered by Harold Macmillan in the early 1960s, by Harold Wilson in the late 1960s and by John Major in the mid-1990s.

The Prime Minister has similar disposition over the membership of Cabinet committees and probably further scope in determining the number and terms of reference of these committees. Yet, as can be seen in Table 1.2, the advent of a new government in May 1997 did not bring a radical change in the Cabinet committee structure.

Comparison between the two lists in Table 1.2 suggests that the pattern of Cabinet committees is less a matter of prime ministerial whim, more a function of circumstance and routine. And although both Major and Blair have chaired the more important committees, they seem less ubiquitous in this role than is sometimes supposed. Moreover under Blair – allegedly the more 'presidential' of the two – the chairing of Cabinet committees is shared among six different ministers (including the Prime Minister), compared with four under Major. Some Cabinet Committees are standing (i.e. regular) committees, while others are *ad hoc* – that is, more specific and usually short term. In the recent past, membership has, in some cases, included civil servants who also used to maintain their own parallel structures, though the latter seem to be less in evidence nowadays. Cabinet committees are supplemented by a number of sub-committees and, since 1997, by a Joint Consultative Committee (JCC). The JCC is chaired by Tony Blair. Its membership is *ad hoc* but includes senior Liberal Democrats and discusses mostly constitutional issues, especially electoral reform. It is sometimes said that Cabinet committees in general are a means by which the Prime Minister can 'divide and rule', dispatching business which proceeds to the Cabinet in sanitised form for approval with little debate. Such is almost certainly true, though it is unlikely that debate could be suppressed indefinitely in this way. In fact, the advent and development of these committees as a regular feature from the earlier decades of the present century has almost certainly helped the Cabinet *as an institution* to keep up with the growing volume of work. At the same time their significance has perhaps been

TABLE 1.2 *Cabinet Committees under the Major and Blair Governments*

Major (January 1997)	*Blair (July 1999)*
Economic and Domestic (Prime Minister)	Economic Affairs (CE)
Defence and Overseas (Prime Minister)	Defence and Overseas (Prime Minister)
Nuclear Defence (Prime Minister)	Constitutional Reform (Prime Minister)
Northern Ireland (Prime Minister)	Northern Ireland (Prime Minister)
Intelligence Services (Prime Minister)	Intelligence Services (Prime Minister)
Environment (DPM)	Environment (DPM)
Home and Social Affairs (LPC)	Home and Social Affairs (DPM)
Local Government (DPM)	Local Government (DPM)
Public Expenditure (CE)	Public Services and Expenditure (CE)
Queen's Speeches and Future Legislation (LPC)	Queen's Speeches and Future Legislation (LPC)
Legislation (LPC)	Legislation (LHC)
Competitiveness (DPM)	Devolution (LC)
Policy Coordination and Presentation (DPM)	

Note: Committee chair indicated in parenthesis.

Key: CE = Chancellor of the Exchequer
DPM = Deputy Prime Minister
LC = Lord Chancellor
LHC = Leader of the House of Commons
LPC = Lord President of the Council

(The above listings exclude sub-committees and miscellaneous ministerial groups.)

exaggerated, as evidenced by the Blair government's creation of some twenty *ad hoc* task forces, covering a range of issues including education standards, NHS waiting lists, creative industries, the disabled and the housing market. Some of these task forces are chaired by Cabinet ministers, others by outsiders. For example, the entrepreneur Richard Branson chairs the Tobacco Sports Sponsorship Task Force, seen by critics as evidence of 'government by crony' and an undermining of the Cabinet and its committees.

The agenda and official records of Cabinet meetings are determined and vetted by the Prime Minister. Most premiers have probably engaged in a certain amount of manipulation. But it is unlikely that even the most assertive Prime Minister could with impunity suppress an issue of importance to Cabinet colleagues – as Margaret Thatcher discovered in 1986 when Defence Secretary Michael Heseltine resigned from the Cabinet, precipitating the resignation (sacking) of another minister Leon Brittan and bringing acute embarrassment to the Prime Minister herself. In what became known as the 'Westland affair', Heseltine had been denied the opportunity to put before the Cabinet his proposals for a European consortium to rescue the ailing British helicopter firm Westland plc (Linklater and Leigh, 1986). He returned to the backbenches from where he remained a brooding presence until the autumn of 1990 when he came forward to help bring Thatcher's premiership to an end. In any event, to accord significance to the Prime Minister's agenda-setting role is to concede the importance of meetings of the whole Cabinet. In fact most observers would agree that, save for exceptional circumstances, the Cabinet has long since ceased to have a deliberative decision-making function, though it may well retain some sort of collegiate role. Even under Thatcher (not a noted enthusiast for collective structures) the whole Cabinet usually met at least once a week when Parliament was in session and under other premiers it has often convened with greater frequency.

Since the 1920s the approval of the Prime Minister has been required for the filling of all the most senior positions in the civil service. The Prime Minister is the political chief of the civil service, and of the security services. Both positions are formal ones in that they are mediated through others who have a more direct, day-to-day responsibility – the Chancellor of the Duchy of Lancaster for the civil service, the heads of MI5 and MI6 for the security services. Some premiers have made fairly active use of their prerogative over civil service appointments, most notably Margaret Thatcher. But even Thatcher only altered the course of events directly in a handful of cases, though in a more general sense she undoubtedly left her mark on the Whitehall psyche. When premiers have intervened in the appointment process it has, as often as not, been to help a departmental minister to get the person of his or her choice, or to deny an unwanted appointee (Barberis, 1996, pp. 124–30). The prerogative has been used sparingly if at all by Prime Ministers as a weapon against departmental ministers. Similarly, it is doubtful whether the premier gains any such advantage as head of the security services, unless the 'surveillance boffins' are set to the task of monitoring other ministers on behalf of Downing Street. From what little is known about the security services, they seem to work to their own agenda rather than that of the Prime Minister. Indeed during the 1960s and 1970s Prime Minister Harold Wilson was himself the subject of their attentions (Dorril and Ramsay, 1991; Pimlott, 1992, pp. 697–723).

Leadership of the civil service and of the security services affords the Prime Minister an overview of certain of the activities of government. This panoramic perspective derives also from other aspects of the Prime Minister's strategic position. It allows the incumbent to see beyond the confines of the departmental briefs within which other ministers are apparently ensnared. It is a point reinforced by three others, each of which are often seen as further strengthening the premier's hand. First, the Prime Minister's role is given sustained prominence by the ever-increasing incursion of the international dimension, not least the extensive cross-national networking that is the product of a more closely integrated Europe. As mentioned in the last section, the Prime Minister is the 'functional' head of state, representing Britain at most of the important international gatherings. Such meetings are more common nowadays than ever before. Of course, other Cabinet ministers are also increasingly drawn under the same spotlight, but the Prime Minister is the 'common denominator'. The international dimension helps to underline the uniqueness of the premiership and certainly keeps the incumbent almost constantly in the public eye. The second point connects with this one. Media attention tends in general to focus on Downing Street, though again not exclusively. Downing Street is equipped to meet this challenge and may in some ways have encouraged the trend, actively engaging to secure more favourable coverage. The Press Secretary is one of the most important members of the Prime Minister's entourage (see next section). And from this observation there arises the third point. Not only is there a corps of press officers, there is also a more extensive bureaucratic structure radiating outwards from the Prime Minister's Office. This structure, too, will be discussed in the next section. Suffice it to say that some commentators see all or most of the more important of Whitehall's 'highways and byways' as leading to Downing Street. On the other hand, the premier does not have a formal department comparable to that of other ministers – possibly as much a deprivation as a liberation! It is partly for this reason that the Prime Minister has sometimes been described as a 'king surrounded by powerful barons' (i.e. ministers). Departments of state are far from impregnable as power bases for their respective ministers, but they can be quite formidable 'baronial fortresses' – especially the Treasury, the Foreign Office and the Home Office. It must be remembered, too, that most statutes confer authority upon a particular secretary of state (or equivalent), hardly ever upon a Prime Minister. Moreover, the premier's role as *de facto* head of state and the focus of media attention may become a liability to an incumbent whose popularity has waned or whose policies are seen to have failed. By no means all publicity is good publicity. The press are apt to blame the Prime Minister for everything that goes wrong (as well as right) in a government, even where the lead role has been played by a Cabinet colleague.

Nowhere is the double-edged position of the Prime Minister more clearly illustrated than in the dissolution of Parliament. As with the appointment of Cabinet ministers, the dissolution of a Parliament prior to its statutory five years' duration is technically the prerogative of the monarch upon the advice of the Prime Minister. In practice and in normal circumstances, if a Prime Minister requests a dissolution the monarch will accede. The more interesting question is the extent to which it constitutes a weapon in the hands of the Prime Minister vis-à-vis other members of the Cabinet. It is unlikely that a premier would seek dissolution without consulting at least the more senior Cabinet colleagues and others outside the Cabinet. Conversely, a Prime Minister may resist pressure to seek a dissolution, as did James Callaghan in the autumn of 1978. Staying his hand, Callaghan kept his inclinations well concealed – as much so as any of his predecessors or successors. He had nevertheless already taken numerous soundings, receiving 'divided counsel' (Morgan, 1997, pp. 636–44). More importantly, the fate of any Prime Minister and of each and every member of the Cabinet are inexorably interwoven. They stand or fall together, especially when an election is in prospect. By the premature dissolution of Parliament the Prime Minister *may* gain advantage for his or her party, hence for himself or herself, in the ensuing election, as did Thatcher in 1983 and in 1987. It is far less clear that it offers any great leverage vis-à-vis other members of the Cabinet.

Three broad points arise from the foregoing discussion. First, that for every argument with which it can be claimed that the Prime Minister 'lords it' over the Cabinet there are almost equally well-founded reasons for doubting the extent of such supremacy. In part it depends upon how much a particular premier really wants to assert himself or herself; and then the prevailing circumstances will offer further or lesser opportunity. The mood of the nation, the strength of the economy, the international climate, the parliamentary arithmetic and the proximity of an election (pre or ante) – all these factors will affect the subtle chemistry of relationships within the Cabinet. Much also depends upon exactly what claim is being made about 'prime ministerial power'. Is it the ability to fend off putative successors from within the party; the ability to keep public opinion 'onside', if necessary at the expense of colleagues; success in initiating and driving through policies, again in the face of opposition from other senior figures; or the capacity to neutralise unwelcome initiatives from other quarters? Second, though, these questions assume an adversarial relationship, a constant battle of wits between the Prime Minister and Cabinet. Such a perspective may sometimes be appropriate but is often simplistic and misleading. It is certainly simplistic to assume a continuous contest, the Prime Minister set at odds with the rest of the Cabinet. More likely there will be a matrix of (shifting) alliances, the Prime Minister having certain allies (though not always the same ones), pitching in alongside one, two or more than two identifiable 'opinion sets'. Besides, a strong Prime Minister may well mean not a weak Cabinet but a strong one and an effective government. But effective government requires more than a strong Prime Minister and a strong Cabinet. It depends also upon the administrative apparatus through which their efforts are directed – the 'undergirding'. For another weakness of the prime ministerial – Cabinet government dichotomy is that it ignores even the more immediate, let alone the wider, institutional totality within which the real game is played out. Third, then, we need a perspective which embraces the Prime Minister and Cabinet as forming part of what has been described as the Cabinet *system*, featuring the core executive, together with the constellation of 'policy networks' through which various inputs are mediated. The next section therefore brings some of these notions into play.

The Cabinet System, Core Executive and Policy Networks

The notion of a Cabinet system implies that the central institutional structures need to be analysed as a totality in themselves and as part of a wider totality (Burch and Holliday, 1996, pp. 1–2). The Prime Minister and Cabinet do not operate in a vacuum. They form the heart of what is nowadays known as the core executive – 'the complex web of institutions, networks and practices surrounding the prime minister, cabinet, cabinet committees and their official counterparts, less formalised ministerial "clubs" or meetings, bilateral negotiations and interdepartmental committees' (Rhodes, 1995, p. 12). The more synoptic perspective implied here emphasises how the Prime Minister and Cabinet operate as part of a wider institutional nexus, forming a fairly well-integrated if not quite seamless web of interrelationships or policy networks. Rhodes and Marsh (1992, p. 13) adopt J. K. Benson's definition of a policy network as 'a cluster or complex of organisations connected to each other by resource dependencies and distinguished from other clusters or complexes by breaks in the structure of resource dependencies'. There thus exist any number of policy networks, each distinct but not necessarily isolated from the others. The policy network approach has had its critics (see Dowding, 1995) but it serves to highlight the dynamics of the policy process, emphasising the linkages between different institutions, actors and groups. Each network constitutes a different mixture of structures, actors and groups, producing varying outcomes. We should not assume that the Prime Minister and Cabinet, either separately or together, monopolise all the levers of power on all issues all of the time. Other participants and groups have their roles to play, within and beyond the immediate core. Power relationships will vary, not only over a period of time but also at any one time in different areas of policy.

The central institutions comprise the Prime Minister; the Cabinet; Cabinet committees; the Prime Minister's Office; and the Cabinet Office. The office of Prime Minister, the Cabinet and Cabinet committees have been discussed above. It remains therefore to say something about the Prime Minister's Office and about the Cabinet Office.

The Prime Minister's Office

There are a number of constituent elements which, since the 1970s, have been described collectively as the Prime Minister's Office (see Lee, Jones and Burnham, 1998; Kavanagh and Seldon 1999):

- Private Office
- Political Office
- Policy Unit
- Press Office

All senior ministers, including the Prime Minister, have long been served by a private secretary, becoming from the inter-war years part of the regular Whitehall bureaucracy. Under Tony Blair there is the Principal Private Secretary (PPS), four private secretaries (each covering a different area of policy), a diary secretary and a planning and visits secretary together with support staff. The PPS is a senior civil servant in his or her own right and probably spends as much time with the Prime Minister as anyone else. Private secretaries have been described as the 'impresarios of Whitehall' (Henderson, 1984, p. 1), the 'fixers', the (prime) minister's 'eyes and ears'. All who work within the Prime Minister's Private Office are among the brightest of Whitehall's brightest lights, united by a common professional (if not personal) loyalty to the premier. It is their job – though not theirs alone – to ensure that the Downing Street view pervades Whitehall. Their efforts are augmented by those of the Chief of Staff, a position which has been a regular feature since Mrs Thatcher's premiership during the 1980s. Tony Blair's Chief of Staff, Jonathan Powell, had been a career diplomat but had also worked with him during Blair's time as Leader of the Opposition. Some have seen Powell's appointment as having changed if not undermined the position of the PPS and the rest of the 'regular' Private Office of which the Chief of Staff is little more than a semi-detached member.

Under Margaret Thatcher, the Chief of Staff was technically part of what has come to be known as the Political Office and which, under Blair, consists of a political secretary (a party partisan) and two parliamentary secretaries (i.e. both MPs). More significant is the Policy Unit, established by Harold Wilson in 1974 partly to provide a counterweight to the official bureaucracy (Donoughue,

1987). It contains eleven policy advisers, headed by David Mili-
band. The Policy Unit has usually been staffed predominantly by
political partisans rather than regular civil servants, though the
precise mix has varied over time (Willetts, 1987). Future Conservative Cabinet ministers John Redwood and David Willetts were both
members of the Unit during the 1980s before they became MPs.
Indeed under Blair's premiership nearly all members have been
active in the Labour cause, a fact seen by some as further evidence
of the deeper party political hue that pervades the Prime Minister's
Office these days.

Similar observations have been made about the Press Office and,
in particular, about the role of the Chief Press Secretary. In fact
there is ample precedent. Clement Attlee in the 1940s employed as
his 'adviser on public relations' Francis Williams, a former editor of
the *Daily Herald* and a known Labour sympathiser. During the
1960s Harold Wilson appointed Thomas Lloyd-Hughes and, in
the 1970s, another ex-journalist and 'Labour man' Joe Haines. In
1978 James Callaghan tried to regularise the position with the
appointment of Tom McCaffrey, a career civil servant who nevertheless departed from Whitehall and continued to work with
Callaghan after the 1979 general election. In 1979 when the Conservatives took office, McCaffrey was succeeded by another career
civil servant, Bernard Ingham. In fact Ingham became one of
Thatcher's most robust defenders, prompting claims that he had
politicised his role. Although a seconded career official (Christopher
Meyer) held the post under John Major between 1994 and 1997, the
partisan nature of the post and the personal stamp of the premier
received renewed emphasis when in May 1997 Blair brought in his
own press secretary, Alistair Campbell. The Press Office is well
established as a mini-bureaucracy. There is not only the Chief
Press Secretary but also a Deputy Press Secretary and five other
press officers (each with a specific remit) as well as ancillary staff.
With the ever greater emphasis upon policy presentation and 'news
management', the Press Office has grown in importance, twice daily
press briefings now being given by 10 Downing Street. Of course,
the Prime Minister's Press Office does not have exclusive control
over the news management function. Alistair Campbell found it
necessary to warn departmental information officers about the
high incidence of leaks and to supervise more closely the relationship between individual Cabinet ministers and the press. For this

purpose a Strategic Communications Unit was established in 1998. It remains to be seen whether this unit will succeed in improving what, despite contrary appearances, Downing Street evidently considers to be a weakness at the centre.

Although not part of the Prime Minister's Office, mention should be made of the Whips' Office. The Chief Whip lives at 12 Downing Street in close proximity to the Prime Minister and, together with the other whips and party managers, he (or she) helps to maintain discipline among backbench government MPs. The whips are rightly seen as agents of the party leadership, especially of the Prime Minister. Given the nature of the British parliamentary system, they play a vital role in transmitting impulses from the core executive to the legislature (and vice versa).

The organisational terrain in and around the Prime Minister's Office is shown in Figure 1.1, including the Cabinet Office and, in lesser detail, the Treasury. Of course, no visual representation can do justice to the richness and complexity of a living reality – especially the many informal and overlapping relationships at the centre of government. Figure 1.1 offers a simple impression, not a faithful reproduction.

At the heart of the Cabinet Office is the Cabinet Secretariat. Established by Lloyd George when he assumed the premiership towards the end of 1916, the Cabinet Secretariat and the wider Cabinet Office are strategically placed at the centre of the Whitehall bureaucracy. Today there are six secretariats – one each for economic and domestic affairs; defence and overseas affairs; joint intelligence; intelligence and security; European affairs; and, since 1997, the constitution. Brief mention may be made of the latter two of these secretariats. The European secretariat has assumed an increasing importance since its creation in the early 1970s. Its job is to ensure that other departments in Whitehall coordinate their responses to the EU, avoiding possible contradictions to overall government policy. The effective discharge of this function involves many painstaking meetings, discussions and, occasionally, 'bloodletting' sessions behind closed doors in order to keep all quarters of Whitehall 'onside'. The European secretariat itself works in tandem with the UK permanent representative (UKREP) to the EU, a key link between the British government and the Brussels bureaucracy. The constitution secretariat is a creation of the Blair government, a further reminder of the adaptability of these central administrative

32

Figure 1.1 Central institutions of the core executive

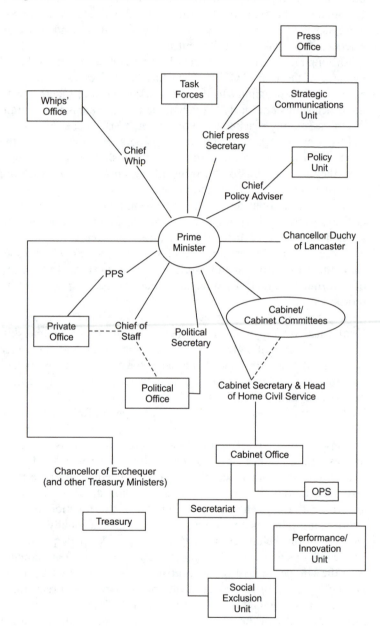

structures. Its role is to coordinate across Whitehall the administrative dimension of constitutional reform, especially devolution
and freedom of information.

Beyond the Secretariat the Cabinet Office embraces the Office of
Public Service (OPS) which, growing out of the Management and
Personnel Office, itself created in the early 1980s following the
demise of the Civil Service Department, has assumed an increasing
role. It has oversight of the general management of the civil service;
better government; the (Citizen's) Charter; deregulation; and standards in public life. In addition, the Better Regulation Unit, established by the Major government, works closely with the independent
Better Regulations Task Force 'to reduce the burden of unnecessary
regulation, particularly on small businesses' (Office of Public Service, 1998, col. 69).

The OPS has its own permanent secretary but the overall official
chief of the Cabinet Office is the Cabinet Secretary who, since 1981,
has also been Head of the Home Civil Service. The Cabinet Secretary serves the entire Cabinet and is not strictly a permanent secretary to the Prime Minister, although the two must of necessity
maintain a close working relationship, the precise nature of which
varies with the personal chemistry. In January 1998 Sir Richard
Wilson succeeded Sir Robin Butler in this post and was almost
immediately asked by Tony Blair to make recommendations for a
strengthening of the central machinery. The most significant ensuing change was the creation of a Performance and Innovation Unit
under the direction of Cabinet minister Jack Cunningham, who
became Chancellor of the Duchy of Lancaster in the reshuffle of
July 1998 before his subsequent replacement in the same position by
Mo Mowlam. Quickly dubbed by critics as 'the enforcer', the function of Cunningham and his Unit was according to the government,
to help achieve 'better co-ordination and practical delivery of policy
and services which involve more than one public sector body' (*Daily
Telegraph*, 29 July 1998, p. 5). The unit operates by means of a series
of reviews, bringing together in closer liaison the Cabinet Secretariat, the Policy Unit and the Treasury. It reports, via the Chancellor
of the Duchy of Lancaster, to the Prime Minister. So, too, does the
Social Exclusion Unit, set up at Blair's initiative late in 1997. This
unit is technically part of the Economic and Domestic Affairs
Secretariat of the Cabinet Office but draws its staff from beyond
as well as within the civil service. Its purpose is to coordinate

policies designed to strike at the roots of social exclusion – unemployment, crime, poor housing, low standards of education, bad health and family breakdown.

Pretty well all the work of the Cabinet Office brings it into contact with one or another part of Whitehall. It does not and cannot work in isolation. The same may be said about the Treasury, of which the Prime Minister remains First Lord but which is in effect the Chancellor of the Exchequer's department. Together, the Cabinet Office and the Treasury are the 'twin towers' of the Whitehall bureaucracy. They are sometimes seen as rivals and may from time to time get at cross purposes. Normally they operate on rather different planes, through different if adjacent and sometimes overlapping axes.

As crucial elements within the core executive, the Cabinet Office and the Treasury are plugged into a complex and far-reaching 'circuitry', transmitting (and receiving) impulses not only within but beyond the confines of Whitehall. These circuits or policy networks are the mechanisms through which the core executive maintains contact with a range of relevant persons and organisations – MPs, opinion leaders, experts, think tanks, pressure groups and the like. The Cabinet system thus stands at the centre of a wider universe. Not all constellations necessarily revolve around the Cabinet system. Sometimes, perhaps quite often, the critical action will take place elsewhere – in the economy, the international community and, increasingly, the European Union. It has become customary, almost obligatory, to see the Cabinet system in this wider context. From such a perspective we can maintain a sense of proportion: there is much more to prime ministerial or Cabinet government than the Prime Minister and the Cabinet, or even the core executive. We can better appreciate the constraints, the relative helplessness and disillusionment often experienced by office-holders as they get closer to the apparent centres of power. Even if authority in Britain is, as Anthony King suggests, highly concentrated and if political gravity has a habit of reclining toward the centre, others can still have their day. Conversely, to those on the outside the opposite may be true: office-holders do not know their own strength. Whatever the reality, patterns can be expected to vary, hence the need for serial case studies, as proponents of the policy network model (and others) have insisted (see, for example, Smith, 1999, p. 255).

Conclusions

With this remark we may make a number of concluding observations, mainly arising from the discussion in the last section. First, Tony Blair's premiership has so far been marked by an attempt to strengthen the centre of government, especially the *political* nerve centre in and around his own office. In so doing, however, he is merely accentuating a trend long since evident. That he and many of his predecessors have felt the need to do so may simply reflect an insatiable power lust. But it my also reflect a genuine weakness at the heart of government – perhaps a long-standing weakness, though no doubt exacerbated by the pace of change and a sensitivity to the ever intrusive mass media. There is nothing new about calls to strengthen the centre of government, including proposals for a full-scale Prime Minister's department (Berrill, 1980). Equally, some observers believe that there is no such need; that the Prime Minister's Office is adequate (Jones, 1985a).

Second, it may be useful to distinguish analytically between, on the one hand, the permeation of policy ideas and, on the other hand, their effective coordination and execution. Some would see the centre – the core executive generally – as being well equipped to disseminate policy ideas. But the capacity for coordination, sustained 'follow through' and effective implementation across a range of initiatives is another matter. There are no more main central government departments now than there were thirty, forty or fifty years ago. This stability largely reflects the dual conventions that each department should be represented by at least one independent Cabinet minister and that there should be no more than twenty-odd ministers in the Cabinet. There are fewer civil servants, though public expenditure has not diminished substantially as a proportion of GDP. Yet there are a greater number and variety of administrative 'outlets' – executive agencies, quangos and fringe bodies of all sorts, not to mention use of the private sector through 'contracting out'. If the 'map of state' embraces no further extremities of territory, then its arterial networks are denser, more convoluted, involving increasingly subtle and delicate sets of dependencies and interdependencies.

There are at least two specific challenges to the future of the core executive. One is to achieve coordination without impairing implementation. It may be necessary to establish coordinating machinery to ensure coherence and drive *from within the centre itself*. But coordinating machinery can 'gum up the works': more progress-chasers may sometimes mean less progress. It need not be so if a lightness of touch can be maintained. This characteristic, though, is not one for which progress-chasers or enforcers are noted. Nor is it one for which they are likely to receive either attention or reward. And if this challenge can be surmounted then another one beckons. It is a matter of how and to what extent effective executive command can be reconciled with the pluralistic canons of liberal democracy, so avoiding charges of elective dictatorship. The way in which government is conducted at its utmost levels is of vital importance here. It would be a delusion to suppose that the Cabinet could or should function as an all-embracing collective decision-making body. But it may still be possible to uphold the integrity of individual ministers, both as members of the Cabinet and as the political chiefs of their respective departments.

Finally, there is the prospect of constitutional reform. Here much depends upon the nature and extent of the changes that unfold under the Blair government's programme. Direct changes to the constitutional role of the Prime Minister or of the Cabinet seem unlikely. But if, for example, electoral reform were to enhance the prospect of coalition government or if there were to be a decisive move towards federalism then there could be indirect yet profound consequences for the core executive, including the Prime Minister and Cabinet. At the same time, both flexibility and the force of tradition are likely to remain powerful features of the British system. History may yet provide its inspiration and the premiership of, say, Lloyd George could turn out to be a convenient model. Such could be the case if constitutional (or other) changes were to render incompatible the marriage of a more presidential, executive-orientated premiership with the day-to-day demands of party leadership. It is improbable but not impossible.

References

Alderman, R. K. (1995) 'A defence of frequent ministerial turnover', *Public Administration*, 73, pp. 497–512.
Barberis, P. (1996) *The Elite of the Elite: Permanent Secretaries in the British Higher Civil Service* (Aldershot: Dartmouth).

Benn, T. (1981) *Arguments for Democracy* (London: Jonathan Cape).

Berrill, K. (1980) 'Strength at the centre – the case for a prime minister's department', *Stamp Memorial Lecture* (London).

Blake, R. (1975) *The Office of Prime Minister* (London: Oxford University Press).

Brazier, R. (1991) *Constitutional Reform: Reshaping the British Political System* (Oxford: Oxford University Press).

Burch, M. and Holliday, I. (1996) *The British Cabinet System* (London: Prentice Hall/Harvester Wheatsheaf).

Crossman, R. H. S. (1963) Introduction to Walter Bagehot's: *The English Constitution* (London: Fontana).

Donoughue, B. (1987) *Prime Minister: The Conduct of Policy under Harold Wilson and James Callaghan* (London: Jonathan Cape).

Dorril, S. and Ramsay, R. (1991) *Smear! Wilson and the Secret State* (London: Fourth Estate).

Dowding, K. (1995) 'Model or metaphor? A critical review of the policy network approach', *Political Studies*, 43, pp. 136–58.

Foley, M. (1993) *The Rise of the British Presidency* (Manchester: Manchester University Press).

Giddings, P. (1995) 'Prime minister and cabinet' in Shell, D. and Hodder-Williams, R. (eds), *Churchill to Major: the British Prime Ministership since 1945* (London: Hurst and Co.), pp. 30–70.

Henderson, N. (1984) *The Private Office* (London: Weidenfeld and Nicolson).

Hennessy, P. (1986) *Cabinet* (Oxford: Blackwell).

Hennesy, P. (1995) *The Hidden Wiring: Unearthing the British Constitution* (London: Victor Gollancz).

James, S. (1999) *British Cabinet Government*, 2nd edn (London: Routledge).

Jones, G. W. (1985a) 'The prime minister's aides' in King, A. (ed.) *The British Prime Minister*, 2nd edn (Basingstoke: Macmillan), pp. 72–95.

Jones, G. W. (1985b) 'The prime minister's power' in King, A. (ed.) *The British Prime Minister*, 2nd edn (Basingstoke: Macmillan), pp. 195–220.

Kavanagh, D. and Seldon, A. (1999) *The Powers Behind the Prime Minister: The Hidden Influence of Number Ten* (London: HarperCollins).

King, A. (1981) 'The rise of the career politician in Britain – and its consequences' *British Journal of Political Science*, 11, pp. 249–85.

King, A. (1991) 'The British prime ministership in the age of the career politician', *West European Politics*, 14(2), pp. 25–47.

Lee, J. M., Jones, G. W. and Burnham, J. (1998) *At the Centre of Whitehall: Advising the Prime Minister and Cabinet* (Basingstoke: Macmillan).

Linklater, M. and Leigh D. (1986) *Not with Honour: The Inside Story of the Westland Scandal* (London: Sphere Books).

Morgan, K. O. (1997) *Callaghan: A Life* (Oxford: Oxford University Press).

Office of Public Service (1998) *Civil Service Yearbook 1998* (London: The Stationery Office).

Pimlott, B. (1992) *Harold Wilson* (London: HarperCollins).

Rhodes, R. A. W. (1995) 'From prime ministerial power to core executive', in Rhodes, R. A. W. and Dunleavy, P. (eds) *Prime Minister, Cabinet and Core Executive* (Basingstoke: Macmillan), pp. 11–37.

Rhodes, R. A. W. and Marsh, D. (1992) 'Policy networks in British politics', in Marsh, D. and Rhodes, R. A. W. (eds), *Policy Networks in British Government* (Oxford: Clarendon), pp. 1–26.

Riddell, P. (1993) *Honest Opportunism: The Rise of the Career Politician* (London: Hamish Hamilton).

Rose, R. (1991a) 'Prime ministers in parliamentary democracies', *West European Politics*, 14(2) pp. 9–24.

Rose, R. (1991b) 'The political economy of cabinet change', in Vibert, F. (ed.), *Britain's Constitutional Future* (London: IEA), pp. 45–72.

Smith, M. J. (1999) *The Core Executive in Britain* (Basingstoke: Macmillan).

Thomas, G. P. (1998) *Prime Minister and Cabinet Today* (Manchester: Manchester University Press).

Willetts, D. (1987) 'The role of the Prime Minister's Policy Unit', *Public Administration*, 65, pp. 443–54.

2

Ministers and Civil Servants

KEVIN THEAKSTON

The relationship between ministers and civil servants is the central hinge of the system of government in Britain – the point where the democratically-elected and the permanent elements in Whitehall come together, the vital connecting link between decision and action, accountability and expertise, change and continuity. This chapter tries to put the relationship between politicians and bureaucrats in Whitehall into historical perspective by discussing developments over the post-1945 period as a whole, starting with the so-called 'consensus' period, then looking at the long years of Conservative rule under Mrs Thatcher and John Major, and finally discussing how the minister/civil service relationship appears to be working out under 'New Labour'. But first, to set the scene, let us hear the top mandarins speak for themselves.

How the Real 'Sir Humphreys' See It

The popular BBC television comedy series *Yes, Minister* and *Yes, Prime Minister* (perhaps now rather dated but still fun to watch), in their depiction of life inside the government machine, created a memorable image of the scheming Sir Humphrey Appleby manipulating the innocent Jim Hacker and pulling the strings behind the scenes, all the time furthering the bureaucracy's own agenda and interests. Not surprisingly, when they lift the lid (in lectures or articles) on the work of government, senior civil servants tend strongly to deny that the *Yes, Minister* version is anywhere near the truth. 'In the Treasury, ministers drive the main policy agenda', insists Lord (Terry) Burns, Permanent Secretary of that department 1991–98. 'In the end the Chancellor decides – just like it says in the textbooks' (Burns, 1994, p. 56). As Burns describes it, 'there is an implicit contract between ministers and officials when it comes to making decisions and implementing them':

> Ministers set the policy agenda, often with help from officials, and make decisions within it. They seek, and officials offer, advice within the framework of this policy agenda. Officials are free to make observations about the likely results of policy proposals and to argue vigorously about the merits of various options until the point that the decision is made. Once a decision is made, it is implemented and defended equally vigorously. In return for the privilege of being involved in the debate and having a chance to put their views, it is expected that officials subsequently keep their private views to themselves. And ministers take responsibility for the decisions they have taken. (Burns, 1994, pp. 57–8)

Researching the Treasury and social policy in the 1990s, Parry and Deakin (1997, p. 3) were, indeed, impressed by 'the centrality of ministerial personality and responsibility. Theories of bureaucratic power would not readily predict the old-fashioned strict constitutionalism that we encountered. Within the Treasury, there is an active search for a policy steer from [ministers]'. 'In the end, we can't do anything without ministerial support', a Treasury spending official remarked, giving an insight into how the system works in practice:

> We don't go to ministers and say, 'what do you want?' We see ministers on various bits of business and you pick up the music – you get a feel for what they want and what their aims are. The present ministers' [in the Major government] social view is that they're not interested in equity, in people at the bottom. That is their view and as good civil servants that's our social view too. We don't invent a social policy – but we interpret it. (Private information)

In day-to-day Treasury–spending department relations, in fact, there is a strong presumption against the personal involvement of ministers (which can raise the stakes), and in favour of business being settled at official level where possible, though with ministerial aims and interests being taken fully into account and with the politically-sensitive matters (not necessarily 'important' in a conventional sense) ending up on ministers' desks (Thain and Wright, 1995, pp. 132, 189, 207).

As Sir Brian Cubbon (Permanent Secretary at the Northern Ireland Office 1976–79, and then at the Home Office 1979–88) put it, 'the implied arrangement is that we [the civil servants], with our experience, will help you, ministers, make the system work in pursuance of your political aims, and you tell us about everything you think and do and listen to us'. Ministers decide on policy, and civil servants advise, but Cubbon maintains that

> policy-making is not a satisfactory term for describing the daily role of ministers. I suspect that it was invented by civil servants to flatter ministers into thinking that ministers' contributions are more coherent and rational than they really are. Ministers think in terms of ideas and prejudices and headlines, rather than policies. Furthermore 'advice' suggests a distancing of the two roles. In practice, civil servants take part in a dialogue with ministers which is often about the political and media handling of the matter as well as the merits. Would it not be better, minister, to get some bad news out of the way, just before some better news? (Cubbon, 1993, p. 9)

The civil service role is not to frustrate ministers, but to 'act as an apolitical and objective ballast when [they] are in full sail'. 'We widen the *objective* base on which are made what must inevitably be *political* decisions. We present arguments and reality to the fevered ambitions and fears of politicians. We concentrate on "what *can* happen", *not* "what *ought* to happen"' (Cubbon, 1993, p. 10).

The mandarins are clear-eyed about their political masters. 'Because the average tenure of a Minister is so short', says Sir Geoffrey Holland (Permanent Secretary at Employment 1988–93 and at Education 1993–4), 'all want to make their mark':

> As one once said to me: 'You are running a marathon; I am in a 100 metre sprint'. So they must introduce – and introduce very quickly – something new, their own initiative, the development for which...they will claim personal credit...This leads to Ministers often ignoring previous Ministers' 'things' (while playing lip service to them), to the all too evident tendency to pull up tender plants before they have taken root, to

lack of interest in anything other than 'my thing' and, not least, to an obsession with the short term. Further, it leads to a confusion between 'presentation' and 'announcements' and action and real effect. It is touching to see Ministers' faith that when they have announced something at the Dispatch Box, it has happened. Of course it has not. The job is only just beginning for Sir Humphrey and the civil servants. (Holland, 1995, p. 42)

All the same, Holland is adamant that Whitehall needs 'Ministers with ideas ... To some it might seem like heaven on earth to have a Minister who has no ideas and is endlessly open to the suggestions or recommendations of officials. But that is not the case ... The burden of responsibility becomes too great if the traffic in ideas is all one way. Officials need stimulus; need leadership; need, on occasion, conflict. No Department will do well unless that flow of ideas comes, day in and day out' (Holland, 1995, p. 43). Lord (Robin) Butler – Cabinet Secretary and Head of the Civil Service 1988–97 – makes a similar point. 'The civil service can keep the show on the road, but if it's to act in a really purposeful sort of way, only politicians can inject that' (Mann, 1995, p. 22). Privately, many of the top officials were dismayed that John Major's government seemed to have little clue about what it wanted to do (except continue in office) and were frustrated by ministerial indecision, the lack of a firm lead, and governmental losses of nerve in relation to backbench protest and external buffeting. 'It's like an orchestra', said Butler in an easily-broken code. 'Unless there's a conductor giving a bit of expression, zest and direction to it, they'll go on playing the notes, but it won't be music.'

The Post-War 'Corridors of Power'

There is a definite sense in the post-war period – from the 1940s up to the 1970s – of the civil service as a powerful estate of the realm. From Attlee to Churchill, through Eden, Macmillan, Douglas-Home, Wilson, Heath and Callaghan, the mandarinate provided a continuous thread running through changing governments, privy to the secrets of all of them, trusted advisers to successive Prime Ministers and ministers from both the main parties. Behind the scenes, some top officials, such as Norman Brook – Cabinet

Secretary for sixteen years (1947–62) – exerted more real power than many of the transient elected ministers. The civil service had had a 'good war'; well into the 1950s it seemed to be an enduring and self-confident (even complacent) institution whose place in society was beyond question, though from the 1960s onwards outside critics and would-be reformers were pushing it off its pedestal. Looking back on this period, a former senior insider likened the permanent secretaries to country-house butlers, referring to the idea of the civil service as the permanent inhabitants of the 'stately home' of government, greeting the new tenants (ministers), being the utterly discreet, indispensable and efficient 'servants', but essentially running the 'house' as they wanted (private information).

Former Labour MP John Garrett once characterised the position since the Second World War in the following way:

> There have been two very radical governments which came in with very clear and novel agendas, one was the Attlee Government in 1945 and the other was the Thatcher Government in 1979. They ... implemented those programmes and ... the Civil Service ... found itself basically in a position of taking orders or executing decisions which had been taken by a Government. In the intervening period, in the 1950s, 1960s, 1970s, the so-called years of consensus politics, it was essentially the Civil Service machine which was managing a relatively stable political picture and ministers tended to be carried by that machine with their agendas fixed by their departments.

In other words, the picture is of a 'normal' period in which officials played a large role in making policy, and 'exceptional' periods in which new governments have had very clear agendas of their own and forced a change of direction. Garrett's argument is, however, open to the objection that the so-called consensus policies may in fact have been just as much the result of conscious political decisions by ministers as the so-called radical policy departures (TCSC, 1993, qs. 286–7).

In the consensus years, the civil service was certainly a powerful force for continuity – the 'automatic pilot', as Churchill once described Sir John Anderson. 'We attempted to moderate the more extravagant demands of ministers' was how Lord Sherfield (Sir Roger Makins, deputy head of the Foreign Office and head of the Treasury in the 1950s) loftily recalled his time in Whitehall (Paxman, 1991, p. 132). The politicians had to be brought face to face with 'ongoing reality', as Sir William Armstrong (Permanent Secretary of the Treasury 1962–8, and Head of the Civil Service 1968–74) put it, explaining that ministers decided the questions officials put to them arising out of the then-dominant neo-Keynesian economic policy framework; they did not question the framework itself (Theakston, 1999, p. 179). Two images of the mandarins' role stand out from this period. One is Labour minister Hugh Dalton's description of them as 'congenital snag-hunters', highlighting the difficulties and problems in following a particular policy (Theakston, 1992, p. 18). The other is Sir Edward Bridges' (Head of the Civil Service 1945–56) acknowledgement of the existence of well-established 'departmental views' shaping the advice given to ministers and affecting the implementation of policy (Bridges, 1950).

Permanent secretaries of the 1980s and 1990s often comment privately that, in the 1950s and 1960s – when they started their careers – the topmost civil servants were important policy figures in their own right, carrying more clout than their successors. The formidable Dame Evelyn Sharp (head of the Ministry of Housing and Local Government 1955–66) frankly admitted that she saw part of her role as to 'act as a brake to the Minister', arguing that a new minister had to 'learn the limits within which he can operate' and that a permanent secretary should produce initiatives of his or her own. For many years, 'the Dame' was a dominating force in the fields of local government and planning policy (Theakston, 1999, ch. 6). Sir Frank Lee, head of the Treasury 1960–2, also stands out as the key official involved in persuading the Macmillan government to apply for membership of the European Community. And another senior and controversial Treasury official, 'Otto' Clarke – 'ruthless in the pursuit of effective solutions, ruthless in the demolition of soft advice, soft decisions, soft colleagues and soft Ministers', according to Lord (Douglas) Allen, former Head of the Civil Service (Clarke, 1978, p. x) – was the driving force behind the important Public Expenditure Survey Committee (PESC) public expenditure planning reforms of the 1960s.

The system was then much more hierarchical and centralised than today. In some departments (most notoriously, the Home Office), up to the mid-1960s, all the advice and recommendations going to the secretary of state were channelled through the permanent secretary – an arrangement which effectively filtered out dissenting views and alternative ideas held lower down the ladder (Barberis, 1996, pp. 38–9). And to a much greater extent than was the case in later decades, there was an elaborate structure of high-powered interdepartmental official-level committees, meeting to go over the ground together before issues were put to ministers and active in developing a 'Whitehall view'. William Armstrong described decision-making inside government as 'a subtle mixture. We [officials] do the thinking. The politicians contribute imagination, intuition, ideas and perhaps above all the *will*' (Theakston, 1999, p. 179). But Sir Edward Bridges was clear that a permanent civil service provided 'a continuity of knowledge and experience' – it embodied institutional memory – and that ministerial ideas had to be tested against the 'practical philosophy' of 'the storehouse of departmental experience' (Bridges, 1950, p. 19).

This is not to deny that all the evidence is that the civil service served post-war Labour and Conservative governments with equal loyalty and efficiency, changing course as necessary when one set of ministers took over the reins of power from another (Theakston, 1995, ch. 1). That successive governments were able to make major policy changes suggests that either the mandarins cooperated fully with ministers, in textbook fashion, or that the political will stressed by William Armstrong could indeed successfully overcome any bureaucratic resistance or sluggishness. In all governments, of course, Whitehall insiders and well-informed observers could draw up two lists: one of those ministers who ran their departments, and the second of those ministers run by their departments (Sampson, 1962, p. 235). But 'except in unusual circumstances', argued Roy Jenkins (Labour Chancellor of the Exchequer in the 1960s), a minister did not have to 'batter his head against a brick wall of determined departmental opposition. If he knows what he wants to do he will not in general have much difficulty in getting his policy carried out' (Theakston, 1992, p. 32). Tony Crosland, another Labour minister, privately told the Fulton Committee of his concerns about the 'political loneliness' of ministers (the need to supplement civil service policy advice with more politically-oriented advice) and about Whitehall's 'tendency to sceptical inertia' (PRO, 1966b), but maintained that 'it's a great mistake to think there's a continuous battle going on' (Theakston, 1992, p. 17).

Richard Crossman's famous *Diaries of a Cabinet Minister* do, of course, give just that impression – 'already I realise the tremendous effort it requires not to be taken over by the Civil Service' (Crossman, 1975, p. 21). Crossman's evidence, as a serving minister, to the Fulton Committee was sensational and damning:

> The higher Civil Service was a coherent and cohesive oligarchy presenting Ministers with narrow alternatives of choice. He was struck by the importance of official committees of which Ministerial committees were mere shadows. The official committees were the effective bodies, working in secret from Ministers. The Cabinet was in danger of becoming what Bagehot had described the Crown, 'the dignified element of the constitution'. The minutes of Cabinet committee meetings recorded not what had been said but what ought to have been said, based on Ministers' briefs; that was necessary because what Ministers said in the absence of their official advisers would often sound like ill-informed rubbish...A Minister had no secrets. His telephone conversations were listened into by his officials.... Civil servants had no loyalty to their Ministers; their loyalty was to their colleagues in the Civil Service, to whom they passed on information about their Minister. For instance, as Minister of Housing and Local Government he had found that his officials passed on everything about what he was planning, including his consultation with his allies in the Cabinet, to the Treasury, that is, from the point of view of a Minister of Housing and Local Government, to the enemy. All this had the effect of separating a Minister from his colleagues, and of preventing any united front of Ministers to counter-balance the united front of civil servants. He did not blame civil servants for the way that they operated. He had no evidence that civil servants treated Labour Ministers differently from Conservative Ministers. If there was a conspiracy it was a conspiracy of the permanent against the impermanent; no doubt civil servants felt that they had to behave as they did in order to preserve a departmental continuity in the face of frequent changes of minister. (PRO, 1966c)

Against this sort of conspiratorial view of how the system operated against radical ministers (which became almost taken for granted on both the Labour left and the Conservative right in the 1970s and 1980s), it is worth quoting another ministerial verdict from inside the 1964–70 Labour Cabinet:

> Take the fear that many socialists still feel that the Civil Service will resist socialist legislation. Broadly speaking I would say that it is quite untrue to believe that Whitehall, if you are firmly committed to anything, would try to stop you doing it. It is my experience that if they know you are determined to do any simple, easily understood, specific measure – they

will do it for you with knobs on. Civil Servants are careful people. They have re-insurance policies, they study the Opposition as carefully as they study the Government and that is why they are always ready for you when you cease to be Opposition and become Government. My Ministry had been at work for months on a contingency plan for carrying out the [relevant] section of our manifesto... So what most Socialists still imagine will be the main problem facing the Labour Government simply is not a problem. Of course your Civil Servants will argue about the exact way of putting your plans into practice. That is their job and any politician should be grateful. But as for the idea that Whitehall is afraid of the jolt caused by a change of Government and is against the prospect of new men with new ideas, I can only give my impression that Civil Servants not only acquiesce in the inevitable – some of them are glad at the prospect of a shake-up in the political stratosphere and quite often complain that the new man does not have enough new ideas. (Fabian Society, 1967, pp. 80–1)

The author of this analysis was also none other than Richard Crossman! Crossman was a notorious intellectual gadfly, who no doubt believed what he said at the time he was saying it. Politically, he was a bull-in-a-china-shop figure. An important – but often overlooked – theme of his diaries is how clever and determined ministers (such as Crossman...) can in the end triumph over White-hall opposition. After he left office in 1970, however, he was adamant that Labour's mistakes and failures could not be blamed on the civil service. Scapegoating the mandarins was an unconvincing alibi. The real problem, he argued, was that the party's policy planning before winning office had been inadequate and that the government did not have a clear enough sense of direction. At the end of the day, the politicians were in charge.

The Mandarins under the Conservatives 1979–97: Politicised Poodles?

'Whitehall will always respond readily to clear direction combined with sustained pressure', insisted Kate Jenkins, one-time head of the Prime Minister's Efficiency Unit, describing the impact of the Conservative government elected in 1979 upon the civil service machine (Jenkins, 1992, p. 212). The Thatcherites scorned Whitehall's consensus outlook and the departmental orthodoxies, and were determined to assert their political authority over the mandarinate. 'Unless we break out of the civil service straightjacket now, we'll never get another chance to rule,' an incoming minister was quoted as saying in May 1979. 'It is beginning to look to many of us that civil servants are a breed who really believe they run the country, and that all they've got to do is to knock new ministers into shape' (Summerton, 1980, p. 402). But it was Mrs Thatcher who was to do the 'knocking into shape' in Whitehall, by virtue of her long tenure in office, her 'conviction-politics' approach to government, and the far-reaching managerial and organisational changes she set in train.

There could be no doubt about the power relationship between politicians and officials, or about who was calling the shots, in the 1980s and 1990s. The insiders' joke about the *Yes, Minister* television programmes was that ministers regarded them as amusing comedy, civil servants regarded them as hilarious farce, and the man in the street regarded them as documentaries. However, the myth that the real-world Sir Humphreys could always resist change or 'see off' elected ministers who had radical intentions and clear priorities was finally laid to rest in the 1980s. But while Conservative politicians maintained that they were simply upholding the constitutional norm of political/ministerial supremacy, outside critics and the opposition parties became increasingly concerned about just what was happening inside the Whitehall 'village community'.

Post-war prime ministers, on the whole, were content to leave civil servants to run the civil service – Mrs Thatcher was not. The allegations that the close personal interest she took in senior appointments and promotions, together with the fact that by the end of her lengthy premiership she had appointed virtually all the officials in the top ranks, meant that she had 'politicised' the higher civil service were understandable but exaggerated. The way in which she made top Whitehall appointments was arguably within the bounds of what an ambitious, active and wilful Prime Minister could properly do in the British system (Richards, 1997, p. 36). In fact, some of her supporters felt that she did not go far enough and were disappointed by the failure to bring in large numbers of politically-committed business outsiders. Rather than a crudely partisan politicisation effect, however, there was a socialisation effect in the sense that a whole generation of officials learned that advancement went to the 'can-do' types – tough-minded managers who could get things done and deliver results – while the traditional, cautious, 'wait-a-minute' bureaucrats (Sir Peter Kemp's term [Kemp, 1996]) languished. By the 1990s the message had been picked up and John Major could stand back from the process, interfering much less than his predecessor in the machine's selections, though his government did open up more top posts to outside competition. However, his ministers showed little compunction in forcing out even their permanent secretaries if they could not get on with them. In the 1960s there had been uproar when Labour minister Barbara Castle had tried to sack her permanent secretary; in the Major years there was one straight sacking (Sir Peter Kemp, Office of Public Service, in 1992), two early retirements after the officials concerned had fallen out with their secretaries of state (Sir Geoffrey Holland, Education, 1993; Sir Clive Whitmore, Home Office, 1994), and one 'engineered' retirement after a departmental merger (Sir Tim Lankester, Education and Employment, 1995 [see Foster and Plowden, 1996, pp. 231–2]). The execution of Admiral Byng to 'encourage the others' comes to mind (and perhaps future governments would feel that they could follow these precedents?).

'Relations between Ministers and senior officials had never been what the textbooks described – objective, non-political advice from officials on which Ministers superimposed the political element', a leading permanent secretary (Sir Eric Roll) had explained to the Fulton Committee back in 1966. 'Indeed, one of the great strengths of the British Civil Service had been the political consciousness of officials ... [though] there were limits to [this] ... Officials fitted in with Ministers but did not identify with them. There was a reticence in going too far; officials often had an almost word-perfect acquaintance with party manifestos, they were ready to give Ministers advice on political tactics, but were unwilling to go behind overt statements of policy to the underlying value judgements and presuppositions' (PRO, 1966a). In the 1980s, however, this detachment or the 'neutral competence' once expected of the mandarins in advising on and then implementing policy was not enough (Barker and Wilson, 1997, p. 223). Mrs Thatcher wanted one hundred per cent commitment, zealous loyalty and total engagement. The real problem was not the fear that this expectation could pull civil servants into a dangerous over-identification with the government of the day and compromise their ability to switch to serving another party after an election – a danger which was probably overstated, the higher civil service on the whole being clearly concerned to preserve its independence and integrity in this sense (Barker and Wilson, 1997, p. 232). Instead – and probably more damaging to their political masters' interests – was the atrophying of the 'snag-hunting' role, as seen most starkly in the failure to alert ministers to policy disasters-in-the-making like the poll tax (Butler *et al.*, 1994). Perhaps the new breed of 'activist' officials were actually too compliant for ministers' own good?

Although the Thatcherites had, on the political or ideological level, a ferocious attitude towards the mandarin class and what it stood for, it is striking how many Conservative ministers praise in their memoirs the ability and quality of the civil servants who worked for them (e.g. Tebbit, 1989, p. 231). Inevitably, ministerial styles and working methods varied. For instance, Kenneth Clarke tended to focus on only the key issues, was a strong believer in delegation and letting people get on with the job, trusted his civil servants and didn't try to second-guess them. In contrast, Michael Howard was reportedly a workaholic 'details' man, ambitious and insecure, preoccupied by tactics and media opinion, and mistrustful of his officials (using his right-wing special adviser as a 'political rottweiler') (Lewis, 1997). Damaging leaks coming from inside the Home Office testified to civil service disaffection and low morale during Howard's period as Home Secretary. From time to time Number Ten obviously suspected some ministers of 'going native' (Hogg and Hill, 1995, p. 203), and as late as 1995 an internal Home Office report suggested that the traditional 'liberal' 'departmental view' on law and order persisted there (Lewis, 1997, p. 25), but on the whole over the 1980s and 1990s the 'storehouses of departmental experience' became less relevant as Conservative ministers successfully strove to dominate the 'Whitehall village' and overturn departments' conventional policy thinking.

Concerns about 'an unhealthy closeness between Ministers and civil servants' after such a long period of single-party rule, and 'a greater willingness to contemplate actions which are improper' were registered by the all-party Treasury and Civil Service Committee in 1994 (TCSC, 1994, para. 78). The Scott Report on arms to Iraq brought these issues into sharp focus, and in truth what was really disturbing about the picture of contempt for Parliament, and ministerial and official cynicism and dissembling, revealed by Scott was that it showed the government machine working normally. There were legitimate opposition fears that the civil service was coming (or being pushed) too close to serving the political interests of the ruling party. In 1983, for example, the shadowy 'DS19' team set up in the Ministry of Defence by Michael Heseltine, using information from the intelligence services to smear CND (and by association the Labour Party, too), pushed at the bounds of constitutional propriety by involving civil servants in a partisan propaganda campaign in the run up to the general election of that year (Crick, 1997, pp. 245–50). In 1995, with another election looming, Heseltine – now Deputy Prime Minister – again blurred the distinction between government and party with his Coordination and presentation of government policy (EDCP) committee, combining ministers, civil servants and Conservative Party staff, established to handle the 'coordination and presentation' of government policies (i.e. spotting banana skins and attacking Labour). His plan to get officials to set up teams of 'cheerleaders' to champion government policies was vetoed by the Head of the Civil Service (Crick, 1997, pp. 422–4). After prolonged pressure the government finally introduced a new code of conduct for civil servants in 1995, enjoining officials to act with 'integrity, honesty, impartiality and objectivity' in their dealings with ministers, and binding them not to act in a way that is 'illegal, improper, unethical or in breach of constitutional convention' (Theakston, 1995, pp. 182–3), but the doubts and uncertainties about the future of the traditional public service values remained.

'The genie of real ministerial control is out of the bottle', argued Peter Kemp in 1996 (Kemp, 1996). But some commentators (and, privately, some senior mandarins) wondered if the price in terms of diminished governing competence might not be proving too high. In their book, *The State Under Stress* (1996) – widely-read and influential at the top of the civil service itself – Sir Christopher Foster and Francis Plowden argued that the 1980s and 1990s saw the breakdown of the traditional relationship of partnership between ministers and mandarins – what they called the 'Haldane model' of a close, almost symbiotic interrelationship between ministers and their official advisers. Ministers seemed to trust civil servants less and not want to listen to their advice on policy (see also Plowden, 1994). Decisions were increasingly taken in more informal ways (with fewer properly-organised committees with supporting minutes and documentation), often at meetings of ministers and special advisers from which officials were excluded. Civil servants were brought in later, to 'tidy up' and implement what had already been decided – a move towards what Foster and Plowden called the 'Woodrow Wilson model', reflecting American notions of a formal separation between politicians and administrators, with the latter concentrating on implementation. When combined with a programme of large-scale management reorganisation and 'delayering' across the main Whitehall departments – eliminating nearly a quarter of top-level staff between 1994 and 1997 – the worry was that the devaluing of the continuity, experience in depth and more objective approach to policy institutionalised in the civil service threatened to undermine the policy-making capacity of government.

New Labour in the Driving Seat

A newly-appointed middle-ranking minister in the Blair government had an early education in the ways of officialdom when he tried to get a new piece of office equipment. He wanted a 'white board' fixed to his wall, which he could use during meetings to highlight key points, and on which he could write things to remind himself of objectives, decisions and matters to chase up. There was a tremendous bureaucratic fuss. All sorts of objections were raised: it would have to be wiped clean before outside visitors came into the minister's office in case they glimpsed secret information; officials from one section of the department might not want the minister to write on it ideas they were not yet letting officials from other sections of the department know about; maybe curtains would have to be hung in front of the board! 'It's a simple thing I want, isn't it?' protested the bemused politician. 'But, minister', came the reply from his civil servants, '*we* are your white board' (private information).

The official story is that May 1997 represented a textbook 'handover'. The then Head of the Civil Service, Sir Robin Butler said that he was proud that the transition to a new party of government after eighteen years of serving their political opponents had taken place so smoothly. The new Prime Minister sent him a memo after the election expressing his 'gratitude for the quite superlative way in which the Civil Service have handled the first change of Government in this country for 18 years', and pledging that Labour intended to 'sustain and build up the tradition of a professional and impartial Civil Service' (see Theakston, 1998). One new minister reported that 'the fabled civil service machine really is as good as its reputation, a "Rolls Royce" service'; another said he was 'struck by the extent to which the civil service had been diminished and down-sized though still as committed and ingenious as ever' (Bennett, 1997, p. 18).

But in other ways it was more of a mixed story. Sir Robin Butler admitted that there were frictional problems and 'some bumpy moments' (Riddell, 1997). 'The civil service is a bit like a curate's egg', one minister said privately. 'Some bits are brilliant, some are terrible; some are fast, others slow'. A Foreign Office minister explained that his department had experienced a 'culture shock':

> There are some doubts... Change was difficult in terms of our new style. They were very comfortable with the Tories. Eighteen years makes a really comfortable relationship. The civil servants knew exactly when to get out the minister's slippers, as it were, and to pour the glass of whisky. It was that sort of relationship. Therefore, there was an uncertainty as to what was going to happen – some [officials] have been able to live more easily with that, others have found it a challenge they cannot manage, and have been difficult. There have been examples of ambassadors trying to redefine what we've been saying... It will take a little time to work through. (Private information)

Used to working in a fairly informal manner and with small personal staffs in opposition, some ministers were also surprised by the size and complexities of the government machine, and the need for extensive departmental and interdepartmental consultations and clearance. 'I want things to happen in two weeks', exclaimed Northern Ireland Secretary Mo Mowlam. 'It takes two months sometimes. I have to consult other departments. I just can't do it. It drives me mad' (Mowlam, 1998).

Civil service reactions to their new political masters have also been mixed. Some officials were glad to see the back of the Conservatives, looked for a transfusion of energy and new ideas, and welcomed the professional challenge of switching to work for a new government. In some quarters though – notably the Treasury – the initial enthusiasm soon turned to disillusion and frustration, tensions being caused mainly by the working methods and style of new ministers and their political advisers. The well-known civil service 'bounce' of *Yes, Minister* fame was tried out in the Social Security

Department, where officials went ahead with a controversial anti-fraud scheme immediately after the election – the Benefit Integrity Project, agreed in principle in 1996 by the Tories but not implemented by them – and only told the new minister about it a month later, over her mobile phone at Preston railway station, when disabled groups were protesting outside Downing Street! At the Home Office, officials hoping for a change of tone were dismayed that the new ministerial team seemed as strongly committed as the outgoing one to a tough law and order stance and a soaring prison population (*The Economist*, 1998b). At the Northern Ireland Office, Mo Mowlam was plagued by damaging leaks apparently coming from disgruntled officials opposed to her policies. And there were reports that some senior Foreign Office officials, disliking Robin Cook and viewing his 'ethical' foreign policy with cynicism, were privately pleased to see him damaged by the political storm over his outsting of the diary secretary in his private office and claims that he had considered appointing his mistress to the job. The Sandline/arms-to-Sierra Leone affair further strained relations between Foreign Office ministers and the diplomats, and raised questions about the running of the FCO, as Cook appeared to distance himself from alleged staff failures. (The official inquiry pointed to 'cock up' not 'conspiracy' by blaiming failures of communication and management, staff overload, and diplomats' lack of understanding of domestic political sensitivities [Legg, 1998].)

Another problem area has been Whitehall's media operation where, for a government committed to freedom-of-information reform, New Labour has had an almost unhealthy obsession about control of information, 'presentation' and 'spin doctoring'. The Prime Minister's Press Secretary, Alistair Campbell – probably one of the government's half-dozen most influential figures – oversaw a tremendous centralisation of communications and briefing which, in many ways, is pretty sensible in the modern media environment. But there has been controversy over the reorganisation of the Government Information Service and of the number of departmental heads of information (at the latest count, nine) forced out after clashing with their ministers, or at least failing to establish the sort of good working relationship required in that crucial post. One of them – Jill Rutter, formerly of the Treasury – argued that civil servants were 'in denial' over Labour's developing politicisation of this part of Whitehall, and the Commons Public Administration

Select Committee split along party lines when it reported on the issue (Select Committee on Public Administration, 1998). Cabinet Secretary Sir Richard Wilson told MPs that, as a political appointee, Campbell was more able than a neutral career civil servant could be 'to present policies in a political context', but that it would be wrong for him to 'go over the top and attack the Opposition with bricks and bottles'. However, the difficulties in establishing and maintaining clear boundaries between party and government roles in this area – between 'information' and 'propaganda' – could well continue to plague the government (Franklin, 1998).

Although some Labour politicians, during their years in opposition, had talked darkly about the 'politicisation' of the civil service by the Conservatives, the Blair leadership was adamant that Labour had no 'hit list' of senior officials they wanted to remove (Mandelson and Liddle, 1996, p. 248). However, the Permanent Secretary at Transport – Sir Patrick Brown, a man closely associated with Conservative privatisation policies – took early retirement when his department was merged into John Prescott's new 'super-ministry', and a number of other long-serving permanent secretaries have also left, including Terry Burns, head of the Treasury and one of the architects of Tory economic policies in the 1980s and 1990s, who had never properly meshed with Gordon Brown's team. There were also claims that some senior officials at the Department of Trade and Industry (DTI) were moved because Labour ministers were finding it hard to work with them. On the other hand, some key figures from the previous 'regime' have prospered under the new one: Michael Howard's former permanent secretary, Sir Richard Wilson, is the new Cabinet Secretary, and John Major's former press secretary, Gus O'Donnell, was picked by Gordon Brown to become the Treasury's top economist and head of the government economic service.

The real problem, some Labour insiders believed, was 'thought colonisation' or the development of a 'Conservative mindset', which had affected Whitehall's policy values and ways of operating. For instance, one described some DTI officials as being 'completely Heseltined – they want to go out and marketise everything... they got encultured by the Conservatives' (private information). 'I felt some [civil servants] found it difficult to believe there'd been a change of government', one minister privately complained about some parts of his department. 'They had an agenda and we had to change agendas, and sometimes we had to change personnel to change agendas – and that's not easy in the civil service. I had to complain to the permanent secretary to get changes made.' He went on:

> I would query now – and I didn't before – the neutrality notion: that the civil servants are there, are neutral, and when the government comes in they start implementing their [ministers'] agenda. I don't think that's true... Some of the people that were appointed by the last lot – who were in a very long time – were almost like place-people for them. They had a hell of an agenda, can't see beyond that agenda... and just want to carry on implementing it – and they rebut you at every turn and say, 'you have no option'... [Getting a change of policy] was like going through a swamp, swimming in mud... I had total resistance to that... We need to change the system so that when there's a change of government, it's accepted that you bring a layer of political advice [sic] in, that there's scope to change the top layers of government, like in other countries. (Private information)

While not suggesting that this minister's views are widely shared inside the government, it is significant that other observers have also picked up signs that 'if Whitehall is unable to deliver the goods, ministers will turn increasingly to other advisers, with unpredictable consequences' (*The Economist*, 1998b). Though speculation about moves towards an American-style politicised system (where whole layers of the bureaucracy change when a new President takes office) is exaggerated, Labour ministers will ensure that key posts are not filled by people unsympathetic to their objectives (Cameron, 1998).

'Good civil servants will be useful to Labour ministers' was Peter Mandelson's view before the election. 'When officials speak up to raise difficulties about policy proposals, this should not be dismissed as troublemaking or obstruction. Officials should be encouraged to do this and not be dismissed as "unsound" when they do, because successful policy implementation depends on robust scrutiny and discussion' (Mandelson and Liddle, 1996, pp. 248–9). One minister did indeed report that his 'civil servants set out reservations [about an initiative], but they performed the task they should perform – to say, "Yes, but have you considered these factors?" – and they did that very well.' Some Labour ministers, however, complain that the civil service policy input has been too weak. One had to insist to his staff that he wanted them to play a role in helping to generate policy: 'Don't just say, "yes, minister – you said this, therefore we'll go and do it, come hell or high water". I want an argument with you... I've got some brackets here, fill them in for me' (private information).

Labour has brought in an increased number of political advisers – over 70, compared with 38 under John Major – with a big increase in the Prime Minister's Downing Street staff in particular. Used properly these can reinforce, not subvert, the political impartiality and integrity of the civil service. But in some parts of Whitehall there has been a definite tendency to take decisions in separate political meetings with a clique of these advisers and to keep officials at arm's length. In the Treasury power has been concentrated in the hands of Gordon Brown's political trusties (economic adviser Ed Balls and – until he resigned in early 1999 – chief 'spin doctor' Charlie Whelan), information tightly controlled, and the regular career officials not particularly trusted or listened to. Critics paint a picture of a Chancellor of the Exchequer unable to manage the powerful administrative and intellectual resources of the Treasury machine to his advantage (Pym and Kochan, 1998). On a wider front, there have been doubts that the long-run consequences of the growing power of ministerial personal advisers and spin doctors may not be altogether helpful for the government as a whole and the cause of coherent policy-making:

> Departmental civil servants, of course, owe a loyalty to their minister, whose wishes they would respect. However, this loyalty goes only so far. It does not extend to personal politics, which are professionally off-limits to civil servants. It co-exists with civil servants' loyalty to the government as a whole. Importantly, civil servants' careers are not advanced by being the creatures of individual ministers, but by the contribution they are deemed by their seniors to have made to the collective enterprise of government. For the advisers and the spin-doctors, imported by Mr Blair's ministers in unprecedented numbers into Whitehall, matters are different. Their loyalty is wholly to their minister. He appoints them. He sacks them. If he rises, they rise. If he goes, they go. Their immediate incentive is thus to further the minister's individual cause. They are lured into promoting their man, which usually means rubbishing somebody else's. Their incentive to further the government's long-term cause is more distant. (*The Economist*, 1998a)

New Labour may discover the hard way that there is still merit in the traditional notion of a permanent and neutral career civil service.

Conclusion

New Labour's impact upon Whitehall (particularly over several terms) is likely to be profound. As far as the relationship between ministers and civil servants is concerned we have so far, as it were, only seen the first couple of episodes of the new *Yes, Minister* series. But already it is clear that, under Blair, the machine will be subject to effective ministerial control and direction. Civil service 'sabotage' or 'obstruction' has never been a convincing alibi for the failures of different British governments, and it most emphatically will not be for this one.

How far will the traditional Whitehall model survive in the future? If we think about the minister–civil service relationship as described by the senior mandarins themselves at the start of this chapter, a number of points can be made.

First, the idea of a 'contract' linking ministers and mandarins together in policy making undoubtedly took a severe battering in the 1980s and 1990s – with ministers not looking to their officials for advice and sometimes seeking to evade responsibility for controversial decisions. The argument that the civil service acted as a sort of 'ballast' also no longer seemed credible. The Blair government has made reassuring noises here but in practice – as seen with the over-reliance on political advisers and 'spin doctors' – may not be putting the clock back entirely on the changed policy-making style associated with the Conservatives (Foster and Plowden, 1996).

Second, top civil servants continue to play a key role at the fulcrum between politics and administration by virtue of their expertise in 'making the system work'. Ministers (Conservative and Labour) do seem to look for and to value the traditional mandarin skills – of 'managing the political interface', political nous, and a thorough knowledge of the governmental and parliamentary process.

And finally, the importance of ministers providing a clear sense of policy direction remains a constant: Whitehall *does* need ministers with ideas and to have clearly in mind the purposes of their government. The challenge for the Blair government is to articulate and then maintain that strong sense of purpose.

References

Barberis, P. (1996) *The Elite of the Elite: Permanent Secretaries in the British Higher Civil Service* (Aldershot: Dartmouth).

Barker, A. and Wilson, G. (1997) 'Whitehall's disobedient servants? Senior officials' potential resistance to ministers in British government departments', *British Journal of Political Science*, 27, pp. 223–46.

Bennett, S. (1997) 'First impressions last', *Fabian Review*, September 1997, pp. 18–19.

Bridges, Sir E. (1950) *Portrait of a Profession* (Cambridge: Cambridge University Press).

Burns, Sir T. (1994) 'Some reflections on the Treasury', in Holly, S. (ed.), *Money, Inflation and Employment* (Aldershot: Edward Elgar).

Butler, D., Adonis, A. and Travers, T. (1994) *Failure in British Government* (Oxford: Oxford University Press).

Cameron, S. (1998), 'Whitehall goes to Washington', *Spectator*, 16 May, pp. 23–4.

Clarke, Sir R. (1978) *Public Expenditure, Management and Control* (London: Macmillan).

Crick, M. (1997) *Michael Heseltine: A Biography* (London: Hamish Hamilton).

Crossman, R. (1975) *The Diaries of a Cabinet Minister*, Vol. 1, *Minister of Housing 1964–66* (London: Hamish Hamilton and Jonathan Cape).

Cubbon, B. (1993) 'The Duty of the Professional', in Chapman, R. (ed.), *Ethics in Public Service* (Edinburgh: Edinburgh University Press).

Economist (1998a) 'Rumour, tittle-tattle and gossip', 24 January, p. 34.

Economist (1998b) 'Tony Blair's mighty servant', 21 February, p. 37.

Fabian Society. (1967) *Socialism and Affluence: Four Fabian Essays* (London: Fabian Society).

Foster, C. and Plowden, S. (1996) *The State under Stress* (Buckingham: Open University Press).

Franklin, B. (1998) 'Tough on Soundbites, Tough on the Causes of Soundbites: New Labour and News Management', in J. Stanyer and C. Dobson (eds), *Contemporary Political Studies 1998* (Keele: Political Studies Association).

Hogg, S. and Hill, J. (1995) *Too Close to Call* (London: Little, Brown).

Holland, Sir G. (1995) 'Alas! Sir Humphrey. I knew him well', *Royal Society of Arts Journal*, 5464, November, pp. 39–51.

Jenkins, K. (1992) 'Organisational Design and Development: the Civil Service in the 1980s', in C. Pollitt and S. Harrison (eds), *Handbook of Public Services Management* (Oxford: Blackwell).

Kemp, P. (1996) 'Whitehall's quiet revolution', *The Independent*, 19 February.

Legg, Sir T. (1998) [and Ibbs, Sir R.], *Report of the Sierra Leone Arms Investigation* (London: The Stationery Office).

Lewis, D. (1997) *Hidden Agendas* (London: Hamish Hamilton).

Mandelson, P. and Liddle, R. (1996) *The Blair Revolution* (London: Faber & Faber).

Mann, N. (1995) 'A very civil servant', *New Statesman and Society*, 17 November, pp. 22–3.

Mowlam, M. (1998) Interview in *The Sunday Times*, 22 March.

Parry, R. and Deakin, N. (1997) *The Treasury and Social Policy*, ESRC Briefing (Swindon: Economic and Social Research Council).

Paxman, J. (1991) *Friends in High Places* (Harmondsworth: Penguin).

Plowden, W. (1994) *Ministers and Mandarins* (London: Institute for Public Policy Research).

PRO (1966a) Public Record Office, Fulton Committee papers BA 1/3.

PRO (1966b) Fulton Committee papers BA 1/4.

PRO (1966c) Fulton Committee papers BA 1/6.

Pym, H. and Kochan, N. (1998) *Gordon Brown: The First Year in Power* (London: Bloomsbury).

Richards, D. (1997) *The Civil Service under the Conservatives 1979–1997* (Brighton: Sussex Academic Press).

Riddell, P. (1997) 'Old hand makes light work of political bumps', *The Times*, 29 October.

Sampson, A. (1962) *Anatomy of Britain* (London: Hodder & Stoughton).

Select Committee on Public Administration (1998) *The Government Information and Communication Service*, HC 770, 1997–98.

Summerton, N. (1980) 'A mandarin's duty', *Parliamentary Affairs*, 33, pp. 400–21.

TCSC (1993) Treasury and Civil Service Committee, *The Role of the Civil Service: Interim Report*, HC 390, 1992–93 (London: HMSO).

TCSC (1994) Treasury and Civil Service Committee, *The Role of the Civil Service*, HC 27, 1993–94 (London: HMSO).

Tebbit, N. (1989) *Upwardly Mobile* (London: Futura).

Thain, C. and Wright, M. (1995) *The Treasury and Whitehall* (Oxford: Clarendon Press).

Theakston, K. (1992) *The Labour Party and Whitehall* (London: Routledge).

Theakston, K. (1995) *The Civil Service since 1945* (Oxford: Blackwell).

Theakston, K. (1998) 'New Labour, new Whitehall?', *Public Policy and Administration*, 13, pp. 13–34.

Theakston, K. (1999) *Leadership in Whitehall* (London: Macmillan).

3

The Civil Service: Structure and Management

TONY BUTCHER

Since the early 1980s, the British civil service has been undergoing a radical transformation in its structure and management. There have been significant changes in the structure of the civil service, particularly as a result of the Next Steps programme, market testing, contracting out and privatisation. The management of the civil service has been recast in response to the business-oriented philosophy introduced by the Thatcher and Major governments and the emphasis on customer care set out in the Citizen's Charter. As a result of such developments, the 'old' civil service associated with British government before the election of the Thatcher government in 1979 has been transformed into a 'new' civil service.

What has been the agenda and early impact of the new Labour government on the structure and management of this 'new' civil service? Are we witnessing a continuation of the initiatives of the Thatcher and Major administrations or does Labour have a different programme for the civil service? Before addressing these questions, however, we need to briefly survey the developments which took place in the structure and management of the civil service under the Thatcher and Major governments.

The Civil Service under the Thatcher and Major Governments

The 1980s and 1990s saw a number of significant initiatives involving the structure and management of the civil service. These developments were part of a wider movement from the traditional bureaucratic model of public administration – with its emphasis on efficient and impartial bureaucracy and public accountability – to what has been described as the 'new public management' – with its focus on a more managerial and consumerist approach to the organisation of the public sector. The central doctrines of the new public management consist of an emphasis on cost-cutting and value for money; the disaggregation of public bureaucracies; a management style which emphasises targets, rewards linked to performance and the 'freedom to manage'; the promotion of competition through the use of market-type mechanisms; and a greater focus on the consumers of public services (see, for example, Hood, 1991, pp. 4–5; Rhodes, 1991, p. 1). These ideas had a significant impact on the structure and management of the civil service under the Thatcher and Major governments.

One manifestation of the impact of the new public management on the civil service during the period of the Conservative governments was the increased emphasis on cost-cutting and value for money. A central plank in this approach was the programme of efficiency scrutinies launched in 1979 by the Prime Minister's Efficiency Unit, headed by Sir Derek Rayner. The programme was concerned with uncovering inefficiency and waste in government departments, and continued throughout the 1980s and 1990s. It resulted in substantial savings – by the early 1990s the Efficiency Unit was claiming that cumulative savings as a result of the programme amounted to over £1.5 billion (Theakston, 1995, p. 127). Another important element in the Conservatives' efficiency strategy was the Financial Management Initiative (FMI), introduced by the Thatcher government in 1982, which aimed to improve management in the civil service by emphasising the need for accountable management in government departments, stressing cost awareness and holding individual officials accountable for the costs under their control (on the FMI, see Pyper, 1995, pp. 62–4).

The increased emphasis on efficiency and value for money launched by the Thatcher administration was continued by the Major government in the 1990s. An important development established in 1995 was the requirement that government departments draw up annual efficiency plans spelling out how they intended to stay within the limits of their running costs. In their attempts to improve performance, departments and agencies were expected to make much more use of private sector management techniques such as priority-based cost management, benchmarking and process re-engineering. A major project involving the benchmarking of the performance of Next Steps agencies against the private sector was introduced by the Major government in 1996. Benchmarking was intended to identify best practice and highlight areas where the civil service could learn from other organisations. It was also believed that peer pressure amongst agencies would act as a substitute for the competitive pressure found in the private sector (Saner, 1997).

The promotion of greater efficiency contributed to the dramatic decline in the size of the civil service during the Thatcher and Major years. Civil service numbers were also reduced as a result of the increased emphasis upon the use of information technology, including the Department of Social Security's operational strategy and the computerisation of the PAYE system by the Inland Revenue. Central government became the country's main user of information technology systems, with many civil service procedures moving from clerically-based operations to ones which were information technology-based (Treasury and Civil Service Committee, 1994, para. 253). The departmental senior management reviews launched by the Major government in the mid-1990s also resulted in some striking staffing cuts – for example, the Treasury shed a quarter of its senior staff. By the election of the Blair government in May 1997, the number of civil service staff had fallen to 495 000 from 732 000 at the time of the election of the first Thatcher government, a decline of some 32 per cent.

The most important set of changes in the structure and management of the civil service associated with the Thatcher and Major governments was the Next Steps programme, widely seen as the most ambitious attempt at civil service reform since the pioneering Northcote-Trevelyan Report of the mid-nineteenth century. Introduced in 1988, the Next Steps programme separated the executive and policy-making roles of central government departments, resulting in the creation of a range of semi-autonomous executive agencies, such as the Employment Service and the Vehicle Inspectorate, responsible for the delivery of public services and given managerial flexibilities in matters of recruitment, pay and conditions. Next Steps was concerned with the break-up of departments into executive agencies and policy-making cores – a manifestation of the disaggregation of large bureaucratic organisations associated with the ideas of the new public management. Although launched by the Thatcher government, the programme was dramatically expanded by the Major government, developing to include such key areas of civil service work as the delivery of social security benefits. By the time of the election of the Blair government, three-quarters of the civil service was working in Next Steps agencies or (in the case of the Inland Revenue, Customs and Excise, the Crown Prosecution Service and the Serious Fraud Squad) operating on Next Steps lines. A number of other areas of civil service work were candidates for agency status (for fuller details, see Cabinet Office, 1997c).

The Next Steps initiative was a manifestation of a management style which emphasised the 'freedom to manage' and a perform-ance-based culture. Agency chief executives – on fixed-term con-tracts and with salaries linked to performance – are given a considerable amount of day-to-day freedom from ministerial and departmental supervision. Framework agreements set out the details of an agency's aims and objectives, its relationship with its parent department, including parliamentary accountability, and its financial responsibilities. Agency chief executives are set specified performance targets covering service quality, financial performance, the efficiency with which the service is provided and the throughput of the agency.

Under the Thatcher and Major administrations, the civil service was also exposed to another element of the new public management philosophy – the promotion of competition through the use of market-type mechanisms. Developments in civil service manage-ment in the late 1980s and early 1990s emphasised the contractual approach, involving the separation of the responsibility for deciding what a service should be from the responsibility for delivering it (Harden, 1992, p. 14). Thus Next Steps agencies were given framework documents, annual business plans and medium-term corporate plans which formed 'contracts' between ministers and agency chief executives, specifying agency objectives, finances and flexibilities.

The development of what has been described as 'management by contract' within the civil service through the Next Steps initiative was followed in the early 1990s by a move to 'management of contract', with the introduction of the Major government's mar-ket-testing programme. Launched in 1992, and following closely on the heels of the *Competing for Quality* White Paper published the year before (HM Treasury, 1991), the market-testing programme required Next Steps agencies and government departments to explore whether the best long-term value for money could be achieved through contracting out work to the private sector (Greer, 1994, pp. 59–80). Described by the former Next Steps project manager as a process of 'shopping around' (Treasury and Civil Service Committee, 1993, para. 370), the programme resulted in a large number of civil service activities – including the Inland Revenue's information technology services – being contracted out to private sector organisations. By spring 1996, £3.6 billion of activities had been reviewed, with expected gross annual savings of £720 million (Cabinet Office, 1997a, p. 11).

In addition to market testing, the privatisation of civil service activities was also an important part of the Major government's efficiency agenda. The Major government emphasised its intentions to consider the privatisation of civil service activities when it announced that Next Steps agencies would be considered for sale to the private sector as part of the regular process of agency reviews. Known as the 'prior options' process, the reviews included a consideration of whether a particular activity should be abolished, privatised or contracted out. Initially, agencies were reviewed every three years, although this was later extended to five years. Following such reviews, certain agencies – including the Recruitment and Assessment Services Agency, Chessington Computer Centre and HMSO – were sold to the private sector. The Major government also introduced the Private Finance Initiative (PFI), intended to encourage private sector investment in large-scale public sector projects. One major contract awarded under PFI was the one signed with the Contributions Agency by Andersen Consulting to develop and operate a replacement for the existing National Insurance recording system.

The new public management also emphasises the needs of the consumers – increasingly described as customers – of public services. The centrepiece of attempts to empower the consumer during the 1979–97 period was the Citizen's Charter introduced by the Major government in 1991, and widely viewed as the Prime Minister's attempt to put his own stamp on public sector reform. As well as requiring Next Steps agencies and government departments to provide much more information about services through the publication of service standards and details of performance, the Charter also emphasised the importance of consultation, helpful staff and well-publicised and easily available complaints procedures. Following the launching of the Charter, a number of agencies and departments – including the Benefits Agency, the Employment Service, the Inland Revenue and Customs and Excise – published their own charters or charter service statements. The concept of customer service was also an important element in agency framework documents and business plans, agencies being required to demonstrate that they had arrangements for customer consultation and complaints. The Charter's principles concerning customer orientation had a major impact on the operations and culture of Next Steps agencies and government departments like the Inland Revenue, notably through the setting of performance targets and the publication of information about performance. Many agencies demonstrated significant improvements in customer service. Agencies and departments were also successful in winning the Charter Mark, the award given to organisations which developed excellence in delivering services (see Butcher, 1997).

The principles of the Citizen's Charter and the various initiatives designed to improve management in central government associated with the Thatcher and Major governments could only be successfully delivered with new kinds of information and information systems (Bellamy, 1995, p. 55). Thus the development of both the FMI and the Next Steps programme depended upon the invention of 'new measures of resource use, performance and output as indicators of service quality and . . . customer satisfaction' (Bellamy and Taylor, 1992, p. 37). The Citizen's Charter programme raised significant 'methodological, technological, design and management' questions about the information systems underpinning the programme (Bellamy and Taylor, 1992, p. 34). As a result, government departments invested more heavily in information and communication technology.

A key, but little noticed, element in the Major government's attempt to provide more user-friendly services to the public was its vision of 'electronic government', whereby people would be able to link with government offices from their home television sets or from kiosks in post offices, libraries and shopping centres (Office of Public Service, 1996). This growing recognition of the potential of the new technology in the delivery of public services was epitomised by the setting up of the Central Information Technology Unit within the Cabinet Office to coordinate information technology strategy within central government. By the mid-1990s, information technology was playing a major role in the reinvention of the civil service, emphasising Hood's view of the new technology as one of the 'megatrends' linked with the development of the new public management (1991, pp. 3–4).

Thus, under the Thatcher and Major governments, many of the traditional ideas and practices underpinning the structure and management of the civil service were being gradually replaced by a new set of ideas and practices associated with the new public management. Such developments went far beyond the use of new management techniques: they were part of what one commentator described as 'a new way of thinking about the state' (Ridley, 1995, p. 387). These developments were part of what many saw as a public service 'revolution', with the fragmentation of the civil service, contracting out and the decentralisation of service delivery contributing to what has been described as the 'hollowing out' of the British state (Rhodes, 1997, pp. 100–1).

The changes associated with this new managerialism aroused a great deal of controversy. A major concern was the implications of such developments for the traditional qualities and values of the civil service, critics maintaining that there was a conflict between the business-oriented values of the new managerial civil service and the traditional public service ethos. Some observers referred to the fragmentation of the civil service, arguing that the development of agencies constituted a threat to the unity of the service (see, for example, Chapman, 1997). Another significant issue was that of accountability, with important questions being raised about the implications of Next Steps agencies for the concept of ministerial accountability. Thus critics pointed to the blurring of responsibilities which made it difficult to distinguish between policy and operations, with talk of a 'bureaucratic Bermuda Triangle' in which accountability disappeared (Treasury and Civil Service Committee, 1994, para. 165). Like the Next Steps programme, market testing and contracting out also raised important questions about the future of the unified civil service and the traditional answerability of ministers to Parliament (see, for example, Butcher, 1995, pp. 26–8; Treasury and Civil Service Committee, 1994, paras 73–7). As we shall see in the next section, such criticisms were strongly voiced by the Labour Party during the Thatcher and Major years.

The Labour Party and the Civil Service 1979–97

Given the ancestry of the Next Steps programme – which can be traced back to the ideas on accountable management and 'hiving off' explored twenty years earlier by the Fulton Committee set up by Harold Wilson's Labour government – it could be argued that the various initiatives introduced by the Thatcher and Major governments were the kind of developments which the Labour Party would have welcomed (Willman, 1994, p. 4). The Major government's Citizen's Charter also had links with the Labour Party, the idea being traceable to earlier initiatives developed in York and other Labour-controlled local authorities. According to Willman (1994, p. 4), however, the Labour Party showed little enthusiasm for issues of civil service management and efficiency during the late 1980s and early 1990s. It was the Conservative Party which 'seized the high ground' and set the agenda on civil service reform (Theakston, 1995, p. 194). Even the Labour Party's policy review exercise of the late 1980s – designed to modernise the party and its thinking – gave little attention to civil service reform (Theakston, 1998, p. 14). Writing in 1994, just after the publication of an important White Paper setting out the Major government's plans for the future of the civil service, one commentator observed that Labour seemed to have formed very few thoughts about the civil service (Walker, 1994).

Although the Labour Party agreed with the general objective of civil service efficiency and value for money underpining the efficiency strategy introduced by the Conservatives in the early 1980s (see Theakston, 1992, p. 198), there was much disquiet about the motives behind the Next Steps initiative launched in 1988 (see, for example, Gould, 1991, p. 4). Thus, one leading front-bench spokesman, Roy Hattersley (*HC Debs*, 18 February 1988, col. 1150), called for all-party talks before any radical changes were made to the civil service. Backbench Labour MPs were critical of Next Steps, expressing suspicions of 'creeping privatisation' and suggesting that the initative was a stepping stone to the eventual sale of parts of the civil service (see, for example, *HC Debs*, 20 May 1991, col. 674). One leading Labour Party figure on the civil service, John Garrett, went so far as to describe the initiative as an 'attack' on the service, which would result in its dismemberment, a change in its ethos, and the reduction of parliamentary accountability (Treasury and Civil Service Committee, 1988, pp. 48–55). Labour criticisms of the Next

Steps initiative also included complaints about reduced ministerial accountability. Criticisms about the arrangements for the handling of MPs' enquiries were highlighted by a former Labour minister, Gerald Kaufman, who engaged in a lengthy campaign concerning the practice whereby agency chief executives (and not ministers) answered letters from MPs and responded to parliamentary questions.

Labour concerns about the issue of ministerial accountability were highlighted in 1995 when the Home Secretary, Michael Howard, dismissed the Director General of the Prison Service, Derek Lewis, following the publication of the critical Learmont Report on prison security. The affair – which led to Labour Party calls for the Home Secretary's resignation – concerned the extent of ministerial involvement in the day-to-day operations of the Prison Service, and highlighted the problem of defining the dividing line between 'operational' and 'policy' matters in Next Steps agencies. Labour felt that the dividing line between prisons' operations and policy was not clear enough, one press report saying that Labour was considering removing agency status from the Prison Service and reincorporating it within the Home Office (Halligan, Wighton and Peston, 1997; see also Lewis's own account of the affair in Lewis, 1997).

Another Next Steps agency which attracted Labour Party criticism was the Child Support Agency (CSA), established in 1993 to operate the system for assessing, collecting and, where necessary, enforcing child support maintenance. The CSA was widely admonished for long delays in deciding maintenance orders, slowness in responding to enquiries and making too many errors in assessments. At one stage, Labour shadow ministers were reported to be considering the abolition of the agency (Theakston, 1998, p. 27).

Despite such misgivings about the Next Steps initiative, however, by the time of the Major government, Labour saw 'no principled reason' why parts of the civil service, particularly those performing well-established and relatively non-controversial functions, should not exist as semi-autonomous agencies. Labour's position on Next Steps was that it would take a 'pragmatic attitude' to agencies: there might be some cases where the agency initiative needed reversing and some where new agencies could be established (Gould, 1991, p. 4). Some Labour MPs, notably those on the House of Commons Treasury and Civil Service Committee, became strong supporters of the agency concept (Giddings, 1995, p. 226). The Committee itself worked very hard to develop the non-partisan nature of the Next Steps initiative, stressing the view that it was always possible to change the objectives of an agency's framework agreement (Giddings, 1995, p. 63; Treasury and Civil Service Committee, 1990, para. 20).

The flexibility of agency framework agreements was acknowledged in 1991 by Labour's Shadow Chancellor of the Exchequer, John Smith (1991, pp. 521–22), who observed that a new government could change the framework documents controlling agencies 'in line with its purposes'. This stance was echoed three years later by another Labour shadow minister, who suggested that new rules should be promulgated in revised framework documents, setting out performance in terms of outputs – particularly customer service – as well as inputs (Meacher, 1994). By 1995, Labour's shadow minister for public services was stating that most Next Steps agencies were 'working reasonably well' and that a future Labour government would want to maintain them (Foster, 1996, p. 261). A year later, one of Tony Blair's major policy advisers stated that in many cases agencies were 'sharper instruments' with which to achieve governmental aims than the machinery they replaced, although more ministerial supervision might be required in other cases (Mandelson and Liddle, 1996, pp. 251–2).

However, as Hennessy (1993, p. 3) has observed, the bipartisanship which existed on civil service management reforms by the early 1990s was lost as a result of the Competing for Quality initiative. Although fairly neutral about the Thatcher government's concept of Next Steps agencies, the Labour Party was much more critical of the Major government's initiatives on market testing, contracting out and privatisation. Labour's reaction to the Competing for Quality initiative was very hostile. Unlike the Major government, Labour did not see these developments as an attempt to improve quality, but as a 'crude exercise in cost competition', and called for a moratorium on the market-testing programme in order that there could be a proper evaluation of its costs and benefits (Mowlam, 1993, quoted in Theakston, 1998, p. 30). Labour described the market-testing exercise as representing 'another major step along the road to the dissolution of a national civil service' and expressed concern about the public and parliamentary accountability of private contractors carrying out work formerly performed by civil servants under ministerial direction (*HC Debs*, 4 November 1993, cols. 527–28).

In 1994, however, just before he became Labour Party leader, Tony Blair (1994, p. 7), stated that it was valid to introduce market mechanisms into the running of the public services. A year later, in an important change of emphasis from earlier policy statements, the party's spokesman on the civil service declared that it was not the managerial reforms – such as market testing – that were endangering the essential qualities of the civil service, but 'the particular way in which they are being carried out' (*HC Debs*, 25 March 1995, col. 561). It was becoming clear that, under a Labour government, some form of contracting out would remain a management tool available to the civil service (see, for example, *FDA News*, July 1995, p. 4).

By the time of the 1997 general election, market testing had been accepted by the Labour Party leadership. In the run-up to the election, two of Tony Blair's policy advisers – one of whom was subsequently appointed a minister attached to the Cabinet Office – declared that the civil service was 'not a paragon of administrative virtue' and 'should not have a monopoly over the delivery of public service'. There was room for private sector involvement (Mandelson and Liddle, 1996, pp. 252–4). As one comentator was later to observe, Labour's acceptance of market testing was the 'inevitable consequence' of the party's embrace of the market and its acceptance of tight controls on public spending (Theakston, 1998, p. 30). It was also reported just before the 1997 election that a future Labour government would set up a review of the scope for privatisation, including the possible sale of such Next Steps agencies as Companies House, the Land Registry and the Ordnance Survey (Grice and Hellen, 1997).

John Major's other significant contribution to the reform of civil service structure and management was, of course, the Citizen's Charter programme. When the Charter was launched in 1991, Labour had accused the Conservatives of stealing their idea, the concept of the Charter having been pioneered by Labour-controlled local authorities through such initiatives as customer service contracts. There was strong support for the customer orientation within the Labour Party, which published its own Charter just before the Major government published the Citizen's Charter. A Labour front-bench spokesman was later to describe the idea of a charter as essential (*HC Debs*, 15 November 1991, col. 1347). In the run-up to the 1997 general election, the Labour Party subsequently promised a 'renewed' Citizen's Charter which would give the Charter 'more bite', and which would develop strategies for publishing individual charters and providing information. Labour also promised to initiate a 'cultural revolution' in complaints procedures by using complaints as an opportunity to improve the design and delivery of service (Public Service Committee, 1997, pp. 49–52).

The Impact of the Blair Government

Following its victory in the May 1997 general election, the Blair government inherited a civil service which, under the Thatcher and Major administrations, had been subjected to radical change in both its structure and management. Since the election of the first Thatcher government in 1979, the size of the civil service had been reduced by nearly one-third. Three-quarters of the service had been hived off to semi-autonomous agencies or worked in departments or offshoots of departments which operated on Next Steps principles. There was an increased emphasis on the delegation of managerial responsibility, the setting of targets and performance measurement. In addition to the impact of the new managerialism, the management and culture of the civil service had also changed as a result of the advent of consumerist approaches through the Citizen's Charter programme. Writing in the mid-1990s, one commentator observed that it would be very difficult for any future government to reverse the most substantial reforms introduced by the Thatcher and Major governments (Pyper, 1995, p. 185).

In the event, the election of the Blair government in 1997 has seen a continuing emphasis on civil service efficiency, value for money and the customer orientation. The need to improve the efficiency and management of the civil service is a key feature of the Labour government's approach to public sector reform. Echoing its Conservative precedessors, the newly-elected government stated at the very beginning of its term of office that it wanted to see public services which were efficient and effective, customer focused and which harnessed 'the best of [the] public and private sector' (Cabinet Office, 1997a). David Clark, Labour's Chancellor of the Duchy of Lancaster, and the minister initially responsible for the civil service, stated that there had to be continued efforts to cut out waste.

According to Clark, the challenge faced by the new government was 'to provide high quality, efficient and customer-friendly services, at the lowest possible cost to the taxpayer'. The results of the new government's comprehensive spending review, published in July 1998, announced the intention to introduce public service agreements between each department and the Treasury, setting out objectives and measurable efficiency and effectiveness targets (HM Treasury, 1998). Given Labour's commitment to cut public spending as a percentage of gross national product, this concern with efficiency and value for money is likely to remain a key feature of Labour's policy towards the civil service.

One important component of the Conservatives' concern with civil service efficiency – Next Steps agencies – has been accepted as an established part of the civil service landscape by the Blair government. In the early years of the Next Steps initiative, commentators had been sceptical about the survival of the programme in the event of the election of a Labour government (Davies and Willman, 1991, p. 77). According to David Clark (1997), however, the new government did not propose to turn the clock back: the delegation of managerial responsibilities to Next Steps agencies was 'here to stay'. Labour did, however, signal a new direction in the agency programme, announcing in early 1998 that the main task of creating agencies was now complete and that the emphasis needed to switch to using agencies in the most effective way (Chancellor of the Duchy of Lancaster, 1998, pp. iv–v). As well as needing to ensure that agency targets were sufficiently demanding and that performance against these targets was reported more clearly and openly, the new government also intended to encourage agencies to compare their procedures with best practice in other agencies and departments, as well as with that in outside public and private sector bodies. One consequence of this was the launching of a new phase in the benchmarking project established by the Major government in 1996.

The Blair government also announced that ministers would attempt to dispel the confusion that had been allowed to grow up about agencies and ministerial accountability under the Thatcher and Major governments. The Next Steps programme had always intended that ministers should remain fully accountable for the work of agencies. In the words of David Clark, the Next Steps revolution 'should be a managerial and not a constitutional one'

(Chancellor of the Duchy of Lancaster, 1998, p. vi). As we saw earlier, serious questions about the relationship of Next Steps agencies with their parent departments and ministers had been highlighted by the dismissal of the Director General of the Prison Service by the Home Secretary in 1995. In the event, the Labour Home Secretary, Jack Straw, announced soon after taking office that Home Office ministers would answer parliamentary questions on the Prison Service, rather than questions being answered by the Director General and other Prison Service staff. Mr Straw viewed this move as the first step to taking 'proper' ministerial responsibility for the running of the Prison Service (Home Office, 1997).

Another Next Steps agency singled out for attention by the new government was the CSA, which had had a chequered history since it was set up by the Major government in 1993. Labour announced a four-year plan to move the routine processing of maintenance claims from the CSA's 250 local offices to six central service units. The planned reorganisation was partly a response to the DSS's requirement to make a 25 per cent cut in its running costs. It was also part of the wider movement towards the use of telephone-based operations in the delivery of services by central government, a development that was seen as simplifying the application process for claimants.

The Blair government continued the five-yearly reviews of Next Steps agencies, upholding the previous government's policy that departments thoroughly consider all of the prior options of abolition, privatisation and market testing. Labour accepted the principle of market testing and contracting out and refused to rule out the possibility of some privatisation of Next Steps agencies (see, for example, House of Lords Public Service Committee, 1998, Q.1882). The public services minister, David Clark, declared that he could not 'turn back the clock' on market testing. Market testing and contracting out would not be followed 'as an article of faith' (quoted in *FDA News*, July 1997, p. 2), but they would be used where they could be shown to offer best value for money. Plans for market testing and contracting out inherited from the previous government were to proceed unless the relevant minister was satisfied that better value for money could be achieved by other means (Cabinet Office, 1997d).

The new government was also interested in asset disposals and the development of public–private partnerships. Labour's 1997 election manifesto had included a section on the possible sale of departmental assets – 'property, land and buildings' – that were surplus to requirements. The possibility of sales of central government assets was reinforced by the publication in late 1997 of a register of national assets – *The National Asset Register* (dubbed by the press as a modern-day Domesday Book), listing the land, buildings, equipment and other assets owned by government departments. The wide range of assets included the Treasury-owned car park used by Ipswich Town Football Club, the barracks owned by the Ministry of Defence, and a stud farm which was the property of the Home Office. Treasury accounting rules were changed in order to allow departments to retain the profits from sales on single items with a maximum value of £100 million during the period 1998–2000, provided that these profits were used to finance capital spending. Press reports indicated that the new government believed that there was no need to retain many of these buildings and property holdings, and plans to sell Ministry of Defence buildings and land were subsequently announced in the summer of 1998. At the same time, the sale of Inland Revenue and Customs and Excise properties and property owned by the Department for Education and Employment was also being considered by the Blair government (Evans, 1997; Waples, 1998).

In addition to the sale of central government assets to the private sector, the Blair government also revived the PFI, with the development of partnerships between the public and private sectors being seen as a way of levering in additional finance for central government activities. Labour had inherited a number of projects designed to involve the private sector in the delivery of social security benefits. In the summer of 1997 it was announced that the Department of Social Security was proceeding with the sale of the ownership and management of its estate to the private sector, with the entire property portfolio being sold to a consortium led by Goldman Sachs, the US investment bank (Mortished, 1997). In April 1998, it was announced that the National Savings Department, the 130-year-old savings bank, was seeking private sector involvement in the delivery of its administration services. Just over two months later, the government announced that it would be seeking private investment for the Royal Mint, a Next Steps agency.

In addition to these developments, the Blair government also extended the customer focus launched by its predecessor. Soon after its election victory, the government announced that it would relaunch the Citizen's Charter as part of its 'Better Government' initiative to modernise and improve government (*HC Debs*, 4 June 1997, cols 378–9). In June 1998, following a wide-ranging consultation exercise, the Charter programme was renamed Service First. Broader-ranging than its predecessor, the Service First programme not only includes charters and the Charter Mark scheme, but also a 'People's Panel', consisting of 5000 members of the public, who are consulted on a range of matters about the delivery of public services.

Shortly after the launching of the Service First programme, the government also announced important changes in the machinery for the central management of the civil service. It was announced that the Office of Public Service, established by the Major government to oversee management initiatives in the civil service, was to be merged with the Cabinet Office, giving the Cabinet Office a new focus as the service's 'corporate headquarters'. The new government's continuing emphasis on management and efficiency within the civil service was also reflected in the inclusion within the revamped Cabinet Office of a Centre for Management and Policy Studies (incorporating the Civil Service College), designed to provide a focus for thinking on new approaches to management.

Future Developments under New Labour

Although initially hostile to many of the initiatives introduced by the Thatcher and Major governments in the structure and management of the civil service, and the ideas and assumptions associated with them, by the time of the 1997 general election, the Labour Party had adopted much of the language, and many of the practices, of the new public management. Under the Blair government, Next Steps agencies have been accepted as an integral part of the civil service, market testing and contracting out have continued where they offer better value for money, and the Charter programme has been relaunched. Labour might have placed a greater emphasis on the effectiveness and responsiveness of service delivery, and be more pragmatic about market testing and privatisation, but there is a great deal of continuity with the approaches of the Thatcher and Major administrations.

Thus the public management revolution has continued under the Blair government, but what of the future? Central to the Labour government's plans for the public sector is the promotion of what they label 'better government', described as 'services which are user-friendly and suited to the way people live their lives' (Cabinet Office, 1998). The aim of 'better government' is to provide high-quality efficient and effective public services which are delivered in an accountable, open, accessible and responsive way (House of Lords Public Service Committee, 1998, p. 151). In developing better government, the Blair government has highlighted two key areas which affect the future structure and management of the civil service: the continued pursuit of the ideals of the Charter programme in improving the quality of services, and the increased use of information technology (House of Lords Public Service Committee, 1998, QQ 1852–1854).

The relaunching of the Charter programme as Service First is central to Labour's approach to 'better government'. The Blair government is committed to looking at government services from the perspective of the consumer, arguing that the Major government's Citizen's Charter programme was very much a 'top to bottom' process (House of Lords Public Service Committee, 1998, para. 1854). In its pursuit of 'better government', it has promised to encourage participation and consultation in the delivery of public services, and to monitor and enforce service standards. An important element in Labour's relaunching of the Charter programme is the use of information technology – including teletext and the Internet – to create a comprehensive information network. Labour's aim is to help the consumers of public services to access information about entitlements, complaints procedures and redress machinery (Public Service Committee, 1997, p. 50).

The use of information technology in the relationship between government and the consumers of services, and in the delivery of government services, is the second, and potentially most significant, element in Labour's approach to the structure and management of the civil service. The Blair government has set itself a target of providing a quarter of public services electronically – through televisions, telephones or computers – by the year 2002. It sees the harnessing of the 'information revolution' in the provision of more efficient and responsive services as the key to 'better government'. According to the government, information technology represents 'an amazing opportunity to restructure government's dealings with citizens...around their needs' (Cabinet Office, 1997b). Thus Labour wants members of the public to deal directly with government through such interactive devices as 'electronic post offices', Internet links down home telephone lines or multi-media kiosks in supermarkets and shopping centres. As a result of such initiatives, government itself would become more responsive to people's needs. In addition to making government more accessible, the Blair government also views information technology as a way of reducing the traditional boundaries between government departments, with people no longer having to work out which department to contact. In the long term there could be 'a radical restructuring' of the government machine 'around the needs of the customers' (Cabinet Office, 1997b).

Using the language of the new public management, it is claimed that government in the information age will 'work better and cost less' (Bellamy and Taylor, 1998, p. 86). The greater use of information technology has enormous significance for the future structure and management of the civil service. Its potential lies in terms of streamlining central government structures, achieving efficiency savings, and enabling public services to become more customer-friendly.

Despite these benefits, the increased use of information technology by central government has certain actual and potential costs, not only for the civil service, but also for the consumers of the services that it provides. In part a response to the need to save on the running costs of government departments, electronic government will inevitably mean further job losses in the civil service (Gosling, 1998, p. 22). Also, despite its contribution to improving civil service efficiency and helping to develop the customer orientation, the greater use of information technology will increase central government's capability for surveillance – with the consequent threats to personal privacy – through the expansion of its ability to integrate and cross-match data between information systems (Bellamy and Taylor, 1998, pp. 86–8).

Long-running issues such as the implications of agencification and contracting out for accountability and the unity of the civil service will continue to play a major part in debates about the structure and management of the civil service. However, the concerns raised by the civil service's greater use of the new technology will also loom large in such discussions.

References

Bellamy, C. (1995) 'Managing strategic resources in a Next Steps department: information agendas and information systems in the DSS', in O'Toole, B. J. and Jordan, G. (eds), *Next Steps: Improving Management in Government* (Aldershot: Dartmouth), pp. 55–73.

Bellamy, C. and Taylor, J. A. (1992) 'Information and new public management: an alternative agenda for public administration', *Public Policy and Administration*, 7(3), Winter, pp. 29–41.

Bellamy, C. and Taylor, J. A. (1998) *Governing in the Information Age* (Buckingham: Open University Press).

Blair, T. (1994) 'The Blair essentials', *FDA News*, January, pp. 5–7.

Butcher, T. (1995) 'The Major Government and Whitehall: the civil service at the crossroads', *Teaching Public Administration*, XV(1), Spring, pp. 19–31.

Butcher, T. (1997) 'The Citizen's Charter: creating a customer-orientated civil service', in Barberis, P. (ed.), *The Civil Service in an Era of Change* (Aldershot: Dartmouth), pp. 54–68.

Cabinet Office (1997a), *Next Steps Briefing Note March 1997* (London: Cabinet Office).

Cabinet Office (1997b) 'Clark outlines vision for electronic government', Press Release CAB 34/97, 18 June.

Cabinet Office (1997c) *Next Steps Briefing Note October 1997* (London: Cabinet Office).

Cabinet Office (1997d) 'Government's 12 Guiding Principles for Market Testing & Contracting Out', Press Release CAB 114/97, 4 November.

Cabinet Office (1998) 'Open for business at the touch of a button', Press Release CAB 139/98, 8 June.

Chancellor of the Duchy of Lancaster (1998) *Next Steps Report 1997*, Cm 3889 (London: The Stationery Office).

Chapman, R. A. (1997) 'The end of the British civil service', in Barberis, P. (ed.), *The Civil Service in an Era of Change* (Aldershot: Dartmouth) pp. 23–37.

Clark, D. (1997) 'The civil service and the new government', speech at the QEII Centre, 17 June (London: Cabinet Office/OPS).

Davies, A. and Willman, J. (1991) *What Next? Agencies, Departments and the Civil Service* (London: Institute for Public Policy Research).

Evans, M. (1997) 'MoD considers selling defence research agency', *The Times*, 7 November, p. 13.

Foster, D. (1996) 'Labour and public sector reform', *Parliamentary Affairs*, 49(2), April, pp. 256–61.

Giddings, P. (1995) 'The Treasury Committee and Next Steps agencies', in Giddings, P. (ed), *Parliamentary Accountability: A Study of Parliament and Executive Agencies* (Basingstoke: Macmillan).

80   *The Civil Service: Structure and Management*

Gosling, P. (1998) 'Future shock?', *Public Service Magazine*, March, pp. 20–2.

Gould, B. (1991) 'Learning to love the service', *FDA News*, 11(13), pp. 3–4.

Greer, P. (1994) *Transforming Central Government: The Next Steps Initiative* (Buckingham: Open University Press).

Grice, A. and Hellen, N (1997), 'Brown steals Tories' privatisation thunder', *The Sunday Times*, 9 March, p. 1.

Halligan, L., Wighton, D. and Peston, R. (1997), 'Labour plans jails shake-up', *Financial Times*, 25 February, p. 1.

Harden, I. (1992) *The Contracting State* (Buckingham: Open University Press).

Hennessy, P. (1993) 'Questions of ethics for government', *FDA News*, 13(1), pp. 3–5.

HM Treasury (1991) *Competing for Quality*, Cm. 1730 (London: HMSO).

HM Treasury (1998) *Modernising Public Services for Britain: Investing in Reform*, Cm. 4011 (London: The Stationery Office).

Home Office (1997) 'Jack Straw announces ministers to answer Prison Service PQs', Press Release 118/97, 8 May.

Hood, C. (1991) 'A public management for all seasons?', *Public Administration*, 69(1), Spring, pp. 3–20.

House of Lords Public Service Committee (1998) Session 1997–98, *Evidence*, HL 55–I (London: The Stationery Office).

Lewis, D. (1997) *Hidden Agendas: Politics, Law and Disorder* (London: Hamish Hamilton).

Mandelson, P. and Liddle, R. (1996) *The Blair Revolution: Can New Labour Deliver?* (London: Faber & Faber).

Meacher, M. (1994) 'An ambitious and broad agenda', *The Times*, 6 October, p. 18.

Mortished, C. (1997) 'US bank acquires DSS buildings for £400m', *The Times*, 1 August, p. 21.

Mowlam, M. (1993) *The Future for Public Services: Labour's Drive for Quality and Accountability* (discussion paper).

Office of Public Service (1996) *government. direct. A prospectus for the Electronic Delivery of Government Services*, Cm 3438 (London: HMSO).

Public Service Committee (1997) Third Report, Session 1996–97, *The Citizen's Charter*, Vol. II, HC. 78–II (London: The Stationery Office).

Pyper, R. (1995) *The British Civil Service* (Hemel Hempstead: Prentice Hall/Harvester Wheatsheaf).

Rhodes, R. A. W. (1991) 'Introduction', *Public Administration*, 69(1), Spring, pp. 1–2.

Rhodes, R. A. W. (1997) *Understanding Governance: Policy Networks, Governance, Reflexivity and Accountability* (Buckingham: Open University Press).

Ridley, F. F. (1995) 'Reinventing British government', *Parliamentary Affairs*, 48(3), July, pp. 387–400.

Saner, M. (1997) 'The question of quality', *Capability*, Issue 4.

Smith, J. (1991) 'The public service ethos', *Public Administration*, 69(4), Winter, pp. 515–23.

Theakston, K. (1992) *The Labour Party and Whitehall* (London: Routledge).

Theakston, K. (1995) *The Civil Service Since 1945* (Oxford: Blackwell).

Theakston, K. (1998) 'New Labour, New Whitehall?', *Public Policy and Administration*, 13(1), Spring, pp. 13–34.

Treasury and Civil Service Committee (1988) Eighth Report, Session 1987–88, *Civil Service Management: The Next Steps*, HC 494–I (London: HMSO).

Treasury and Civil Service Committee (1990) Eighth Report, Session 1989–90, *Progress in the Next Steps Initiative*, HC 348 (London: HMSO).

Treasury and Civil Service Committee (1993) Sixth Report, Session 1992–93, *The Role of the Civil Service: Interim Report*, Vol. II, Minutes of Evidence and Appendices, HC 390–II (London: HMSO).

Treasury and Civil Service Committee (1994) Fifth Report, Session 1993–94, *The Role of the Civil Service*, Vol. I, Report, HC 27–I (London: HMSO).

Walker, D. (1994) 'Labouring over the civil service', *Public Finance*, 5/12 August, p. 7.

Waples, J. (1998) 'Brown opens his property jewel box', *The Sunday Times*, 22 February, p. 3.11 (Business section).

Willman, J. (1994) *Labour and the Public Services*, Social Market Foundation Memorandum No. 6 (London: Social Market Foundation).

4

Parliament in Transition

PHILIP NORTON

With the return of a Labour government in May 1997, Parliament faced two challenges. One was long standing, though in many respects exacerbated by the size of Labour's majority. The other was essentially specific to the return of the Labour government.

Inherent Conflict

The first challenge was how to reconcile a conflict basic to the institution. The government is chosen through elections to the House of Commons. MPs of the government party are elected under a party label and are expected to sustain the government in office. At the same time, the House of Commons is expected to subject government to scrutiny. Bills have to be scrutinised, the policies and actions of government questioned. For most Members of Parliament there is thus a potential conflict between loyalty to one's party in government and loyalty to the institution of which one is a member.

This conflict has generally been resolved in favour of government. Commitment to party usually takes precedence over commitment to the institution. As a result, government has been able to dominate and this dominance has found institutional expression. Government business has precedence on most occasions in the House of Commons. Procedure, such as the use of *ad hoc* committees for scrutinising bills, tends to favour government. The House of Commons has variously been seen as a vehicle at the disposal of government and almost customised to meet its requirements.

However, the conflict has not been resolved totally in favour of government. The House has not wholly discarded procedures and practices that permit of debate and scrutiny. Time has been devoted to debate, though the emphasis on debate on the floor of the House has tended to favour government, squeezing out the opportunity for more sustained and extensive scrutiny through the medium of committees. The House has usually been a world-beater in terms of the number of hours it sits. The House has developed new procedures for scrutinising government, such as Question Time and the opportunity to table written questions (see Franklin and Norton, 1993). Question Time developed especially in the nineteenth century. Prime Minister's Question Time is a recent innovation, dating from 1961.

The developments favouring the House over government were more than matched by the developments favouring government. So much so that by the 1960s a highly critical literature developed, bemoaning the limited capacity of Parliament to exert influence over the government of the day. 'Well, it's dead', declared Conservative MP Humphry Berkeley in 1963, 'power has now bypassed the House of Commons' (quoted in Butt, 1967, p. 10). MPs had the option of accepting the situation or seeking to do something about it. The 1960s and 1970s saw various attempts to resolve the conflict a little more in favour of parliamentary scrutiny. A notable finding of Donald Searing's magisterial analysis of members' roles in the early 1970s was that a substantial proportion of MPs – just over 40 per cent of backbenchers – fell predominantly into the category of policy advocates, that is, wanting to influence public policy (Searing, 1994). The opportunities to have an impact on policy were extremely limited and subsequent years saw various attempts to strengthen parliamentary means of influence. Those attempts bore fruit notably in the early years of Conservative government under Margaret Thatcher, especially but not exclusively with the creation of the departmental select committees.

The period of Conservative government exemplified the conflict between the demands of party and the demands of the House. The government used whatever means it could to ensure the passage of often controversial legislation. At the same time, there was pressure from members in different parts of the House to strengthen the means of scrutiny in order to give them a greater influence over public policy. These conflicting pressures lent themselves to two views of Parliament: one emphasised the government's hold on its majority and thus subscribed to the 'elective dictatorship' thesis of British politics. The other emphasised the structural and behavioural changes within the House, thus stressing the development of the House into a stronger policy-influencing legislature (see Norton, 1997a, pp. 155–76).

This struggle has been marked since the return of a new Parliament in 1997. On the one hand, a party that was the 'out' party for eighteen years was returned to office, committed to strengthening Parliament. The House saw an unprecedented proportion of new MPs elected – just over one-third of the House, roughly double the usual new intake. Most of the new Labour MPs had experience of local government, where the emphasis is on decision-making through committee. It was assumed that many would, in Searing's terms, be policy advocates (see Norton, 1997b, pp. 17–31). There was also the realisation that, given the size of the parliamentary party, most Labour MPs would not get their foot on even the first rung of the ministerial ladder. It was thought that many would thus seek to find some other means of fulfilment through parliamentary activity, such as service on select committees, and make a name for themselves through such activity.

On the other hand, there was the sheer size of Labour's majority, making it unlikely that the government would ever be vulnerable to defeat. The government's overall majority of 179 exceeded the size of the parliamentary Conservative party. Under Tony Blair's leadership, the parliamentary party had already adopted stronger standing orders limiting independent voting behaviour by members. There were also changes in the whipping arrangements. Instead of being elected, the Chief Whip was appointed by the leader. The composition of the Whips' Office also underwent something of a transformation. New techniques of keeping MPs 'on line' were also introduced, including the use of pagers. There was also the prospect of new MPs being ultra loyal to the leader who had delivered such a stunning electoral victory.

This conflict – between the needs of a government and of a scrutinising House – did, indeed, become a feature of the new Parliament. In fulfilment of a manifesto pledge, the government recommended to the House the appointment of a Select Committee on the Modernisation of the House of Commons. The committee was chaired by the Leader of the House, Ann Taylor. She sought consensus in order to produce recommendations that strengthened the House and, in some respects, improved the House for the purposes of public perception or for the convenience of members. Under her leadership, the committee produced seven reports within one year. Much of this chapter will be devoted to assessing those reports.

At the same time, the government was elected on a programme of reform and it had a heavy legislative schedule in the first session. The task of the whips was to ensure that the measures were passed and, if possible, passed expeditiously and in the form in which they were introduced. The Chief Whip, Nick Brown, adopted a no-nonsense approach to getting the government's business through and was reputedly not enamoured of attempts to strengthen the House in any way that might threaten the government's position. The Leader of the House and the Chief Whip thus adopted conflicting positions. Ann Taylor had a responsibility to get the government's business through but, as Leader of the House, had a responsibility to the House as a whole. The Chief Whip simply had a responsibility to get the government's business through.

Constitutional Change

The second challenge came as a consequence of the new government's commitment to constitutional change. Whereas the first challenge came essentially from within, this derived from developments external to the House. The government had a manifesto commitment to various measures of constitutional reform and the first session of the Parliament was notable for the number of measures that were introduced and passed. The components of constitutional change are covered elsewhere in this volume and so it is sufficient to merely adumbrate here the principal measures passed by Parliament. Parliament enacted measures providing for referendums in Scotland, Wales and London; for the creation of an elected parliament in Scotland, an elected assembly in Wales, an elected mayor and authority in London; for the incorporation of the European Convention on Human Rights into British law; and for an elected assembly and different consultative bodies in Northern

Ireland. It also passed the European Communities (Amendment) Act, giving legal effect in the UK as necessary to the Amsterdam treaty and ratifying those parts of the treaty requiring ratification by Parliament. In the second session, it introduced a House of Lords Bill to remove hereditary peers from membership of the House of Lords.

These changes set the Parliament apart from earlier Parliaments. They did so because of their cumulative effect. The period from 1979 to 1997 had seen some important measures of constitutional change, including the passage of two European Communities (Amendment) Acts – one in 1986, giving effect in domestic law to the provisions of the Single European Act, and the other in 1993, giving effect to the Maastricht treaty – but there was no package of measures designed to reshape the British constitution. Rather, the period had been notable for the opposition by the government to reform of the basic constitutional framework of the United Kingdom.

There are, though, two elements of similarity between the measures passed occasionally during the period of Conservative government and the several measures passed under the new Labour government. First, the measures have had important implications for Parliament. Second, those implications were not fully grasped at the time the measures were passed. There were various motivations for the constitutional changes, and the reasons were at the core of the debate during their passage. Relatively little consideration was given to their impact upon the House of Commons, especially at the practical level. There was some debate on the broad constitutional implications for Parliament but little on how the changes would impact upon the actual workings of the House of Commons.

Given this background of inherent conflict and constitutional change, the purpose of this chapter is to assess the attempts made by the House of Commons to acquire a greater critical capacity of government – especially at a time when government enjoys political hegemony in the House – and the consequences of constitutional change for the position and working of the House. Only by doing so can we assess the likely position of Parliament in the British polity in the new millennium. Is the House of Commons likely to be so marginalised as to be essentially irrelevant? Or is it adapting to the changed conditions in such a way that allows it to fulfil some useful role in the political system?

Parliamentary Reform Pre-1997

During the 1960s and 1970s, MPs on both sides of the House pressed for reform of parliamentary structures and procedures in order to enable them to have a greater impact on the government and its measures. The period witnessed experimentation with new procedures, some of which were short-lived and others of which were made permanent or built upon in later Parliaments. The most significant reforms were those introduced during the time that Richard Crossman was Labour Leader of the House of Commons (1966–8). There was a greater use especially of investigative select committees and a failed experiment with the use of morning sittings (see Norton, 1981, pp. 204–5).

The most significant and lasting reforms of the latter half of the century were to come later, in the 1979–83 Parliament. Foremost among the reforms was the introduction of a near-comprehensive series of departmental select committees. Within a matter of years, they had established themselves as a permanent feature of the parliamentary landscape. They were the most prominent but not the only changes introduced. Provision was also made, among other things, for Opposition Days (replacing Supply Days), Estimates Days (to discuss specific estimates), the use of special standing committees (SSCs) to scrutinise bills, with the committees being empowered to take evidence, and the creation of the National Audit Office, to improve scrutiny of spending by government departments (Norton, 1986a, pp. 69–98). The changes were such as to merit the Parliament being dubbed 'the reform Parliament' (Norton, 1986b).

The reforms helped reshape the House of Commons. The departmental select committees, in particular, gave the House a structured and specialised means of scrutinising government on a consistent basis. The nature of that scrutiny is considered by Michael Rush in the next chapter. The committees have been at the heart of a greater institutionalisation of the House of Commons: the use of permanent committees reflects a greater specialisation by the House, as does the development of a degree of specialisation within the committees themselves (Norton, 1998a, pp. 143–62). Since their introduction, they have been variously adapted to meet changes in departmental structures, and extended in scope. They have also been supplemented by a number of other committees, thus further highlighting a shift of emphasis from the chamber to the committee room (Norton, 1998a).

The reforms of the 1979–83 Parliament have been sustained by the House, but subsequent Parliaments of Conservative government (1983–97) saw no reforms comparable to those of the 'reform Parliament'. Rather, the period was one of consolidation and modest advances. The period was thus not exceptional. What was clearly exceptional, and in need of explanation, was the introduction of such a major reform as the departmental select committees in 1979. If we can identify the reasons for that then we have the basis for assessing the likelihood of parliamentary reform in the Parliament elected in 1997.

I have elsewhere suggested that the successful introduction of the departmental select committees in 1979 was the product of four variables (Norton, 1994a, pp. 80–7). All four were necessary but none by itself was sufficient.

First, the *sine qua non* of effective parliamentary reform, there has to be the political will on the part of MPs to achieve change. That means that MPs have to want reform and to be prepared to press for it. Without that, there is little likelihood of change. Why should government consider reform, entailing effort and potential problems for itself, if MPs are not pushing for it?

Second, there has to be a window of opportunity. The parliamentary agenda is usually crowded. We have already noted that the House of Commons has been a world leader in terms of the number of hours it sits. The more crowded the parliamentary timetable, the more difficult it is to find time to debate what are essentially domestic items for the House. It would also be plausible to hypothesise that a party newly-elected to office – as with the Conservatives in 1979 or Labour in 1997 – will have a substantial legislative agenda, which may serve to squeeze out consideration of other issues. For substantive reform to be achieved, a window of opportunity has to be found and exploited and such windows are likely to be narrow during the lifetime of a Parliament.

Third, there has to be a coherent reform agenda behind which MPs can unite. Even if there is pressure for change from MPs, there has to be some clear proposal, or package of proposals, for which they can vote. If they are to enhance parliamentary scrutiny of government, then the reforms have to be clearly designed for the purpose. Various changes have been proposed and made to procedures and practices of the House which are designed to achieve other goals. These have included the convenience of MPs and improving the public face of the House. These are not undesirable goals but the means of achieving them may not have the effect of improving the scrutinising capacity of the House and, indeed, in certain circumstances could limit rather than enhance it.

Fourth, there has to be leadership in order to ensure the demands are met and that a clear proposal or set of proposals is brought before the House of Commons. Though it is possible to envisage a situation in which the demand is so great that no Leader of the House of Commons could resist it (a situation in which Michael Foot was beginning to find himself in the 1978–79 session), a leader is almost certainly necessary in order to facilitate the acceptance by government of substantial proposals for reform. Ministers stood in the way of various reform proposals in the 1960s and various members of the new Conservative Cabinet in 1979, including the Prime Minister, were known to be sceptical or hostile to the introduction of the new select committees. Leadership is needed and, in practice, that means leadership by the Leader of the House. The Leader of the House is in a position to introduce the motion or motions necessary to achieve change and also to ensure that the introduction takes place at an opportune time.

All four of these conditions were met in 1979. Demand for more effective means of scrutinising government came from both sides of the House – this had been demonstrated in debate at the end of the 1974–9 Parliament. There was a clear window of opportunity right at the beginning of the Parliament – before the legislative agenda became too demanding on time and before ministers were too well entrenched and committed to a 'departmental' view of reform. There was a clear reform proposal before the House. The Procedure Committee of the House had produced an authoritative report in 1978 (Select Committee on Procedure, 1978), recommending the creation of departmental select committees, and it was this report that formed the basis of the recommendations placed before the House. Finally, there was leadership. The new Leader of the House, Norman St John Stevas, moved quickly to introduce the motions necessary to give effect to the recommendations. In this, he was aided by the fact that the House was already flexing its muscles over the issue of MPs' pay, with backbenchers giving him a difficult time at the Dispatch Box. In those circumstances, the Cabinet was reluctant to stand up to an assertive House.

The House of Commons thus achieved the most significant reform of its procedures for many decades: indeed, in terms of enhancing its capacity to scrutinise government, the most important reform of the century. There were reforms in subsequent Parliaments but nothing on the scale of the 1979–83 Parliament and a number were not, in any event, designed primarily to enhance parliamentary scrutiny of government. In 1992, for example, a Select Committee on the Sittings of the House made recommendations to limit the time the House spent sitting, especially late at night (Select Committee on Sittings of the House, 1992). In 1994 the House agreed to implement recommendations made in the report. The effect of the change, though, was to enable MPs to get home earlier and to limit the occasions when they might have to be at Westminster on a Friday. (As a result of the report, the House introduced ten non-sitting Fridays each session.) These effects were not undesirable but they contributed little of substance to the capacity of the House to question and check government.

Reform under a Labour Government

The Labour manifesto in the 1997 election supported modernising Parliament, as had the Labour manifesto in 1966. Ann Taylor, shadow Leader of the House in Opposition, was appointed Leader of the House. She moved quickly to ensure that the manifesto commitment to recommend the appointment of a Select Committee on the Modernisation of the House of Commons was implemented. The committee was approved by the House on 4 June. It was set up 'to consider how the practices and procedures of the House should be modernised'. It was also charged 'to make a first report to the House before the summer adjournment with its initial conclusions on ways in which the procedure for examining legislative proposals could be improved'.

The committee held a number of meetings before issuing its first report on 29 July (Select Committee on Modernisation, 1997a). The report, entitled simply *The Legislative Process*, made several substantial recommendations. Foremost among these were

- The programming of legislation, to ensure that each part of a bill received scrutiny, with a standing committee having power to decide a programme for the bill it is considering.
- Providing greater opportunities for pre-legislative scrutiny and consultation, with more bills being published in draft form and with some possibly being considered by select committees or by *ad hoc* committees.
- Allowing some bills to carry over from one session to the next, instead of being killed off automatically once the end of the session is reached, thus allowing for a more staggered introduction of bills and a more balanced legislative workload.
- Making greater use of different types of committee, including more use of special standing committees, which have the power to take evidence from witnesses.
- More post-legislative scrutiny, with select committees being encouraged to monitor legislation newly in force.
- Improving the explanatory material published with bills and introducing a daily agenda to replace the rather complex Order Paper.

The recommendations, if implemented, had the potential to change significantly the capacity of the House of Commons to scrutinise legislation.

Publication of the report on the legislative process was followed by six others within a year. All seven are listed for convenience in Table 4.1. The most significant after that on the legislative process was the seventh on scrutiny of European legislation. Parliament has no formal role in the law-making process of the European Union but it has sought to engage in pre-legislative scrutiny, the House of Commons going for breadth (looking at every EU document prior to its submission to the Council of Ministers) and the House of Lords for depth (looking at selected documents in detail) (Norton 1996). The Modernisation Committee drew on previous reports from the Select Committee on European Legislation in order to recommend an extension of existing scrutiny procedures – especially through the creation of more European Standing Committees, which have the capacity to question ministers – as well as proposing the setting up of a UK Parliament office in Brussels, thus strengthening the capacity of the House to monitor developments in EU institutions independent of government. The other reports served to

TABLE 4.1   *Reports from the Select Committee on Modernisation of the House of Commons 1997–98*

First Report: The Legislative Process, HC 190
Recommended, among other proposals, the timetabling of bills, more pre- and post-legislative scrutiny, greater use of special standing committees, and the carry-over of bills from one session to another.

Second Report: Explanatory Material for Bills, HC 389
   Contained proposals on how explanatory material accompanying bills can be improved.

Third Report: Carry-Over of Public Bills, HC 543
Contained proposals on how bills may be carried over from one session to another and recommended the use of *ad hoc* motions for the purpose.

Fourth Report: Conduct in the Chamber, HC 600
Recommended, among other things, that privy councillors should not necessarily have precedence in being called in debate, that the wearing of an opera hat to raise a point of order during divisions be abolished, that a motion to move next business should replace that allowing members to 'spy strangers', that members named by the chair should lose their parliamentary salary for the period of suspension, and that the Speaker should have discretion to impose a variable time limit on speeches.

Fifth Report: Consultation Paper on Voting Methods, HC 699
Outlined a number of options for voting by electronic methods and invited members to complete a questionnaire on the subject.

Sixth Report: Voting Methods, HC 779
Reported the results of the survey of members on the various options on voting methods: 53 per cent preferred the existing method of voting and 70 per cent deemed it acceptable. Only 13 per cent preferred the use of fingerprint readers and 13 per cent the use of smart cards. In the light of these findings, the Committee stated that it proposed to pursue the matter no further.

Seventh Report: The Scrutiny of European Business, HC 791
Recommended an increase in the number of European standing committees (to consider EU documents) from two to five, an extension of the scrutiny reserve (under which a minister cannot agree to a proposal in the Council of Ministers until parliamentary scrutiny is complete) to the second and third pillars of the EU, and the creation of a UK Parliament Office in Brussels.

---

demonstrate both the wide range of the Committee's remit as well as the sheer extent of its activity. In July 1998, the Committee indicated that it planned to look at ways to make the House a more family-friendly institution.

The work of the Modernisation Committee, and the approval by the House – without a vote – in November 1997 of its first report give some credence to the thesis that the House of Commons is adapting to changing conditions and seeking to maintain, or strengthen, its position as a policy-influencing legislature. This thesis gains further support from the work of the departmental select committees and the behaviour of members in the chamber.

The select committees have proved active bodies of investigation and scrutiny, being prolific – as in past Parliaments – in their output. A number have issued critical reports – critical of departments or publicly-funded bodies – and attracted media attention. A particularly notable example was the report of the Select Committee on Foreign Affairs in 1999 on the government's handling of the supply of arms to Sierra Leone; the committee was scathing in its criticism of the 'appalling failure in the briefing of Ministers' (Select Committee on Foreign Affairs, 1999, p. xxix). Others have issued less controversial but nonetheless solid reports with recommendations for action. Some ministers and civil servants have been subjected to intense questioning: some have found themselves in difficulty in answering, others have had little difficulty in fending off questions. The work of the departmental select committees has been supplemented by that of other investigative select committees, not least the Public Accounts Committee, under the chairmanship – as is traditional – of a senior Opposition MP.

Nor has the critical scrutiny been confined to committees. Despite the government's overall majority, Opposition members have variously used the chamber to engage in critical questioning of government. The new Leader of the Opposition, William Hague, soon achieved a reputation for forcing the Prime Minister onto the defensive during Prime Minister's Question Time and various backbenchers acquired reputations for subjecting ministers to sustained and sometimes difficult questioning. (Their number included three former ministers: Virginia Bottomley, Eric Forth and Ann Widdecombe, the last-named being promoted to the Shadow Cabinet in 1998.) On the government benches, a number of backbenchers proved willing to disagree with their front bench and on occasion defy the whips. On 10 December 1997, 47 Labour MPs voted against the government, and several abstained, over a reduction in lone-parent benefits. The size of the rebellion was unusual, especially for the first session of a Parliament. Within the first year of the Labour government, at least 76 Labour members – almost one in five of all Labour members – had voted against the government on at least one occasion (Cowley, 1998, p. 5). Some of the rebels formed their own dining club and auctioned off the letters of condemnation they had received from the whips (*The Sunday Times*, 6 September 1998). The level of rebelliousness in the first session – traditionally lower than in subsequent sessions in Parliaments where a new government is returned to office – was greater than that in the first sessions of eight other post-war Parliaments. Drawing on analysis of voting behaviour of past Parliaments, one analyst was thus able to write in September 1998: 'Whilst there is no guarantee that this PLP will behave as PLPs (and Conservative parliamentary parties) have in the past, the data strongly suggest that this first session of the parliament has been atypical of what is to come: not only will future sessions of this parliament be likely to see further dissent . . . but they are likely to see disproportionately more dissent' (Cowley, 1998, p. 5).

These developments have to be set against others which lend weight to the alternative thesis, that of the marginalisation of the House in the political process. The departmental select committees continue to labour under various constraints (see Norton, 1994b, pp. 29–33), including difficulty in acquiring information – a point conceded by various committee members, including the Labour chairman of the Defence Committee (George and Morgan 1999), and by the Foreign Affairs Committee in its 1999 Report on Sierra Leone – and by the fact that a government secure in a massive parliamentary majority may simply ignore whatever a committee recommends. Removing a member from a committee, or preventing an appointment, is one of the powers now employed by government whips against rebels (*The Sunday Times*, 6 September 1998). Rebellions by backbenchers may embarrass the government politically but few expect them ever to reach a level where they threaten to rob the government of a majority. The extent of rebellion in the first session, even though greater than in many post-war Parliaments, was less than in the first session of recent Parliaments (Cowley, 1998, p. 4). And those MPs who did rebel were more likely to be long-serving members rather than members of the new 1997 intake (Cowley, 1998, p. 6).

If members are not able to utilise existing procedures to engage in effective critical scrutiny of a determined government, then much rests on the reports and recommendations of the Modernisation Committee. The likelihood of significant parliamentary reform being achieved can be assessed using the four criteria identified as making possible the 1979 reforms: political will, a window of opportunity, a reform agenda, and leadership.

Political Will

In introducing the first report from the Modernisation Committee, Ann Taylor declared: 'Members of the House want to see a more effective legislature, more input into the legislative process and to be able to use their time more constructively' (Select Committee on Modernisation, 1997b). Members may want those things but the evidence that the political will exists to press for them – especially the first (a more effective legislature) – is limited. One survey of new MPs in the summer of 1997 found that 71 per cent had a favourable reaction on first arrival at Westminster. When asked what they would like to change about the institution, most directed their comments to procedure and matters more directly affecting their work (such as office accommodation and having to stand around waiting to vote). Few comments were directed at significant change in the relationship of the House to government. 'The responses indicate that, while the new MPs are not averse to change, they have not entered Parliament with a clear agenda of parliamentary reform in mind. If there is to be significant reform, the new MPs will have to be rallied to the cause rather than be the vanguard that some have claimed them to be' (Norton and Mitchell, 1997, p. 13). Although the responses to the survey on voting methods, reported in the sixth report of the Modernisation Committee, showed that new MPs were more likely than longer-serving members to favour a change in voting procedures, just over half of all new members found the existing method acceptable (Select Committee on Modernisation, 1998, Annex). There is little overt evidence of a clear demand for reform on the part of MPs: if anything, the attention of parliamentary sketchwriters has been caught by the degree of loyalty on the part of government backbenchers rather than by a demonstrable and widespread demand for reforms that would enable the House to engage in more effective scrutiny of government.

Window of Opportunity

The evidence of the 1979 reforms suggests that a window of opportunity exists at the beginning of a new Parliament but thereafter it is more likely to be closed or at least barely ajar. Once a Parliament is under way, the government's legislative programme tends to be time-consuming. Ann Taylor moved to ensure an early debate on the first report from the Modernisation Committee but thereafter the opportunity for taking issues of reform to the floor – or of reform engaging members' attention – was limited. The first session proved a busy as well as a long one, necessarily extended because of legislation on Northern Ireland; by the latter half of the session, there was little time to squeeze any additional items onto the timetable. The programme for the subsequent session was also crowded, encompassing another of the government's constitutional reform measures: that for removing hereditary peers from the House of Lords. As a Parliament progresses, the time and attention of members is absorbed by business brought forward by government. There is less time to stand back and think about the processes and structures of the House itself. By the end of the first session, there was little or no evidence that the work of the Modernisation Committee was being followed eagerly by MPs; two reports had been discussed in the House but both occasions attracted little interest. A similar lack of interest was apparent in the subsequent session: debates on Committee reports in November and December 1998 drew relatively few members to the chamber; the December debate was notable principally for the intervention of the former Labour Chief Whip, Derek Foster, who conceded that he had agreed to the recommendations of the Select Committee on the Sittings of the House (published in 1992 but agreed by the House in late 1994) 'only when it was obvious that my party would win the election, and that it would be to our advantage to have shorter hours' (*House of Commons Debates*, vol. 322, col. 1022, 16 December 1998). There were fewer than thirty MPs in the chamber when he made his remarks.

Reform Agenda

The first report from the Modernisation Committee provided a useful reform agenda in terms of strengthening the House as a body of legislative scrutiny. However, the report made recommendations without providing clear guidance on how its proposals were to be locked into the system. By approving the report, the House was agreeing to what should be done rather than agreeing new rules introducing the proposed reforms. Though some action was taken, as on a new daily agenda and the publication of some bills in draft form, the House made no provision for the regular or automatic use of special standing committees nor for the regular carry-over of bills; instead, much was to be left to government. Furthermore, the other reports of the Modernisation Committee lacked a clear focus. Only the seventh report, on the scrutiny of European legislation, was essentially directed at strengthening the House as a scrutinising body. Recommendations embodied in other reports were designed for cosmetic or tidying-up purposes (such as abolishing the use of an opera hat for raising a point of order during divisions) or for the convenience of members (such as ending privy councillors' precedence or looking at how the House may be made more family-friendly). Though these aims may be desirable, they are not central to strengthening the House in its relationship to government and at times the proposals to give effect to them may actually clash with the goal of strengthening the House as a scrutinising body. The unfocused nature of the Modernisation Committee's agenda has served to detract attention from the central purpose of strengthening the House as a body for scrutinising government.

Leadership

The Leader of the House, Ann Taylor, sought to achieve consensus in the Modernisation Committee. This approach resembled that of her immediate Conservative predecessor, Tony Newton, who sought general agreement before bringing proposals to the House. As Newton found, reaching agreement can take time and in his case some of the most entrenched opposition to change – as with the Select Committee on Sittings of the House – came from within the Labour Whips' Office. Given the somewhat heterogeneous composition of the Modernisation Committee, Taylor – and her successor, Margaret Beckett – discovered that agreement was not always easy to achieve. The Conservatives were wary of some proposals, the principal Liberal Democrat on the committee wanted to go further, and one of the Labour members – one of the new 1997 intake – was apparently more concerned with more practical matters affecting members – in other words, the convenience of members – than the basic relationship of the House to the executive. The outcome was, as we have seen, a disparate array of reports and by the end of the session the Committee appeared to have lost its way. The seventh report on European legislation was useful but said little or nothing that had not been said in the previous Parliament by the Select Committee on European Legislation.

What this analysis lends itself to is the conclusion that, in the push and shove between the demands of government and the need to strengthen the House as a body of scrutiny, the latter has tended to lose out to the former. This is not to say that reform may not be achieved incrementally. Some of the recommendations of the Modernisation Committee have borne fruit, a number being approved at different points in 1997 (first report) and 1998 (the most important being that on the scrutiny of European legislation, approved without a vote in November) and others may be implemented at some point in the future. However, the opportunity for a 'big bang' approach to reform, of the sort witnessed in 1979, has been lost. Unless MPs demand reform, it is not likely to happen, at least not on a scale that strengthens significantly the House of Commons. It may be that growing frustration on the backbenches may generate more calls for reform, but the precedents are not strong: the 1983–87 Parliament was characterised by the then Speaker as a 'frustration Parliament' (Norton, 1985, p. 32), but that frustration generated no dramatic change in the structures and procedures of the House.

Impact of Constitutional Change

Though the House of Commons may not be reformed – at least not on any large scale – because of pressures from within, it will be affected – and, potentially, quite dramatically – as a consequence of changes to the constitutional framework of the United Kingdom. Each of the constitutional changes introduced or intended by the

Labour government have implications for the powers and workings of the House of Commons. The effects on the House can be subsumed under the headings of size, power, business, and structures.

Size

The House of Commons has 659 members – making it one of the largest elected legislatures in the world – remaining unchanged during the lifetime of the Parliament elected in 1997. However, the size of the House will be reduced as a consequence of devolution. With Scotland being given its own elected parliament, the Labour government agreed in 1997 that the number of parliamentary seats in Scotland should be reduced. In the next Parliament, when there is a review of constituency boundaries, the Boundary Commission is to be asked to bring the electoral quota in Scotland in line with that for England, in other words ensuring that the number of electors per constituency – at present smaller per constituency in Scotland than in England – is the same in the two countries. This is expected to reduce the number of constituencies in Scotland from 72 to just under 60. An equal electoral quota in Wales – also over-represented at Westminster – would reduce the number of seats in Wales from 40 to about 33.

Devolution is thus likely to produce a modest reduction in the number of MPs, reducing some of the pressures on the resources of the institution. Potentially, an even greater change may occur if the UK acquires a new method of electing MPs. Depending on the type of electoral system employed, the UK could end up with a smaller or (less likely) larger House of Commons, or one roughly the same size as at present. For example, the use of 'Alternative Vote Plus' (single-member constituencies plus a top-up of members to ensure greater proportionality) – as recommended by the Independent Commission on the Voting System (the Jenkins Commission) in October 1998 – could, if there was a demand to retain existing constituencies, produce a larger House. The additional member system (AMS) would have the same effect unless existing single-member constituencies were substantially reduced in number.

The more members there are, the greater the demands made of space, staff time, library resources, and time on the floor of the House. A smaller House allows each member to have a greater share of resources. Given that MPs themselves generate work, usually for career purposes (tabling the maximum number of questions permitted, getting to their feet whenever possible in the chamber), a reduction in numbers would produce a notable 'value added' dimension.

Power

In constitutional terms, the effect of constitutional changes on the powers of the House is more significant. Parliament has already imposed limitations on itself by passing the European Communities Act 1972 and subsequent acts giving approval to later treaties. Under the terms of the 1972 Act, the force of law is given to all existing and future European regulations. Thus, once European law is promulgated it has effect in the UK: the assent of Parliament is not required. Under the 1972 Act, disputes are resolved by the courts and the ultimate arbiter is the European Court of Justice (the ECJ). The ECJ has already flexed its muscles by asserting the power of the courts to suspend an Act of Parliament.

Formally, Parliament retains the power to repeal the 1972 Act and to pass measures expressly overriding European law and, in that sense, it has not divested itself of parliamentary sovereignty. In practice, overriding European law – or repealing the 1972 Act – would create such enormous legal and political problems that it is not regarded as politically feasible. A similar though not quite identical situation is created by devolution, primarily by devolution of legislative powers to the Scottish parliament. The new parliament is empowered to legislate on matters other than those reserved to Westminster. The 1998 Scotland Act asserts the principle of parliamentary sovereignty and Parliament at Westminster could, if it wished, legislate on matters not reserved to it as well as repeal the 1998 Act. However, repealing the Act is not regarded as politically possible and it is unlikely that Parliament would seek to interfere in those areas that it has not reserved to itself. The effect is thus to devolve some of its powers to a body that is elected and thus has an electoral legitimacy of its own. Some limitation is also created by devolving powers to other elected assemblies in Northern Ireland and Wales.

The principle of parliamentary sovereignty is also maintained in the 1998 Human Rights Act, which incorporates the European Convention on Human Rights (ECHR) into British law. As a result of the doctrine of parliamentary sovereignty, the courts are denied the power to strike down a measure of UK law which is found to be inconsistent with the provisions of the ECHR. Instead, the courts have to make a formal declaration of incompatibility. As the Government's White Paper on the Bill put it: 'A declaration that legislation is incompatible with the Convention rights will not of itself have the effect of changing the law, which will continue to apply. But it will almost certainly prompt the Government and Parliament to change the law' (Home Office, 1997, p. 9). In other words, the formal power to ignore the declaration of the courts is maintained while recognising that, in practice, Parliament will change the law to comply with the court's interpretation.

Parliament thus retains the formal power to enact whatever measures it wants, by virtue of the doctrine of parliamentary sovereignty. However, it has imposed self-denying ordinances as a consequence of the passage of the 1972 European Communities Act and, now, by the enactment of the Scotland Act and the Human Rights Act. The effect of these measures is to introduce a new judicial dimension to the constitution (see Craig, 1999), one that effectively limits the capacity of Parliament to impose its will through a simple majority in the two chambers. Critics would point out that the difference all this makes is, in practical terms, limited, given that the House of Commons has little capacity to exercise a judgement independent of government.

There are also implications for the power of the House if there is a new electoral system or a new second chamber. If there is a new electoral system, then this may have dramatic effects on the power of the House to affect legislative outcomes. However, no one can be sure whether the effect would be to strengthen its powers – bargaining having to take place between parties, and/or with individual members having greater scope for independent action – or weaken it further, with parties having to be united in order to deliver on deals done by party leaders. Supporters of electoral reform point to the German Bundestag as an example of the former (the legislature being the site of negotiations and compromise between parties) and opponents point to neighbouring Belgium, where parties in the parliament are so rigidly cohesive that the legislature is regarded as being of little consequence (see Norton, 1998b).

The 1997 Parliament is expected to see a significant change in the House of Lords. The Parliament opened with a House of Lords containing approximately 750 hereditary peers. In December 1998 the Government introduced the House of Lords Bill, with one principal clause: 'No one shall be a member of the House of Lords by virtue of a hereditary peerage'. The bill was given a Second Reading by the House of Commons on 2 February 1999. The Government indicated it would consider accepting an amendment to retain 92 hereditary peers but that it remained committed to ending the dominance of the predominantly Conservative hereditary peers in the Upper House. According to Labour's 1997 election manifesto, 'This will be the first stage in a process of reform to make the House of Lords more democratic and representative' (Labour Party, 1997, p. 32). In January 1999, the Government published a White Paper on Lords Reform (Cabinet Office, 1999) and appointed a Royal Commission, under Tory peer Lord Wakeham, to make recommendations for the second stage. The Commission was asked to report by 31 December 1999, with the Report of the Commission then going to a Joint Committee of the two Houses.

Critics feared that the end result would be that the first stage of reform (the House shorn of its hereditary peers, bar the 92) would prove to be lasting, leaving a House that was predominantly appointed and thus vulnerable to swamping by life peers created by the incumbent Prime Minister. The government insisted that it would proceed to the second stage of reform once the recommendations of the Royal Commission had been considered by the Joint Committee of both Houses. It was widely expected that the proposals for stage two would include at least some element of election. The White Paper outlined various options (nominated, elected, mixed) but notably failed to list any disadvantages under the heading of a mixed chamber. If the second-phase of reform entails a part or wholly elected second chamber, then this has implications for the power of the House of Commons. Although there are no proposals – at least not on the part of government – to increase the powers of the Upper House, a chamber with some electoral legitimacy of its own is likely to be more willing to exercise its formal powers, and even to press for more, than is the case with a chamber that does not have that legitimacy. The experience of the European Parliament, which has pressed continuously for more powers since it made the transition from an appointed to an elected body in 1979, stands as an exemplar of what can happen. A substantial reform of the second chamber may thus serve as something of a threat to the first, especially if the political will exists to challenge decisions of the Commons. That is especially likely to be the case if the governing party does not enjoy a majority in the second chamber. A government, elected through elections to the House of Commons, could thus find itself challenged by an elected or part-elected second chamber.

Business

The business of the House of Commons will also be affected by the various changes to the constitution. The devolution of powers to elected assemblies is likely to reduce some of the burden of the House of Commons with measures that otherwise would be discussed by the House now being within the purview of the new assemblies. There will be few bills devoted to Scotland and the effect of an elected assembly in Northern Ireland should reduce the time spent by the House on Northern Ireland orders. Though the Scottish and Welsh Secretaries will still answer questions at the Dispatch Box, 'they will do so less frequently, and they will answer on a much narrower range of subjects' (Hazell, 1998, p. 17).

There will also be a change in the scope of parliamentary discussions. During the period that Northern Ireland had its own parliament at Stormont (1922–72), the Speaker ruled that matters delegated to the Stormont parliament should be the subject of questioning in Stormont and not in the House of Commons. It is likely that a similar ruling in respect of matters within the remit of the Scottish parliament will limit discussion in the House.

Structures

The structures of the House of Commons will also change, especially as a consequence of devolution (Hazell 1999). The Scottish and Welsh Grand Committees, created to hold general discussions on matters affecting the respective countries, are likely to disappear – there will be little for them to do – and it is also possible that the departmental select committees covering Scotland, Wales and Northern Ireland may go (especially the first); one proposal is that they be subsumed within a wider Select Committee on Devolution (Hazell, 1998, p. 17). Given that there will be less legislation devoted to Scotland, there will be less need for standing committees for Scottish bills.

The effect will thus be to reduce, albeit modestly, the committee work of the House, freeing the time of those members who otherwise would be appointed. However, there is the possibility of the House making use of committees in other areas. Given devolution, the House may make use of a Standing Committee on Regional Affairs to discuss matters affecting English regions. Provision for such a committee exists under standing orders, but one has not met since 1978.

Conclusion

The House of Commons is in a transitional phase, but essentially as an indirect consequence of legislation passed by Parliament rather than as a direct consequence of MPs' deliberating and taking decisions on their own structures and procedures. The various changes to the constitutional framework of the United Kingdom serve essentially to constrict the scope of the House of Commons. Legislative powers have been passed to other bodies and the House defers to the judgement of judicial bodies in determining human rights and the meaning of European treaties. Given these changes, the task of the House is to adapt its existing procedures to meet the changed conditions and to strengthen its capacity to scrutinise and influence government in those areas where government retains responsibility for acting. Though there is some evidence that some members recognise the need to consider the consequences for Parliament of the various changes to the constitution – in 1998, the Commons Procedure Committee began looking at the consequences for the House of devolution – the House of Commons has demonstrated little recognition of the need to look systematically, and with some urgency, at those consequences. And, though some reforms are likely as a consequence of the work of the Select Committee on Modernisation, there is again little evidence that the House as a whole is demanding change in order to strengthen its capacity to scrutinise and to influence the measures and actions of government. If a powerful government and significant constitutional changes are likened to a raging tiger, then the House of Commons may be likened to an inattentive, and poorly armed, hunter.

References

Butt, R. (1967) *The Power of Parliament* (London: Constable).

Cabinet Office (1999) *Modernising Parliament: Reforming the House of Lords*, Cm 4183 (London: The Stationery Office).

Cowley, P. (1998) 'In Place of Strife? New Labour's Parliamentarians', Paper presented at the EPOP Conference, Manchester, 11–13 September.

Craig, P. (1999) 'Constitutionalism, Regulation and Review', in Hazell, R., (ed.), *Constitutional Futures* (Oxford: Oxford University Press).

Franklin, M. and Norton, P. (eds) (1993) *Parliamentary Questions* (Oxford: Clarendon Press).

George, B. and Morgan J. D. (1999) 'Parliamentary Scrutiny of Defence', *Journal of Legislative Studies*, 4(4).

Hazell, R. (1998) 'Westminster and Whitehall', in P. Norton (ed.), *The Consequences of Devolution* (London: Hansard Society).

Hazell, R. (1999) 'Westminster: Squeezed from Above and Below', in R. Hazell (ed.), *Constitutional Futures* (Oxford: Oxford University Press).

Home Office (1997) *Rights Brought Home: The Human Rights Bill*, Cm 3782.

Independent Commission on the Voting System (1998) *The Report of the Independent Commission on the Voting System*, Cm 4090–I, (London: The Stationery Office).

Labour Party (1997) *New Labour: Because Britain Deserves Better* (London: Labour Party).

Norton, P. (1981) *The Commons in Perspective* (Oxford: Martin Robertson).

Norton, P. (1985), 'Behavioural Changes', in P. Norton (ed.), *Parliament in the 1980s* (Oxford: Basil Blackwell).

Norton, P. (1986a), 'Independence, scrutiny and rationalisation: A decade of changes in the House of Commons', *Teaching Politics*, 15(1).

Norton, P. (1986b) 'The Reform Parliament', *The Parliamentarian*, 67(2).

Norton, P. (1994a), 'Independence without entrenchment: The British House of Commons in the post-Thatcher era', *Talking Politics*, 6(2).

Norton, P. (1994b) 'Select committees in the House of Commons: Watchdogs or poodles?' *Politics Review*, 4(2).

Norton, P. (1996), 'The United Kingdom: Political Conflict, Parliamentary Scrutiny', in P. Norton (ed.), *National Parliaments and the European Union* (London: Frank Cass).

Norton, P. (1997a) 'Parliamentary Oversight', in P. Dunleavy, A. Gamble, I. Holliday and G. Peele, *Developments in British Politics 5* (London: Macmillan).

Norton, P. (1997b) 'Roles and Behaviour of British MPs', in Müller, W. C. and Saalfeld, T. (eds), *Members of Parliament in Western Europe* (London: Frank Cass).

Norton, P. (1998a) 'Nascent Institutionalisation: Committees in the British Parliament', in Longley, L. D. and Davidson, R. H. (eds), *The New Roles of Parliamentary Committees* (London: Frank Cass).

Norton, P. (ed.) (1998b) *Parliaments and Governments in Western Europe* (London: Frank Cass).

Norton, P. and Mitchell, A. (1997) 'Meet the New Breed', *The House Magazine*, 13 October.

Searing, D. (1994) *Westminster's World* (Cambridge Mass.: Harvard University Press).

Select Committee on Foreign Affairs (1999) *Sierra Leone: Second Report from the Foreign Affairs Committee*, Session 1998–99, HC 116–I.

Select Committee on Modernisation (1997a) *The Legislative Process: First Report from the Select Committee on Modernisation of the House of Commons*, Session 1997–98, HC 190.

Select Committee on Modernisation (1997b) *Select Committee on Modernisation of the House of Commons, Press Notice, No. 3*, 29 July.

Select Committee on Modernisation (1998), *Voting Methods: Sixth Report from the Select Committee on Modernisation*, Session 1997–98, HC 799.

Select Committee on Procedure (1978) *First Report from the Select Committee on Procedure*, Session 1977–78, HC 588.

Select Committee on Sittings of the House (1992) *Report from the Select Committee on Sittings of the House*, Session 1991–92, HC 20.

5

Parliamentary Scrutiny

MICHAEL RUSH

Ministerial Responsibility and Parliamentary Scrutiny

It is the distinguishing feature of parliamentary government that not only is the executive drawn from the legislature but, crucially, it is constitutionally responsible to it. The fact that almost without exception all ministers are members of either the House of Commons or the House of Lords clearly facilitates Parliament's ability to render them accountable to the legislature, but it is the doctrine of ministerial responsibility that is the constitutional basis of parliamentary scrutiny.

Ministerial responsibility takes two forms – collective and individual – and the ultimate sanction in both cases is the forced resignation of the government as a whole or of an individual minister respectively (Marshall, 1989, Woodhouse, 1994). In practice, however, governments rarely fall through being defeated in the House of Commons. The last to do so was the minority Labour government led by James Callaghan, which was forced into and lost the general election of 1979. The last occasion before that was in 1924 and before that 1895, although Neville Chamberlain resigned as Prime Minister in 1940 after his normal majority fell drastically. Resignations by individual ministers are more common, either because a minister is unwilling to accept government policy on a particular matter or range of matters – collective responsibility – or because the minister regards resignation as an appropriate response when an error of policy or administration has occurred – individual responsibility. However, the former are far more common than the latter and remarkably few resignations take place on the grounds of individual responsibility, in main because disagreement over policy from time to time is inevitable, but admissions of error to the point of resignation are embarrassing and unpalatable to governments.

Does this mean that ministerial responsibility is largely a constitutional fiction? The short answer is, not necessarily: it is a matter of opinion whether the House of Commons in general and government supporters in particular are unduly supine, but bringing down a government or forcing the resignation of a minister are only the ultimate forms of enforcing ministerial responsibility. The longer and more important answer is that in the context of day-to-day politics and policy making ministerial responsibility is the foundation of parliamentary scrutiny. It is precisely because of ministerial responsibility that members of both Houses of Parliament can demand that the government publicly explains and defends its actions and policies. Ministers are answerable to Parliament for their conduct of public policy and administration. The doctrine therefore underpins all debates, all parliamentary questions, all committee activity – the means by which Parliament seeks to exercise its scrutiny.

The Means of Parliamentary Scrutiny

Parliamentary scrutiny is exercised by both Lords and Commons using essentially the same tools, though to different degrees and effect. The great bulk of parliamentary business – more than four-fifths – is nowadays devoted to government business, either in the form of specific legislation or the scrutiny of government policy and administration. Furthermore, the government has considerable control over parliamentary business, not only because it normally has an overall majority in the Commons, but also because, with or without a majority, it retains substantial powers of initiative. Governments commonly secure the passage of well over 90 per cent of their bills through Parliament, occasionally even 100 per cent as in 1992–93 and 1993–94. Thus, even the minority Labour government of 1976–79 achieved success rates of well over 80 per cent. More often than not when government bills do not complete their passage it is because the parliamentary timetable has become

TABLE 5.1   *Division of Time on the Floor of the House of Commons,*
1985–86

	Hours (%)
Business initiated by the government	55
Business initiated by the opposition	10
Business initiated by backbench MPs	35
Total	100

Source: Adapted from Griffith, J.A. and Ryle, M. (1989) p. 12.

too crowded. Government legislation may be modified while it is
going through Parliament, but in most cases the government accepts
changes rather than having them forced upon it. Similarly, the
government normally wins any divisions that take place during or
at the end of debates on policy and administration, but it is misleading to measure parliamentary scrutiny in terms of votes won
and lost. Ultimately, parliamentary scrutiny is about exposing the
government and its activities to public debate and is therefore a
more complex and subtle business than counting members through
the division lobbies. Moreover, the opportunities for scrutiny are
more widespread than the government's ability to secure the passage of its programme would suggest, as the division of time on the
floor of the House of Commons shows in Table 5.1.

Parliament has at its disposal four major means of parliamentary
scrutiny: legislative procedure, debates on non-legislative business,
parliamentary questions, and investigatory committees. Through
these the government is subject to scrutiny by the official opposition
(normally the second largest party in the House), which offers itself
as a government-in-waiting, by other parties in opposition, and by
all backbench MPs, including its own supporters.

Legislative Procedure

Legislation includes all primary legislation, that is bills tabled in
either House which, if passed through all the necessary stages,
become Acts of Parliament, and secondary or delegated legislation,
that is regulations issued by ministers (or, since Britain's accession to
the EU, by the European Commission) under the authority granted
by Acts of Parliament (or in the case of European legislation,

Britain's signature of the Treaty of Rome). Unless it is passed under the provisions of the Parliament Acts 1911 and 1949, all primary legislation must be passed by both Houses of Parliament. The Parliament Acts allow the Commons to override the rejection of a bill by the Lords, but only five Acts have become law in this way: two in 1914, the 1949 Act itself and, more recently, one in 1991 and one in 1999. In addition, the Parliament Act 1911 requires the Upper House to pass financial legislation within one month of its passage through the Commons. The fact that no party has an overall majority in the House of Lords does not generally cause undue difficulties for governments and the Lords normally gives way to the Commons if the Lower House persists in its views on legislation.

Bills go through a fairly elaborate procedure, basically the same in both Houses, at all stages of which (except a formal introduction) they are subject to varying degrees of scrutiny. How effective that scrutiny is undoubtedly varies. The more strongly the government is committed to a bill the less likely it is to accept any but the most limited of amendments. Few bills are subject to a formal allocation of time motion or guillotine, which is only possible in the Commons, but all are normally subject to a timetable negotiated with the opposition.

Following a second reading, which deals with the principles of the bill, it goes through a committee stage in which it is debated in detail clause by clause. The committee stage may be taken on the floor of the House or by a standing committee. Up to two-thirds of all government bills each year are referred to a standing committee. Standing committees, however, are miniatures of the House both in membership and, more importantly, procedure in that they mirror the confrontation of government versus opposition. They are therefore largely a device to enable the Commons to deal with several bills simultaneously, thus freeing the floor of the House for other business. The House then debates the results of the bill's passage through the committee in what is called the report stage, which is followed by a final look at the bill as a whole in a third reading. The House of Lords follows a similar procedure, except that it does not make extensive use of committees for the committee stage of bills, but usually takes that stage on the floor of the House.

Commons debates on government legislation are often partisan, which tends to militate against effective scrutiny, but such debates expose bills to wider examination than they would otherwise receive and force ministers to defend their legislative proposals publicly. Though less partisan than in the Commons and not subject to formal timetabling, legislative debates in the Lords are otherwise subject to similar limitations in that scrutiny is as effective as the expertise, the number of participants, and the time available allows.

Both Houses have the power to appoint a select committee to take the committee stage, which would allow ministers, civil servants, pressure groups, and independent experts to submit written evidence on the bill's proposals and be called to give oral evidence. This procedure is seldom used, however, and debate is therefore normally confined to the members of the House concerned and extra-parliamentary expertise can only be brought to bear informally. Commons Standing Orders also provide for the setting up of special standing committees to take the committee stage of a bill and these have the power to take oral and written evidence. However, such committees have only been used seven times since their inception in 1980, the last two occasions in 1994–95 and 1995–96, although reformers have long pressed for their general or more extensive use (Hansard Society 1993).

A similar situation prevails in the scrutiny of delegated legislation, mostly in the form of statutory instruments. The House of Commons spends only some 5 per cent of the time on the floor of the House on secondary legislation, including that from Brussels, although more time is spent in committees and the Lords devotes more time to delegated legislation than the Commons. But again, with the important exception of the Lords Committee on the European Communities, evidence from the policy-makers and people outside Parliament is not taken by parliamentary committees dealing with delegated legislation. Moreover, statutory instruments may not be amended, only rejected, and most are subject to negative procedure, that is they will come into force unless Parliament specifically rejects them. More recently, following the passing of the Deregulation and Contracting Out Act in 1994, which was designed to reduce the amount of government regulation, the Commons set up a Deregulation Committee to scrutinise regulations proposed for repeal.

Non-legislative Debates

The Commons spends between a quarter and a third of its time on government legislation, but nearly twice as much debating other matters. Some of these debates take place on the initiative of the parties in opposition, although the official opposition understandably has the lion's share of such initiatives. Other debates are initiated by backbenchers on subjects of their choice, but most debates are initiated by the government, relating either to necessary business, such as the debate on the Queen's Speech outlining the government's annual programme, or on financial matters, or debates on particular policy areas. Not all debates end with a division, but those that do normally see the government prevail through its majority. All debates, however, provide MPs, whether supporters of the government or not, with the opportunity to evaluate government policy and administration and to that extent at least are an important contribution to parliamentary scrutiny. How effective they are is a matter of judgement: much depends on the quality of the input by members, an inevitably variable factor, and partisanship sometimes obfuscates more penetrating scrutiny. A former Speaker of the House of Commons has estimated that a backbencher is likely to be called to speak four times a year and experiments have been conducted in placing limits on the length of speeches. The general adoption of such limits might be welcome, but it should not be assumed that the number of speakers able to participate is directly proportionate to the quality of scrutiny. What is more important is to allow and encourage the participation of those who have something useful to contribute to a particular debate, an objective more easily stated than achieved.

Parliamentary Questions

The third means of parliamentary scrutiny is the parliamentary question, sometimes seen as the most potent weapon in the hands of the individual parliamentarian. Certainly, the well-judged question can be used with devastating effect, though not always strictly as a means of parliamentary scrutiny. Furthermore, Question Time in the Commons, especially the once-a-week Questions to the Prime Minister, is undoubtedly the aspect of Parliament most familiar to the public, particularly since the broadcasting of parliamentary proceedings began, first on radio and later on television. The reality of parliamentary questions is, however, more complex.

In the first place those questions which receive an oral answer at Question Time constitute only the tip of the iceberg: in the 1995–96 parliamentary session they amounted to only 13.7 per cent of all questions tabled; the rest received a written reply. This is partly explained by that fact that there are always more questions tabled for oral reply than can be answered in the time available, but the main explanation is that most questions seek a written not an oral answer. All written answers are printed with the day's proceedings in Hansard. Thus, spectacular as Question Time sometimes is, it is certainly quantitatively and probably qualitatively less important as a means of parliamentary scrutiny than questions tabled for written answer. There is no doubt that the latter provide a most effective means of extracting information from the government, often information which the government would not otherwise reveal. This is sometimes simply because it has not been asked to disclose particular information, but also because governments seek to retain as much control over information as possible. Nonetheless, parliamentary questions are a major and generally effective means of scrutiny. Moreover, their use has grown considerably since the 1946–47 parliamentary session, when a total of 16 930 were answered; in 1995–96 the total had more than doubled to 40 388. The pattern of questions has also changed significantly: in 1946–47 not only were more questions answered orally, but questions put down for oral answer were twice as numerous as those put down for written answer. In 1995–96 questions for written answer outnumbered those tabled for oral answer by a ratio of more than six to one; in short, questions for written answer had become immensely more important as a means of parliamentary scrutiny (Franklin and Norton, 1993).

Investigatory Committees

The fourth and final means of parliamentary scrutiny is that of investigatory committees, that is, select committees which have the power 'to send for persons, papers and records' – to take oral and written evidence from anyone or any organisation they wish. In practice, this means they can question ministers, civil servants, independent experts and interested individuals, and organisations from outside the governmental apparatus, including, of course, pressure groups. Oral evidence is presented by invitation and is limited by the time available, but written evidence may be submitted by any individual or organisation and provides an important channel for pressure groups to put their point of view (Rush, 1990).

In addition to select committees, the House of Commons also uses other types of committees which play a part in parliamentary scrutiny. The use of standing committees for the committee stage of bills has already been noted, but business relating to Scotland, Wales and Northern Ireland may also be dealt with by the Scottish Grand Committee the Welsh Grand Committee, and the Northern Ireland Committee respectively, which consist principally of MPs from those parts of the United Kingdom. These arrangements will change to varying degrees with the setting up devolved legislatures in those parts of the UK. The second reading of some bills – four in 1994–95 and two in 1995–96 – is taken in a second reading committee, rather than the floor of the House, and standing committees also examine domestic and European delegated legislation. All these committees provide additional opportunities for scrutiny, but it is investigatory select committees which provide the House of Commons with the most systematic means of parliamentary scrutiny. However, before turning to these in more detail, a brief word should be said about the House of Lords.

The House of Lords and Parliamentary Scrutiny

The House of Lords contributes significantly to Parliament's ability to scrutinise the executive. The membership of the Lords covers a remarkable range of expertise and legislation is often discussed more thoroughly in the Upper House than in the Commons, especially where a bill has been subject to a tight timetable in the lower chamber. It is widely acknowledged that the House of Lords deals more effectively with delegated legislation emanating from Brussels, principally through its Select Committee on the European Communities. Operating through six sub-committees, the European Communities Committee issues between twenty and thirty reports a year. It differs from its Commons counterpart in two important respects: first, whereas the Commons committee concentrates on drawing attention to proposals from Brussels of legal and political importance with a view to their being debated on the floor of the House, the Lords committee produces substantive, investigatory reports; second, the Commons committee does not normally take evidence, but the Lords committee takes a wide range of oral and written evidence. Most of the committee's reports, however, are not debated, but, as Donald Shell (1993, p. 280) points out, 'work by osmosis, transferring information and ideas around the body politic'. Strictly speaking, of course, the scrutiny involved here (and in the Commons) is of the European Commission in Brussels, rather than the government in Whitehall, although the latter bears responsibility for the British response to EU policy initiatives and for those responses to the UK Parliament. Shell (1993, p. 280) concludes that the European Communities Committee provides 'a serious and well-defined response to the practicalities of Community policy-making'.

The House of Lords also plays a major part in dealing with domestic delegated legislation through the Joint Committee on Statutory Instruments and extended its role significantly in 1993 by establishing a Delegated Powers and Deregulation Committee to 'give closer and more systematic scrutiny to the delegated powers sought in bills' (House of Lords, 1991–92, para. 33). This has added a further dimension to the parliamentary scrutiny of delegated legislation, which was subsequently adopted by the Commons.

Although the Upper House has considerably fewer select committees than the Commons, those it has are regarded as effective instruments of scrutiny and, moreover, they do not normally duplicate the inquiries conducted by Commons committees. Apart from the Select Committee on the European Communities and the Joint Committee on Statutory Instruments, the House of Lords has only one other permanent select committee – that on Science and Technology but it also makes use of *ad hoc* select committees, recent examples being those on Central–Local Relations and on the Public Service. In essence the Lords has developed its own distinctive committees and this applies to other forms of scrutiny. Questions for oral answer, for instance, are often more penetrating and less partisan in the Lords and may, unlike the Commons, lead to short debates.

The House of Lords should therefore been seen as supplementing the scrutiny provided by the Commons and not as an alternative to the latter (Shell, 1992; Shell and Beamish, 1993). That parliamentary scrutiny would be seriously damaged by the abolition of the House of Lords, leaving Parliament as a single-chamber legislature, cannot be doubted. Abolition, however, is unlikely, but the Labour government elected in 1997 has already taken steps to remove the hereditary members of the House of Lords and institute a more democratic second chamber, either wholly elected or partly elected, partly nominated (as with existing life peers). This, however, raises other questions: anachronistic and undemocratic as the House of Lords may be, it is incumbent on those who seek its replacement to ensure that parliamentary scrutiny is not weakened as a consequence (Rush, 1994; Constitution Unit, 1996; Cabinet Office, 1999).

Select Committees and Parliamentary Scrutiny

The Public Accounts Committee

Select committees have long been part of the parliamentary scene, but came to particular prominence during the nineteenth century when they were frequently used to investigate particular problems and to produce draft bills. The oldest surviving investigatory select committee, however, is the Public Accounts Committee (PAC), established in 1861 to examine departmental accounts and ensure that the expenditure approved by Parliament has been properly and effectively spent. The PAC has always stood apart from the other select committees, partly because it has the assistance of a full-time official, the Comptroller and Auditor-General (C&AG) and his staff in the National Audit Office (NAO), and partly because its role is one of ensuring financial rectitude and seeking value for money. Put another way, the PAC is regarded as a financial watchdog, not as a critic of the government's policy objectives. The PAC therefore epitomises parliamentary scrutiny, but in practice the line between financial scrutiny and criticising policy is less easily drawn: criticising the implementation of policy, however closely allied to its financial aspects, can frequently lead to or imply criticism of the policy itself. Nevertheless, the PAC has built up a formidable reputation, often being described in the media as 'powerful' or 'highly influential', and it is said that civil servants (including permanent secretaries) do not relish the prospect of appearing before it.

The PAC has undoubtedly produced many penetrating, sometimes scathing, reports on a wide range of government policies. Its criticisms are detailed and widely regarded as authoritative; its recommendations are invariably accepted by the government; and, through the C&AG and, if necessary, subsequent hearings, the committee checks whether its recommendations have been carried out. In the 1980s, for example, the PAC produced highly critical reports on the dispensing of drugs in the NHS, government control of capital expenditure by local authorities, the production costs of defence equipment, home improvement grants, and the cost of storing EC food surpluses and in the 1990s on the Pergau Dam and aid to Malaysia, the Welsh Development Agency, and the Development Board for Rural Wales. The NAO, of course, plays a vital role in all this: with a staff of some 800 the C&AG is able to make detailed analyses of departmental accounts and direct the PAC to those matters which merit its attention. The number of staff at the NAO has fallen slightly in recent years, but this has been compensated for by the growing use of consultants, whose expertise in particular fields can be brought usefully to bear.

Experimental Committees

The PAC apart, however, the use of select committees declined during the twentieth century until their substantial revival in the 1960s and later, culminating in the establishment in 1979 of the then fourteen departmental select committees. As early as the 1930s select committees were seen as a major means of adjusting the balance between the executive and the legislature. That balance, it was argued, had shifted markedly in favour of the executive in the latter part of the nineteenth century and early part of the twentieth with the growth of disciplined parties in Parliament. Increasingly the initiative in parliamentary business fell to the government, most legislation that found its way onto the statute book was government legislation, and Parliament became dominated by the confrontation between government and opposition. The opposition saw itself and was seen as an alternative government and therefore had a strong incentive to cooperate with the government it hoped to replace in managing parliamentary business – the so-called 'conspiracy of the front benches'.

The period after 1945 into the 1960s could be said to mark the zenith of two-party domination in Britain: the Conservative and Labour parties were responsible for more than three-quarters of the candidates standing at general elections between 1945 and 1970, regularly secured 90 or more per cent of the votes cast, and 98 per cent of the MPs elected. Moreover, in the same period the government was defeated only eleven times on the floor of the House of Commons, none of which resulted in the downfall of the government or the calling of a general election. The late 1950s and early 1960s, however, were marked by a growing chorus of criticism of national institutions, including Parliament (Hill and Whichelow, 1964; Crick, 1964). This coincided with an influx in the general elections of 1959, 1964 and 1966 of new members on both sides of the House who were more reform-minded than many of their predecessors. They were not content to be lobby-fodder and expected a more active role. In addition, appalled at the low level of the parliamentary salary (from which they were expected to meet most of their expenses) and the lack of services and facilities at Westminster, they demanded better pay and conditions. In the second edition of his *The Reform of Parliament* Bernard Crick (1968, pp. 66–7) bluntly stated: 'clearly a Member should be able to draw on public funds, or be reimbursed from them, for those essentials he needs to do his job properly: secretary, office, postage, telephone and travel'. Within a short time significant advances had been made on all these fronts: from 1972 a clear distinction was drawn between a member's salary and the expenses incurred in carrying out parliamentary duties and the costs of secretarial assistance, office accommodation, postage, telephone, subsistence, and travel are now met substantially from the public purse (Rush and Shaw, 1974; Rush, 1983, 1996).

Reformers both inside and outside Parliament regarded select committees as offering the most effective way of improving the ability of the House of Commons to scrutinise the government's activities. A survey of MPs conducted in 1967 found that Members elected in 1959 or later were more likely to support such committees than their longer-serving colleagues (Barker and Rush, 1970, pp. 378–84). A limited experiment had been started in the 1950s with the setting up of a Select Committee on Nationalised Industries, which was cited as a successful role-model. In the early 1960s the Estimates Committee, operating through a series of sub-committees, provided further evidence that select committees could usefully investigate policy and administration in a bipartisan manner without undermining the wider partisan conflict in the House of Commons. There followed more experimentation, first with a series of specialised committees, commonly known as the 'Crossman committees' after the then Leader of the House responsible for introducing them. These covered areas such as science and technology, agriculture, education, and Scottish affairs. Then, in 1970, following a major report from the Select Committee on Procedure, the old Estimates Committee and several of the Crossman committees were replaced by a Select Committee on Expenditure using specialised sub-committees to cover a wide range of government departments and policy areas. All these committees demonstrated the viability of investigatory select committees as instruments of parliamentary scrutiny, but they also showed the need for a comprehensive system of committees to cover the full range of government responsibilities.

It was such a system of departmentally-related committees that a further Procedure Committee report recommended in 1978. Its recommendations were accepted by the newly-elected Conservative government in 1979, which, following the rejection of devolution proposals for Wales and Scotland, added committees on Welsh and Scottish Affairs to the twelve departmental committees advocated by the Procedure Committee. The departmental select committees have therefore been in existence since 1979 and remain a vital part of the process of parliamentary scrutiny. They now number seventeen, the number varying according to the number of government departments. The growth in parliamentary scrutiny by investigatory select committees can be gauged by examining committee activity in selected parliamentary sessions between 1956–57, when the Nationalised Industries Committee was properly established, and 1995–96, the last complete session of the 1992–97 Parliament.

Although the figures in Table 5.2 on the number of committees in existence are misleading to the extent that greater use was made of sub-committees before 1979, the overall picture remains clear, especially when it is noted that the number of meetings, including

TABLE 5.2 *Select Committee Activity, 1956–96*

Session	No. of investigatory committees	No. of meetings[a]	No. of inquiries[b]
1956–57	3	120	11
1968–69	9	371	27
1977–78	6	456	51
1985–86	16	555	148
1995–96	21	630	174

Notes: [a] Including sub-committees.
    [b] Including inquiries completed in a subsequent session and those not resulting in a report.

sub-committees, increased by more than five times between 1956 and 1996 and that the number of inquiries rose by a ratio of nearly sixteen to one. In terms of meetings the PAC was a fairly constant factor – 31 meetings in 1956–57 and 38 in 1995–96, but the number of inquiries it conducted rose from three to fifty. This was a consequence of a change of policy from that of conducting a small number of major inquiries to pursuing a much larger number of short, sharp inquiries, though by no means to the neglect of the former. This was further facilitated by increased staffing at the NAO. Inevitably, the number of backbench MPs involved in investigatory select committee activity increased from about seventy to more than three hundred. Lastly, and most important of all, this activity constituted an enormous quantitative increase in and extension of the scope of parliamentary scrutiny.

The Departmental Select Committees

Few observers have argued that the departmental select committees are a failure: MPs, such as Enoch Powell and Michael Foot, who opposed them (and the earlier specialised committees) did so mainly on the grounds that they would undermine the role of the chamber of the House of Commons and encourage consensus politics (Granada, 1973, pp. 159–60 and 193), in short, that select committees are a distraction from the basic role of Parliament as the forum for what Powell called 'the great clash of politics'. Even among supporters of the committees there are those who regard them as only a qualified success. Certainly, the exaggerated hopes of some reformers have not been realised, nor could they have been without a fundamental change in the British political system. The idea that a range of adequately funded and well-staffed select committees could emulate congressional committees in the United States reflects a failure to understand both the congressional and parliamentary systems: the separation of powers and the loosely organised American party system combine to make congressional committees extremely powerful, just as the fusion of powers and the tightly organised British party system combine to prevent select committees from becoming powerful. Indeed, media descriptions of the most effective select committee, the PAC, as 'powerful' are inaccurate in so far as its power is limited, but its influence is considerable because of the authoritative nature of its reports and the wide respect in which it is held. Select committees can do no more than make recommendations and cannot force the government to accept them: all parliamentary committees are creatures of their respective Houses and, as far as the Commons is concerned, the government normally has the last say through its majority.

Assessing the impact of select committees is no easy task: various quantitative measures can be used, but the final judgement must be qualitative. Nonetheless, those statistics available provide a crucial basis for any qualitative judgement (Table 5.3).

In terms of meetings and reports it is clear that some committees are considerably more active than others. For example, the Foreign Affairs, Treasury, and Defence Committees have always been among the more active in both respects, whereas Scottish Affairs, Welsh Affairs, and Agriculture have been among the less active. On the other hand, some committees have varied in their level of activity over the four Parliaments, notably Education, Trade and Industry, and Environment. However, the relationship between the number of meetings and number of reports is variable – Home Affairs, for instance, held 145 meetings in 1987–92 and produced 31 reports, compared with 178 meetings and 21 reports in 1992–97. Thus, in spite of being subject to common procedures, the committees do not operate in a uniform fashion. Each committee decides its own agenda and a great deal depends upon who chairs the committee. The chairing of the committees is shared between the parties: in 1992–97 there were ten Conservative and six Labour chairs and from 1997 fourteen Labour (including sub-committees), four Conservatives and one Liberal Democrat. Who chairs a committee, however, rather than which party, shapes the level of activity and style of a committee. For example, between 1979 and 1983 the Education Committee was one of the most active committees and also ranged very widely in its inquiries (including areas beyond the scope of government responsibilities, such as the future of *The Times* supplements and of the Promenade Concerts, when both were affected by strike action). Informal sub-committees were used, chaired by another member of the committee. All this owed much to Christopher Price (Labour), the committee's chairman, but under his successor in the 1983–87 Parliament, Sir William van Straubanzee (Conservative), the committee was less active and changed markedly in style. Other active chairmen have been

TABLE 5.3 Numbers of Meetings and Reports Presented by Departmental Select Committees, 1979–97

Committee	1979–83		1983–87		1987–92		1992–97	
	Meetings	Reports[a]	Meetings	Reports[a]	Meetings	Reports[a]	Meetings	Reports[a]
Agriculture	99	6	78	10	134	17	128	18
Defence	159	13	176	18	161	50	149	47
Education[b]	166	19	126	10	129	14	106	17
Employment[b]	112	11	102	13	152	16	128	12
Education & Employment[b]	–	–	–	–	–	–	50	8
Energy[c]	150	11	123	29	151	31	–	–
Environment	116	9	131	16	136	25	187	23
Foreign Affairs	249[d]	21	192[d]	20	203	17	212	19
Health[e]	–	–	–	–	45	7	190	19
Home Affairs	218[d]	20	125[d]	16	145	31	178	21
National Heritage[f]	–	–	–	–	–	–	175	24
Northern Ireland[g]	–	–	–	–	–	–	75	5
Public Service[h]	–	–	–	–	–	–	40	5
Science & Technology[i]	–	–	–	–	–	–	131	15
Scottish Affairs	118	8	72	7	[j]	[j]	111	13
Social Security[e]	–	–	–	–	44	6	165	25
Social Services[e]	154	11	135	18	86	26	–	–
Trade & Industry	119	19	141	12	189	17	194	28
Transport	137	15	136	14	132	16	168	23

Treasury & Civil Service[h]	226[b]	24	178[b]	30	157[b]	33	237	30
Welsh Affairs	117	6	74	5	104	17	133	14
Totals	2 140	193	1 789	218	1 968	323	2 748	366

Notes: [a] Excluding special reports, mostly government responses to substantive reports.
[b] Merged in 1995–96 to form the Education and Employment Committee.
[c] The Department of Energy was merged with Trade in 1992.
[d] Including meetings of sub-committees.
[e] The Department of Health and Social Security was divided in 1988.
[f] Department of National Heritage was created in 1992 and renamed Culture, Media and Sport 1997.
[g] The Northern Ireland Committee was set up in 1994.
[h] The Public Service Committee (now Public Administration) was set up in 1995, taking over the responsibilities of the Civil Service Sub-Committee of the Treasury and Civil Service Committee.
[i] The Science and Technology Committee was set up in 1992, following the creation of the Office of Science and Technology.
[j] The Scottish Affairs Committee was not set up in 1987–92 because the government and opposition could not agree on its membership, following the election of only ten Conservatives in Scotland.

Sources: Drewry, G. (ed.), 1989, p. 334 & Annex 22.2; House of Commons Sessional Returns.

Terence Higgins (Conservative – Treasury and Civil Service 1983–92), Frank Field (Labour – Social Services 1987–90 and Social Security 1991–97), Nicholas Winterton (Conservative – Health 1991–92), and Gerald Kaufman (Labour – National Heritage 1992–97 and Culture, Media and Sport from 1997). In a number of cases those chairing committees have developed close working relationships with senior members of the opposite party and the departmental committees are noted for a high level of bipartisanship, including agreeing on reports, as are select committees generally. The number of divisions per meeting was 0.267 in 1979–83, 0.228 in 1984–85, 0.284 in 1985–86, and 0.054 in 1995–96. These figures are both low in number and remarkably consistent, invariably being concentrated on very few matters or particular draft reports and by no means always on strict party lines.

The most obvious statistical measure of the impact of the departmental committees is the extent to which their recommendations are accepted by the government.

The data shown in Table 5.4 are inevitably far from conclusive, especially given the impreciseness of the term 'main recommendations' in section B of the table. A favourable interpretation is that the number of recommendations accepted is surprisingly high given the dominance of the government in the British parliamentary system; a less favourable interpretation is that the proportion of recommendations accepted is very low and that 'keep under review' is a euphemism for rejection. Even if this latter view is adopted, however, the figures suggest some influence and therefore impact on the part of the departmental committees.

An alternative approach is to examine specific claims. Griffith and Ryle (1989, pp. 430–3) in their major study, *Parliament: Functions, Practice and Procedures*, cite twelve 'claimed successes' for the committees. These include Home Affairs and the 'sus law', Transport and the privatisation of HGV testing, Education and the new British Library building, Agriculture and animal welfare, and Energy and North Sea oil taxation. The Procedure Committee has claimed other successes: Foreign Affairs on the future of Hong Kong, Treasury and Civil Service on the publication of the annual reports of government departments, and Trade and Industry on the effect on overseas trade with Asian countries, particularly Malaysia, of the raising of overseas student fees (House of Commons, 1989–90, para. 358). More recently, critical reports from the Social

TABLE 5.4   *Government Responses to Recommendations by Departmental Select Committees*

(a) *The Education, Science and Arts and the Social Services Committees, 1979–83*

Response[a]	Education, Science & Arts %	Social Services %
Accepted	26.5	35.1
Keep under review	46.4	45.2
Rejected	27.1	19.7
Totals	100.0	100.0
	n=181	n=188

Note: [a] Excluding recommendations not directly the responsibility of the government.

(b) *Main recommendation of departmental committees accepted by the government, 1983–86[a]*

	1983–84[b]	1984–85	1985–86	Total
No. of main recommendations accepted	37	143	144	324

Notes: [a] From March to March in each year.
[b] The figures for the period March 1983 to March 1984 were affected by the holding of the general election in June 1983 and the delay in reconstituting the departmental committees until December 1983.
Sources: Rush, M. (1985) 'The Education, Science and Arts Committee' and 'The Social Services Committee' in Drewry, 1989, pp. 100 and 249; *HC Debs*, vol. 101, 15 July 1986, cc. *460–78* (written answers).

Security Committee and the Select Committee on the Parliamentary Commissioner for Administration (the Ombudsman) have been a factor in changes in the operation of the Child Support Agency. Similarly, the Treasury Committee has made a significant contribution to changes in the way in which government expenditure plans are presented to Parliament. On the other hand, Griffith and Ryle also provide instances of the government firmly rejecting major recommendations: by several committees on the Westland affair, by the Treasury and Civil Service Committee on the future of the Civil Service Department (abolished by the government), by

Employment on the dismissal of miners following the coal dispute of 1984–85, by Defence on the privatisation of naval dockyards, by Foreign Affairs on Britain's withdrawal from UNESCO. Similarly, in 1999 the government gave an immediate and brusque rejection to the Foreign Affairs Committee's criticism of the Foreign Office over arms to the government of Sierra Leone. But Griffith and Ryle place the matter firmly in perspective: 'Select committees have not made a general impact on government policies' (Griffith and Ryle 1989, p. 430).

These claims and counter-claims raise a further question, however: should select committees be judged simply on their success or failure to influence government policy? And underlying that question is a more fundamental one: should select committees be seeking to influence government policy? Thus George Jones has argued that the departmental committees were misconceived in that their principal target should be the scrutiny of administration not policy (House of Commons, 1989–90, pp. 195–203). However, given the recommendatory role clearly ascribed to select committees, there is no reason why they should not seek to influence government policy if their inquiries and deliberations suggest that it is appropriate. But influencing policy is not their sole objective, only a by-product of their scrutinising role. In assessing the impact of the departmental select committees over the 1979–83 and 1983–87 Parliaments, Gavin Drewry (1989, p. 426) concluded, 'select committees are, and can realistically only aspire to be, in the business of scrutiny, not of government'.

Judging the effectiveness of the departmental committees as instruments of parliamentary scrutiny should not be limited to assessing their influence on government policies – far more has been achieved in this sphere by the growth of backbench assertiveness since the early 1970s (Norton, 1975, 1978, 1980, 1985; Norton and Cowley, 1999). Committees need to be judged by additional criteria, many of which do not lend themselves to quantification or only partly so.

First, and perhaps most important, all government departments now come under scrutiny by the departmental committees. Second, the sheer volume of information published by the committees brings government policy and administration more fully into the public domain than ever before. Third, ministers and senior civil servants are subject to public questioning more frequently than ever before.

Fourth, the longer-term impact on policy and administration is likely to be significant, especially as committees increasingly review earlier inquiries and return to particular policy areas. Fifth, more MPs are involved in select committee activity, enabling the House of Commons to develop and increase its pool of specialised knowledge and scrutinising skills. Sixth, the departmental committees are much better staffed than their predecessors: in 1995–96 the number of administrative staff was 79 and the number of specialist advisers 108. Nonetheless, problems remain, but these are best considered in the wider context of parliamentary scrutiny.

Parliamentary Scrutiny: An Overview

Ministerial responsibility itself came under considerable scrutiny as a result of the 'arms-to-Iraq' affair and the subsequent inquiry conducted by a senior judge, Sir Richard Scott. However, although the Scott Report provides much fascinating detail about the workings of British government, whether it and the debates that ensued inside and outside Parliament have clarified or clouded the meaning of ministerial responsibility remains a matter of opinion.

Scott strongly criticised two ministers – William Waldegrave, when Minister of State at the Foreign Office, for misleading the House of Commons, and Sir Nicholas Lyell, the then Attorney-General, over issuing Public Issue Immunity Certificates to limit legal access to government documents. Neither minister accepted the criticism and neither resigned, although the government only won the division at the end of the debate on the Scott Report by a single vote (House of Commons, 1995–96; Bogdanor, 1996; Hansard Society, 1997).

Scott also sought to clarify the meaning of ministerial responsibility by arguing that the key to the doctrine lies in the supply of information to Parliament, not whether ministers resign. In turn, Sir Robin Butler, the then Secretary to the Cabinet, offered a further clarification by drawing a distinction between responsibility – meaning accepting the blame, the consequence of which might appropriately be resignation – and accountability – meaning providing information. The distinction is not a new one (Finer, 1956) and it is easy to see where one begins and the other ends, but at what point does rendering an account become a matter of accepting blame?

The absence of resignations over the 'arms-to-Iraq' affair is not an isolated case: no ministerial resignations followed prison escapes from the Maze in Northern Ireland in 1983, Brixton in 1991, Parkhurst in 1995 and a near escape from Whitemoor Prison in 1994 (Barker, 1998); nor did the Chancellor of the Exchequer, Norman Lamont, resign in the aftermath of 'Black Wednesday' and Britain's withdrawal from the ERM. Arguably, some, possibly all, of these cases should have resulted in resignations; certainly, over the same period other ministers resigned for 'lesser offences'. Nor is this a recent development: it is no less true of other governments, other parties and other times (Finer, 1956). The explanation is fairly straightforward, however: governments and governing parties usually rally round the offending minister and political solidarity, usually expressed through the government's majority, rules the day. Of course, the 'offending' minister may lose office in a subsequent government reshuffle, or be 'honourably retired' to the House of Lords, and so political expedience supersedes ministerial responsibility. The paucity and unevenness of ministerial resignations is to be deplored, but it should not be allowed to obscure the much more mundane operation of ministerial responsibility as the foundation of parliamentary scrutiny.

Ministerial responsibility may be the foundation of parliamentary scrutiny, but it can also be used to blunt that scrutiny. In giving evidence to select committees, for example, civil servants use ministerial responsibility to justify a refusal to divulge what advice they have given ministers and ministers refuse to disclose details of intra- and inter-departmental discussions, unless, of course, it suits them. On occasion, in response to parliamentary questions or requests from committees, ministers refuse to disclose information on the grounds that it is not in the public interest to do so, but retain the right to decide the public interest. The role of the whips in determining the membership of select committees and who chairs them was highlighted in the bitter wrangle over the exclusion of Nicholas Winterton (Conservative) from the Health Committee, when the departmental committees were re-established after the 1992 election, although there is little evidence that the whips play a significant part in the subsequent operation of committees.

It is undeniable that parliamentary scrutiny has increased quantitatively from the 1960s onwards, most notably in the number of parliamentary questions asked and in the range and level of select committee activity. But is it effective? Ministers and civil servants are forced to explain and attempt to justify their proposals and actions far more than their predecessors ever were. This can only help to increase the effectiveness of parliamentary scrutiny. Moreover, some of that public exposure – potentially all of it – now reaches a wider audience than ever through the broadcasting of parliamentary proceedings, especially on television. Events like the Falklands War and policies such as the future of Westland Helicopters came under much greater scrutiny than would have been the case in the 1950s; there was, for instance, no parliamentary inquiry into any aspect of the Suez affair in 1956. More does not necessarily mean better, but the more Parliament is able to subject government policy and administration to public examination the more effective parliamentary scrutiny is likely to be.

Effectiveness, however, also needs to be measured qualitatively and that judgement is considerably more difficult to make. The predominance of party normally ensures not only the government's survival, but the survival of its policies. In circumstances other than normal retirement, the fate of leaders lies with their party rather than Parliament, as Edward Heath and Margaret Thatcher know to their cost. This is sometimes true of ministers as well, as could be argued in the cases of David Mellor in 1992 and Norman Lamont and Michael Mates in 1993. A small government majority (or the lack of a majority as in February–October 1974 and 1976–79) can be a crucial factor, considerably enhancing the influence of government backbenchers in particular, but also increasing the potential for greater influence by Parliament. But much depends on perception: the Conservative majority of sixteen after the 1951 election was regarded as a comfortable working majority and so it proved; the slightly larger Conservative majority after 1992 was initially seen in a similar light, but both the perception and the reality quickly changed, as serious divisions emerged, particularly over Europe, and the government's majority was gradually whittled away by by-election losses and defections. A small majority renders the government vulnerable to pressure from its own backbenchers and therefore likely to make concessions on policy, but it also places those same backbenchers under pressure to support their government.

The party, however, is not Parliament but at national level operates largely through Parliament as one of a number of factors influencing policy and with it the scrutiny process. Ministers and civil servants are fully aware that policy is subject to parliamentary scrutiny and take it into account in its formulation; they are aware that they must explain and defend policy and administration to Parliament; and they are aware that they may later be called to account by Parliament. In the absence of parliamentary scrutiny the policy process would be less open and the government less account-able than would otherwise be the case. The fact that policy is largely formulated behind closed doors and that political accountability is far from perfect should not be used to suggest that parliamentary scrutiny is of no significance.

Parliamentary scrutiny, however, must itself be the subject of continuing scrutiny and the Procedure Committee must be prepared to take as dispassionate a view as possible of the efficacy of parliamentary procedures. The various instruments of parliamentary scrutiny need to be seen not as alternatives but as a complementary package, seeking to fulfil different types of scrutiny. Question Time and certain debates, for instance, should be seen as a form of ideological accountability, part of what Crick called 'the continuing election campaign'; questions for written answer and much of what select committees do should be seen as the extraction of information and an efficiency audit; and legislative procedure as a combination of justifying and explaining proposals and subjecting them to detailed examination. None of these is entirely effective and there remain other important gaps in the scrutiny process. The House of Commons is still a long way from providing systematic and effective scrutiny of financial policy and public expenditure; scrutiny of EU legislation has improved, but remains inadequate; domestic de-legated legislation is subject to only limited scrutiny. However, it is the reorganisation of the civil service through the creation of executive agencies under the Next Steps programme that presents Parliament with its greatest challenge in parliamentary scrutiny. A broader challenge awaits the devolved legislative bodies in the pro-cess of being established in Scotland, Wales and Northern Ireland. They need to develop effective means of scrutinising the executive and, though they can and will learn from Westminster, in due course Westminster should be prepared to learn from them.

At the beginning of the 1997 Parliament the Labour government set up a Select Committee on the Modernisation of the House. By the end of February 1998 it had produced seven reports, the most im-portant of which was its first, on the legislative process. The committee generally proposed a more flexible approach to the handling of legislation, with different bills or parts of bills being dealt with by varying procedures. For example, it suggested that, like the annual Finance Bill, the committee stage of some parts of bills could be taken by a special standing committee, which could take evidence, leaving the rest of the bill to a normal standing committee or to be taken on the floor of the House. More bills could be dealt with by second reading committees if non-committee members interested in the bill could attend and take part in debate, but not vote. Major bills should also normally be subject to agreed timetables through 'programme motions' and it should be possible to carry over bills from one parliamentary session to the next. The committee also proposed greater use of pre-legislative consultation of Parliament and more systematic post-legislative scrutiny. In a further report the committee suggested that more comprehensive explanatory material on bills should be provided (House of Commons, 1997–98).

Not all of these proposals require formal changes in procedure. For example, in the 1997–98 session the government published five draft bills, although this is fewer than the number tabled by the previous Conservative government in its last two parliamentary sessions. Similarly, programme motions on bills can be imposed by the government's majority, but are more likely to operate effectively if supported by all or most of the opposition parties. Thus, before the 1998 summer recess ten bills were the subject of twelve programme motions, of which only two were tabled solely in the names of ministers – the other ten had Conservative and Liberal Democrat support and, in two cases, Nationalist support as well. The proposal regarding the carry over of bills, however, required the approval of the House and it remains to be seen to what extent it will be used and how useful a change it is, but it is a potentially double-edged sword. Carry-over may improve the scrutiny of bills in the inevitable queue that builds up towards the end of each parliamentary year by allowing more time for them to be discussed, but the government will probably be reluctant to allow carry-over bills to encroach too much into the next parliamentary session and the opposition may be tempted to use carry-over to delay bills it strongly opposes, especially in the eighteen months or so before the next general election is anticipated.

There have also been changes to the parliamentary week, and changes to the parliamentary year are under consideration (House of Commons, 1998–99). Some debates initiated by backbenchers now take place on Wednesday mornings, leaving about half the Fridays in each session to be non-sitting days to allow MPs to deal with matters in their constitutencies. This practice of having 'constituency days' is further boosted by ending Thursday sittings at 7.30 p.m., rather than the normal 10.30 p.m. There is strong pressure, especially from the Labour benches, to introduce normal working hours for the House and to reorganise the parliamentary year so that the House of Commons meets for the same number of days each year, but for shorter periods with more frequent breaks. In February 1999 the House took its first step in this direction by introducing the two 'mid-term' breaks, one in early Spring and the other in Autumn. Increasingly, in fact, the parliamentary week has been concentrated on Tuesdays, Wednesdays, Thursdays, especially since the introduction of a single Prime Minister's Question Time on Wednesdays.

Potentially significant steps have also been taken strengthen the scrutiny of EU policy proposals. The Commons European Legislation Committee has been renamed the European Scrutiny Committee and is now allowed to examine a wide range of areas without the subject being linked specifically to legislative documents produced by the European Commission. It is also hoped that the European Scrutiny Committee will work more closely with the departmental committees by holding joint sittings on particular matters.

Other, lesser changes, have also taken place, such as giving the Speaker more discretion to limit the length of speeches, but the suggestion that the traditional form of divisions be replaced by electronic voting was firmly rejected in a survey of members conducted on behalf of the Modernisation Committee.

The rejection of electronic voting demonstrates clearly that, ultimately, improving parliamentary scrutiny depends in turn on the attitudes of Members of Parliament, a point which is highly pertinent to another proposal being considered by the Modernisation Committee (House of Commons 1998–99). This is that business should be divided between the House and a 'Main Committee', to which all MPs would belong. It would be able to take any business in which no division is anticipated, such as debates on select committee reports, additional scrutiny of European legislation, government 'green papers' presenting policy alternatives for discussion and, possibly, some white papers presenting firm government proposals. This procedure is used in Australia, but is essentially an extension of the use of the grand committees for some Scottish and Welsh business, but with no restriction on membership. Such a procedure would be attractive to the government, easing the pressure on the floor of the House, but its success as a means of parliamentary scrutiny would depend on enough members taking it seriously.

Ultimately, a balance needs to be maintained between the ideological confrontation of government and opposition and rendering the government accountable. For backbenchers these are conflicting roles – sustaining the government or the opposition, on the one hand, and acting as public watchdogs, on the other – and it is flying in the face of the realities of British politics not to recognise that the conflict between the parties is a more powerful behavioural factor than the demands of parliamentary scrutiny. Nonetheless, procedural and attitudinal changes in the House of Commons have resulted in a limited but significant modification of the partisan confrontation, as a comparison with the 1950s and earlier amply illustrates, and the sharper ideological conflict which characterised the 1980s should not be allowed to obscure that modification. Indeed, the 1990s have seen a distinct softening of the ideological clash, especially with Labour moving to occupy the centre ground. There is, however, a further potential conflict between such ministerial ambitions as backbenchers may have and their watchdog role: upsetting the whips, as that latter role sometimes involves, is hardly likely to smooth the path to ministerial office. In short, backbenchers are no longer willing to be taken largely for granted by the whips, but they, or enough of them, must also be willing to undertake the more mundane tasks of parliamentary scrutiny if the House of Commons is to maintain and improve one of its most important roles.

Parliamentary Scrutiny and UK Governance

It is also important to see parliamentary scrutiny in the wider context of governance – what is Parliament's place in the way in which we are governed? Once the electorate has given its verdict at a general election, Parliament – more particularly the House of Commons – legitimises the actions and policies of the government, but

Parliament is expected to call the government to account between general elections. Government expect and are expected to govern, but the balance between effective and efficient government and accountable government is a fine one: parliamentary scrutiny is not simply about ensuring that the government functions effectively and efficiently; it is also about ensuring that the policies proposed and pursued by the government are exposed to public examination to the point that the policies themselves can be questioned.

There are, however, two other important dimensions – the devolving of power to the regions of the UK and the growing importance of the EU. The creation of new power centres in Edinburgh, Belfast and Cardiff is potentially one of the most significant changes in the governance of the UK since 1832. The responsibilities of the Westminster Parliament will be lessened, particularly in respect of Scotland and Northern Ireland. That may allow Westminster more time and space to enhance its scrutiny role, but it may also hasten the atrophying of Westminster which some commentators inside and outside Parliament already detect. The procedures and practices adopted by the devolved bodies will likely provide food for thought at Westminster and stimulate further change there. Moreover, what Scotland and Northern Ireland have today, Wales will almost certainly and England may demand tomorrow and English regional assemblies on the Scottish model would present a major challenge to the hegemony of Westminster. Yet another challenge is that or proportional representation, which is used for elections to the devolved bodies and might add to the pressures to adopt it for Westminster elections. Were this to happen the party balance might change in the House of Commons (and possibly in a reformed House of Lords) to the point that single-party majority government might no longer be the norm and this too could have a profound impact on how Parliament performs its scrutiny role.

Europe already constitutes a challenge to Westminster, but that challenge is likely to become greater as the EU adopts common policies on an increasingly wide range of matters. Where does this leave national Parliaments? That is a complex question, not least because the European policy net has spread and continues to spread incrementally rather than in broad, clearly-defined policy areas. There is a widespread view that the EU suffers from a serious 'democratic deficit', which the European Parliament neither currently fills nor looks likely to fill in the foreseeable future. This places a considerable onus on national parliaments (*Journal of Legislative Studies*, 1995). Westminster has only slowly come to grips with its European scrutiny role, but doubts continue to be cast about its effectiveness.

Logic demands that parliamentary scrutiny itself needs to be the subject of continuing scrutiny, but that can only be sensibly done within the broader context of governance (Riddell, 1998).

References

Barker, A. (1998) 'Political responsibility for UK prison security – ministers escape again', *Public Administration*, 76, pp. 1–23.

Barker, A. and Rush, M. (1970) *The Member of Parliament and His Information* (London: Allen & Unwin).

Bogdanor, V. (1996) 'The Scott Report', *Public Administration*, 74, pp. 593–611.

Cabinet Office (1999) *Modernising Parliament: Reforming the House of Lords*, Cm. 4183.

Crick, B. (1964; 2nd edn 1968) *The Reform of Parliament* (London: Weidenfeld & Nicolson).

Constitution Unit (1996) *Reform of the House of Lords* (London: University College London).

Drewry, G. (ed.) (1989) *The New Select Committees: A Study of the 1979 Reforms* (Oxford: Clarendon Press) repr. of 1985 Edition with a supplementary chapter on the 1983–87 Parliament.

Finer, S. E. (1956) 'The individual responsibility of ministers', *Public Administration*, 34, pp. 377–96.

Franklin, M. and Norton, P. (1993) (eds) *Parliamentary Questions* (Oxford: Clarendon Press).

Granada Television (1973) *The State of the Nation: Parliament* (London: Granada Television).

Griffith, J. A. G. and Ryle, M. T. (1989) *Parliament: Functions, Practice and Procedures* (London: Sweet & Maxwell).

Hansard Society (1993) *Making the Law: Report of the Commission on the Legislative Process* (London: Hansard Society).

Hansard Society (1997) 'Under the Scott-Light: British Government seen through the Scott Report', *Parliamentary Affairs* (special issue), 50.

Hill, A. and Whichelow, A. (1964) *What's Wrong with Parliament?* (London: Pelican).

House of Commons (1989–90) *Second Report of the Select Committee on Procedure: The Working of the Select Committee System*, HC 19–1.

House of Commons (1995–96) *Report of the Inquiry into the Export of Defence Equipment and Dual-Use Goods to Iraq (the Scott Report)*, HC 115.

House of Commons (1997–98) *The Select Committee on the Modernisation of the House*, First to Seventh Reports, HC 190, 389, 543, 600, 699, 779 and 791.

House of Commons (1998–99) *The Select Committee on the Modernisation of the House: Second Report – 'The Parliamentary Calender – Initial Proposals'*, HC 60.

House of Commons (1998–99) *The Select Committee on the Modernisation of the House: Minutes of Evidence on the Proposals for a 'Main Committee'*, HC 119.

House of Lords (1991–92) *Select Committee on the Committee Work of the House: Report*, HL 35–I & II.

Journal of Legislative Studies (1995) Special Issue: 'National Parliaments in the European Union'.

Marshall, G. (ed.) (1989) *Ministerial Responsibility* (Oxford: Oxford University Press).

Norton, P. (1975) *Dissension in the House of Commons, 1945–7* (London: Macmillan).

Norton, P. (1978) *Conservative Dissidents: Dissension within the Parliamentary Conservative Party, 1970–74*, (London: Temple Smith).

Norton, P. (1980) *Dissension in the House of Commons, 1974–79* (Oxford: Clarendon Press).

Norton, P. (1985) 'The House of Commons: Behavioural Changes' in Norton, P. (ed.), *Parliament in the 1980s* (Oxford: Basil Blackwell), pp. 22–47.

Norton, P. and Cowley, P. (1999) 'Rebels and rebellions: Conservative MPs in the 1992 Parliament', *British Journal of Politics and International Relations*, 1.

Riddell, P. (1998) *Parliament Under Pressure* (London: Gollancz)

Rush, M. (ed.) (1983) *The House of Commons: Services and Facilities, 1972–1982* (London: Policy Studies Institute).

Rush, M. (1990) 'Select Committees' in Rush, M. (ed.), *Parliament and Pressure Politics* (Oxford: Clarendon Press), pp. 137–51.

Rush, M. (1996) 'The Pay, Allowances, Services and Facilities of Legislators in 18 Countries: A Comparative Survey', Top Salaries Review Body, *Report No. 38: Parliamentary Allowances*, Cm. 3330–II, pp. 38–59.

Rush, M. (1994) 'The House of Lords: End it or Mend it?' in Wale, W. (ed.), *Developments in Politics: An Annual Review*, Vol. 5 (Ormskirk: Causeway Press), pp. 21–38.

Rush, M. and Shaw, M. (eds) (1974) *The House of Commons: Services and Facilities* (London: Allen & Unwin).

Shell, D. (1992) *The House of Lords*, 2nd edn (London: Harvester-Wheat-sheaf).

Shell, D. (1993) 'The European Communities Committee' in Shell, D. and Beamish, D. (eds), *The House of Lords at Work: A Study of the 1988–89 Session* (Oxford: Clarendon Press), pp. 247–81.

Shell, D. and Beamish, D. (eds) (1993) *The House of Lords at Work: A Study of the 1988–89 Session* (Oxford: Clarendon Press).

Woodhouse, D. (1994) *Ministers and Parliament: Accountability in Theory and Practice* (Oxford: Clarendon Press).

6

The Governing Parties

RICHARD KELLY

In recent years, political parties have received a rather bad press, with our attention being drawn to declining party membership (Whiteley, Seyd and Richardson, 1994); public disenchantment with party activity (Baggott, 1995); the growing 'irrelevance' of parties to a modern, diverse society (Hall and Jacques, 1988); the parties' 'failure to deliver' once in government (Marr, 1995), and the consequent movement towards a new, 'post-party' style of democratic politics involving pressure groups and referendums (Acherson, 1994).

Amid this growing, post-party culture, it is easy to forget that political parties remain central to any understanding of British political life. Of course it is undeniable that pressure groups have, to a considerable extent, usurped the role of parties as vehicles for political participation. It is also incontestable that the capacity of parties to 'make a difference' in government has been eroded through a loss of sovereignty to the European Union and the globalisation of Britain's economony (Gummett, 1996; Kelly, 1999). The greater use of public referendums, skipping over exhaustive debate both within and between the main parties, is also difficult to ignore – a trend illustrated perfectly within the first years of the Blair government (Draper, 1997).

But such developments require perspective. Any account of modern British politics which ignored them would certainly be defective. Yet any account which managed to ignore the role of political parties would be nothing short of surreal. For the fact remains

138

that parties still play a vital part in the governance of the UK – in terms of making parliamentary government cohesive, of allowing voters a choice of policy packages at general elections (and, as in 1997, to change thereby the personnel and arguably the direction of British government), of introducing new policies (*vide* Thatcherism), and of enabling thousands of ordinary party members to participate more fully in the political system.

In view of this lingering reality it is important to understand the way in which Britain's main parties of government – chiefly the Labour Party and the Conservative Party – conduct their internal affairs. Are they 'oligarchic' as R. T. McKenzie argued over fifty years ago? Or have constituency party members acquired more influence? And are the main party leaders significantly hindered by the views of their party rank and file? These are the basic questions which will be addressed in the course of this chapter, paying particular attention to developments since the 1997 general election.

The Labour Party

New Labour: The Background

Under the leadership of Tony Blair, the concept of 'New Labour' has been a ubiquitous feature of Labour Party language; indeed, it was introduced to the public and the party generally by Blair himself, in his first speech as leader to Labour's annual conference in 1994. However, the concept of New Labour is misleading, for so many of the policy and organisational trends seen during the Blair era were instigated in the decade before Blair's accession, with the nine-year leadership of Neil Kinnock (1983–92) proving especially formative (Hughes and Wintour, 1990; Shaw, 1994). Blair's regime has therefore accelerated, rather than ignited, the sort of changes which distinguish Labour in 1998 from the unelectable outfit of 1983. Consequently, students should resist New Labour's implicit message that 1994 represents a kind of 'Year Zero' inside the party.

Revising Clause IV

Tony Blair was declared Labour Party leader on 21 July 1994, having secured 57 per cent of votes cast in Labour's electoral college – 33 per cent more than his closest rival, John Prescott. More important perhaps was that, owing to the college's 'democratisation' after 1993, Blair was able to collect support from roughly half a million individual members of the Labour movement – a remarkable mandate unavailable to any previous Labour leader (Kelly, 1995). It was unsurprising that Blair was emboldened to pursue his own, radical vision of Labour's future.

The first indication of what this would involve came at Labour's 1994 conference where, as already mentioned, the 'New Labour' slogan was unveiled. But it was only towards the end of his first conference speech as leader that Blair disclosed how far he wanted to go, advocating the revision of Clause IV – the supreme symbol of 'Old' Labour values – and a new, formal statement of Labour's ideology.

Aware that this would not be easy, Blair preceded the vote on Clause IV's future with a six-month period of consultation throughout the party. Questionnaires were duly sent out to all CLP and affiliated members, making it quantifiably the largest single-issue consultation ever carried out inside a British political party. The response rate was equally impressive, with Labour claiming that nearly 18,000 members answered the questionnaires. Of these, 60 per cent agreed that the existing Clause IV was 'no longer an accurate expression of Labour's aims' (Labour Party 1995).

The outcome was that, in April 1995, Labour's National Executive Committee unfurled a proposed replacement to Clause IV, confident that it would be approved formally at a special Labour conference later that month (see Table 6.1). That confidence was not misplaced: the result of the Clause IV ballot was a clear vindication of the new leader's nerve (Table 6.2). It also proved a cue for other, far-reaching reforms within Labour's organisation.

Expanding the Membership

The CLPs' enthusiasm for changing Clause IV was a particular relief to the leader. Although he had not expected them to reject the new Clause IV, he had not dared hope they would support it so emphatically (Anderson and Mann, 1997). Blair's pleasant surprise was to have a crucial effect upon his strategic view of the membership and the part it could play in his planned overhaul of the party structure.

TABLE 6.1 *Clause IV – Ancient and Modern*

The 1918 version

To secure for the workers by hand or by brain the full fruits of their industry and the most equitable distribution thereof that may be possible upon the basis of the common ownership of the means of production, distribution and exchange, and the best obtainable system of popular administration and control of each industry or service.

The 1995 version

The Labour Party is a democratic socialist party. It believes that by the strength of our common endeavour we achieve more than we achieve alone, so as to create for each of us the means to realise our true potential and for all of us a community in which power, wealth and opportunity are in the hands of the many, not the few, where the rights we enjoy reflect the duties we owe, and where we live together, freely, in a spirit of solidarity, tolerance and respect.

Source: Kelly, R. (1998) 'Power in the Labour Party', *Politics Review*, 8(2).

TABLE 6.2 *Labour Party Ballot on the Proposed Rewording of Clause IV, Special Labour Conference, 29 April 1995*

Constituency party members *(accorded 30% of votes)*
Supporting proposal: 90%   Opposing proposal: 10%

Turnout: 41%

Affiliated trade unions *(accorded 70% of votes)*
Supporting proposal: 55%   Opposing proposal: 45%

Notes: [a] Unlike in the 1994 leadership contest, the constituency members' votes were cast by CLP conference delegates rather than by members themselves in a separate and inclusive ballot. However, about 500 of the 633 CLPs did conduct OMOV ballots before the conference, with turnout ranging from 91% in North Wiltshire to 24% in Nottingham East. In all these pre-conference ballots, a 'yes' vote was recorded, the highest majority being in West Worcestershire (97%), the lowest being in Leicester South (66%). The CLPs did not cast 'block' votes at the conference; instead their votes were split so as to reflect the minority as well as majority view.
[b] The unions did not ballot their members beforehand, preferring instead various methods of 'consultation'.
[c] The unions voting against change were TGWU, UNISON, RMT, GPMU, NUM, FBU, EPIU, BFAWU, ASLEF, UCATT.
Source: Kelly, R. (1998) 'Power in the Labour Party', *Politics Review*, 8(2).

Blair had always enjoyed a warm and constructive relationship with his own CLP in Sedgefield (Rentoul, 1995, pp. 30–55). Yet, until the Clause IV ballot, he had never been sure that Labour members in Sedgefield were typical of CLP members nationally. After 1995, Blair had no such doubts, and surmised that 'ordinary' Labour members could prove a vital counterweight to the leftist and electorally damaging tendencies of which trade union and CLP officials were still suspected – again, an analysis which first surfaced during the leadership of Neil Kinnock (Seyd, 1987, pp. 32–64).

Blair and his New Labour allies thus decided to increase the number of 'ordinary' Labour members by using the same sort of recruitment techniques used in Sedgefield. The resulting 'Labour Regeneration Project', headed from London by Nick Smith, aimed to 'transform the experience of party membership' by 'reaching out to largely non-political people who just want a Labour government': this entailed a shift away from 'boring committee work and heavy political debates' towards 'jumble sales, coffee mornings, quiz nights and so on' (*New Statesman*, 28 April 1995).

This semi-political recruitment drive had no small measure of success, enrolling over 100,000 new members between 1994 and 1996 and giving Labour a constituency membership of almost half a million by the 1997 general election – something which enabled Labour to target 100 marginal seats, and encourage tactical voting where necessary, with an extra degree of energy (Butler and Kavanagh, 1997, pp. 210–23). But it was a membership which generally seemed less politically active and much less politically aware than in previous decades – just as New Labour's strategists had planned.

In March 1996, it was announced by the NEC that the autumn party conference would debate the leadership's draft manifesto (*New Life For Britain*), after which it would be submitted to a ballot of all party members. This duly occurred, with the ballot in November 1996 recording a huge 19–1 majority for Blair's 'five key pledges' (Table 6.3). This overwhelming endorsement was consistent with the tone and conduct of recent Labour conferences, which seemed light years away from the theatrical fractiousness which was once their hallmark; at the 1995 conference, the leadership had won all of the 90 issues put to a vote, an almost unprecedented feat in conference history.

There was some concern inside the party, however, that the ethos of Labour's organisation was being subtly yet significantly changed,

TABLE 6.3   *Labour Party Ballot on Draft Manifesto, November 1996*

Individual (CLP) members	
Supporting the manifesto	218,023 (95%)
Opposing the manifesto	11,286 (5%)
Turnout	*61%*
Affiliated (trade union) members	
Supporting the manifesto	577,102 (92%)
Opposing the manifesto	50,182 (8%)
Turnout	*24%*

Note: As with the 1994 leadership contest, all CLP members and all levy-paying
members of affiliated unions were entitled to vote, with the votes aggregated
nationally.
Source: Kelly, R. (1998) 'Power in the Labour Party', *Politics Review*, 8(2).

with its traditional, delegatory system of policy-making giving way to
a barely-discussed version of plebiscitory politics. The construction
of the 1997 manifesto, for example, seemed to short-circuit conference, the NEC and, *inter alia*, Clause V of Labour's constitution.

The leadership's claim that all this was an extension of party
democracy seemed disingenuous. Instead of fulfilling some noble
idea of Athenian democracy, the 1996 manifesto ballot was probably inspired by memories of previous Labour governments and the
problems they faced from a fractious extra-parliamentary party
(Richards, 1997, pp. 3–5). By getting the membership's 'finger-
prints' over an essentially centrist manifesto, the leadership was
skilfully pre-empting party dissent once Labour reached office – a
strategy dubbed 'getting our betrayal in first' by one Blairite adviser
(Draper, 1997, p. 16).

Further Centralisation

New Labour's emphasis upon the 'empowerment' of ordinary members has, ironically, been harnessed to a remarkable centralisation
of decision-making in the interests of ensuring 'moderate' policy
outcomes and 'sensible' campaigning methods – another echo of the
'social democratic centralism' marking the Kinnock era (Shaw,
1988). In September 1995 after prompting from Blair and arch-
adviser Peter Mandelson, the NEC released £2 million towards the
renting of a new 'media and communications centre' at Millbank

Tower, London. It immediately became 'almost shrouded in secrecy' and 'inaccessible to all but a bright, young Blairite elite' (*The Guardian*, 24 March 1997).

Yet it would be wrong to say that Blair's 'Millbank stormtroopers' took an insular approach to policy and strategy, for they made extensive use of voters' 'focus-groups' (assembled by Labour's General Secretary, Tom Sawyer) and a wealth of polling data collated by Millbank's specialised 'task forces'. However, the Labour Party generally was not much involved in ongoing policy formation.

Suspicion that power in the Labour Party was passing upwards, albeit in the guise of 'empowering ordinary members', was not confined to the field of policy-making. In candidate selection, too, there seemed to be an erosion of CLP authority. Between 1994 and 1995, roughly half of those CLPs in winnable seats but without a sitting Labour MP were ordered by the NEC to choose candidates from all-women shortlists. Resistance to this form of positive discrimination was especially marked in the non-metropolitan areas, with CLPs like Slough having to have candidates virtually imposed upon them by national and regional officials (Kelly 1996).

In fairness to New Labour, the all-women policy predated Blair's leadership (it was approved by the 1993 conference) and there were no complaints from the leader when the policy was declared illegal by an industrial tribunal in 1996. However, there were still other areas of candidate selection which saw blatant examples of central interference. In September 1995, the NEC overruled the candidature of Liz Davies, the choice of the Leeds NE CLP, the decision being upheld simply on the grounds of Davies's politics – variously described as 'disloyal' and 'oppositionist' (Kelly 1996).

The 1997 Campaign

In view of what had gone on in the preceding few years, it was unsurprising that Labour's 1997 general election campaign proved a tightly disciplined affair, carefully orchestrated by Peter Mandelson's Millbank team, and meticulously ensuring that all candidates and canvassers stayed 'on message' (Jones, 1997, pp. 235–71).

However, when assessing the technical brilliance of Labour's campaign, a measure of caution is still required. Although Labour owed a huge debt to the organisational flair of Mandelson, and though it benefited from the 'Rapid Rebuttal Unit', the 'Excalibur' computer and so on, the efficacy of Labour's campaign owed most to the discipline and determination of the party generally, with any doubts or differences over policy being wholly eclipsed by a thirst for power. This was illustrated when Gordon Brown hinted during the campaign that Labour might after all privatise air traffic control, a flagrant repudiation of the line taken by the 1996 party conference. Yet the media could still not find a spot of dissent from anyone involved in Labour's campaign (Williams, 1997, p. 76).

Labour in Office

Labour's landslide was seen by party officials as a triumphant vindication of the centralising measures practised in opposition. Furthermore, any argument for decentralising power in future was weakened by a study of voting patterns in Labour's target seats, where constituency-based campaigning was intense in the year leading up to the election. Yet the swing to Labour in these seats seemed no greater than elsewhere, implying that if Labour did indeed 'win' the election (as opposed to the Tories losing it), then the bulk of credit belonged to Labour's national leaders, its national organisation and its national campaign.

Having entered government using strong, centralised disciplines, Labour's attachment to top-down practices and party regimentation became almost obsessive. This was to be demonstrated in the leadership's dealings with Labour MPs, MEPs, councillors, activists and the trade unions.

Regimenting MPs

Despite his majority of 179, Blair showed no sign of complacency in his dealings with Labour MPs (the PLP). Once Parliament had resumed, he immediately summoned the swollen PLP to a special meeting to 'remind' them that their 'prime task' was to 'extol this Government's achievements' (*The Guardian*, 8 May 1997). In other words, dissent would not be tolerated. A harsh approach was also taken towards those MPs suspected of legal or financial improprieties: Mohamed Sarwar, Bob Wareing and Tommy Graham were all suspended from the PLP pending official party inquiries.

Yet 'off message' MPs have alleged other, less formal methods designed to impose discipline. Llew Smith claimed that the then Welsh Secretary Ron Davies threatened him with expulsion from the party if he continued to campaign against the proposed Welsh assembly, while fellow 'devo-sceptic' Ted Rowlands implied that his CLP had been asked by Labour HQ (now fully transferred to Millbank) to threaten him with deselection (*Western Mail*, 4 September 1997).

Prior to the election, Cowley and Norton (1996) asserted that Labour MPs were more likely to rebel than Conservative MPs, especially when backbenchers sensed they were closer to party opinion than the government. This was to be demonstrated within six months of achieving office, when the government proposed cutting benefits to lone parents – 47 Labour MPs voting against the government, while junior Scottish minister Malcolm Chisholm and three private secretaries resigned from the front bench. With a seventh of the PLP already blooded as rebels, further outbreaks of dissent did not seem unlikely.

Regimenting MEPs

Strict discipline has also been imposed on Labour's Euro-MPs. Having refused to accept the Code of Conduct being extended to MEPs in Strasbourg, Ken Coates, Alex Falconer, Hugh Kerr and Michael Hindley (the 'Strasbourg Four') were all barred from meetings of the Labour group. It was claimed by these MEPs that the new closed list system of proportional representation for Britain's European elections in 1999 was carefully designed to punish mavericks like themselves – allowing disliked MEPs (like Christine Oddy in the East Midlands) to be placed in unwinnable positions on their respective regional lists, determined by a panel of NEC members and regional officials.

Regimenting 'the Locals'

Away from both parliaments, Westminster and European, Labour's national hierarchy has been equally unforgiving. In the autumn of 1997, the entire district Labour Party in Doncaster was suspended amid allegations of corruption, while prominent Labour councillors in Camden and Islington endured lengthy disciplinary proceedings.

The prospect of an elective mayor for Greater London, a key part of the government's 'decentralisation' reforms, also led to internal party disputes and a somewhat brutal assertion of central authority. It had long been recognised that a likely outcome of a Labour Party 'primary', among Labour's London members, would be the emergence of Ken Livingstone as official Labour candidate. New Labour officials were horrified by such a prospect, and tried to overcome the difficulty by insisting that Labour's London members could only choose from a shortlist assembled by the NEC, from which Livingstone would be conspicuously absent. During 1998 Labour officials seemed equally heavy-handed in trying to ensure that Rhodri Morgan did not emerge as Labour leader in the new Welsh assembly – despite strong evidence that he was the choice of most Welsh Labour members.

When it came to selecting Parliamentary candidates, national organisers remained equally sceptical of local democracy. At the Uxbridge by-election of July 1997, NEC by-election rules – introduced in 1989 to secure 'suitable candidates for high profile elections' – were again applied, enabling Labour's candidate at the general election to be dumped in favour of an 'identikit Blairite with no local connections' (*The Guardian*, 15 July 1997). Although the Tories unexpectedly held the seat, there were no obvious signs that the by-election ruling would be relaxed in future.

Emasculating Conference

During previous Labour governments, the annual Labour conference had seldom been an enjoyable event for Labour ministers. A clash between activists' ideals and the realities of power often sparked conflict on a grand scale – as when Chancellor Denis Healey was drowned out by jeers in 1976. Given New Labour's penchant for 'control', it was unsurprising that steps should have been taken to prevent a repetition of past traumas after 1997.

Shortly after the election, the NEC endorsed the *Partnership in Power* document, which aimed to overhaul policy-making in the extra-parliamentary party (see Table 6.4). The conference was to be downgraded in favour of Labour's National Policy Forum, supported by policy commissions and a Joint Policy Committee – all contributing to a 'rolling programme' of policy-making, with conference apparently limited to just ratifying or rejecting the finished product.

The proposals did not escape criticism: 107 motions submitted to Labour's 1997 conference asked for *Partnership in Power* to be deferred. But conference duly rejected these demands by a majority of three to one, leading many to wonder if they had just witnessed the last traditional Labour conference.

TABLE 6.4 *Making Labour Policy, Revised Procedures, 1997*

1 National Policy Forum[a] appoints various policy commissions.[b]
2 CLPs, trade unions, MPs, MEPs, affiliated societies and regional policy forums[c] submit policy ideas to policy commissions.
3 Policy commissions prepare reports.
4 Reports considered first by National Policy Forum, second by Joint Policy Committee[d], and finally by National Executive Committee.
5 NEC publishes amended reports for wider discussion within party.
6 Reports discussed further at Party conference.
7 NEC and JPC make further amendments to reports, reflecting ideas which emerged at stages 5 and 6, and release revised reports for wider discussion.
8 Various party sections (see 2) consider revised reports and again submit responses to relevant policy commissions.
9 Final policy commission reports assimilated by JPC and NPF, then submitted to NEC[e].
10 NEC publishes final policy reports for conference discussion and endorsement/rejection[f].

Notes: [a] The National Policy Forum was set up following decisions taken at the 1990 and 1992 Labour conferences, as were the policy commissions and Joint Policy Committee (see below). The Forum comprises about 175 representatives from various sections of the party.
[b] Each policy commission deals with a specific policy area. They comprise about 20 members, drawn equally from the parliamentary and extra-parliamentary parties.
[c] Regional policy forums were set up following a decision taken at the 1996 Labour conference.
[d] The Joint Policy Committee has 'strategic oversight' of the new procedures. It is chaired by the leader and comprises representatives from Cabinet, NEC, MEPs and local government.
[e] Formalised voting and 'rigid procedures' will not be used by either the commissions or the JPC and NPF. They will instead proceed on the basis of 'flexible, small group discussions' and arrive at decisions 'by consensus'.
[f] It is hoped that conference will become 'a showcase not just for the party but for the Labour government'. As such, conference endorsement is assumed to be a formality.
Source: Labour Party (1997) *Partnership in Power*, Labour Party Publications, pp. 2–6.

Distancing the Unions

At the heart of New Labour's ideology was an appeal to the 'enlightened consumerism' of the 'progressive middle class' (Mandelson and Liddle, 1995, pp. 35–70). This, in turn, questioned

Labour's historic links with blue-collar, producer-based interest groups. Unlike previous Labour leaders, Blair had a weak emotional attachment to Labour's union links and had been more inclined to see them as a hindrance (Rentoul, 1995, p. 102). As a result, there were attempts to slacken those links, with certain Blairites, such as minister Stephen Byers, talking of complete cessation (Jones, 1997, pp. 39–40).

At the 1995 conference, the leadership had engineered a further 20 per cent reduction in the union share of conference votes (bringing them down to just half the votes cast). At the same time, there was a concerted effort to reduce Labour's financial reliance upon the unions, soliciting alternative donations from businessmen like Bernie Ecclestone and Matthew Harding, while setting up a special 'Thousand Club' for generous individual donors. By 1997, only 46 per cent of Labour's income came from union sources, a 20 per cent fall from 1987 (Butler and Kavanagh, 1997, p. 55).

By the end of 1997, there was talk from some union leaders, like Lew Adams of ASLEF, of disconnecting themselves from a party which now seemed to view them with such suspicion, an idea which seemed to elicit little complaint from ministers (*The Sunday Times*, 14 December 1997). Party modernisers might bear in mind, however, that Blair, like most Labour leaders, has already had to rely on union block votes during tricky debates at conference. Indeed, had it not been for their support in 1996, he could well have lost conference votes on child benefit and minimum wage policy. In its enthusiasm for OMOV and policy forums, New Labour might give more thought to this aspect of party management: 'individualistically' arranged parties are much harder for their leaders to control.

The Blair Effect

As this chapter's conclusion will affirm, the establishment of a New Labour doctrine always required a New Labour structure. By the summer of 1999, this restructuring was well advanced.

In political science terms, it has involved changing Labour from a 'federal-delegatory' organisation into an 'elite-plebiscitory' organisation. Under the former system, thousands of active party members, delegated by their various unions and CLPs, would make a regular contribution to party policy via sundry committees and conferences. Under the new system, however, around half a million semi-passive members are involved in occasional 'take it or leave it' ballots – ballots which simply ask them to approve or reject policy packages assembled by the leadership. Whether this represents an advance for party democracy, as New Labour would have us believe, is questionable. What is unquestionable is that it marks a paradigm shift in the organisation of Britain's main centre-left party (Kelly, 1997).

It remains to be seen whether this New Labour system will survive any serious decline in New Labour's popularity. It should be remembered that most of the party only accepted Blairism as a short-term electoral calculation; if there is ever cause for a recalculation, Blair's new structures and the disciplines behind them may come to appear fragile. As Tony Benn reminded conference in 1997 'You cannot organise perpetual unity. When dissent exists, dissent will out, irrespective of party rules' (*The Guardian*, 2 October 1997). The state of the Tory Party by 1997 – scarcely democratic yet chronically divided – offered ample proof of Benn's warning.

The Conservatives

As the recent history of the Labour Party has shown, defeated parties tend to look inwards; indeed, they tend to be much more rigorous in self-examination than in their attacks upon the government. This 'iron law' certainly seems to have applied to the Conservative Party since 1997.

For those who followed the 1997 Tory leadership contest, this should have come as no surprise: all five candidates promised an overhaul of both policy and organisation, with William Hague proving keener than most for a 'root and branch' assessment (Norton, 1998). By 1999 a significant reorganisation of the party did seem to have taken place – even though its implications are still unclear. This second section will examine the Tories' new rules, while gauging the effect they might have upon power inside the party.

A Divided Party: The Tories at Westminster

During the second Major government, dissent among Tory MPs seemed to reach new and damaging levels. However, as Cowley (1997) has shown, Tory MPs between 1992 and 1997 were much more cohesive than many observers supposed, rebelling on fewer occasions than during either the Heath government of 1970–74 or the second Thatcher government of 1983–87.

This false impression of dissent owed much to the fact that Tory divisions tended to take place on the high-profile issue of Europe, one division leading to the withdrawal of the whip from eight back-benchers, with another resigning it voluntarily. Nevertheless, it would be equally wrong to argue that dissent was confined to Europe; it was a more general dissatisfaction which led, for ex-ample, to the defection of four MPs between 1995 and 1997, the resignation from Cabinet of John Redwood in the summer of 1995 and a subsequent challenge to John Major's leadership.

The Tories entered the 1997 general election campaign widely perceived as incompetent and divided, with the campaign itself only underlining these perceptions. Two ministers (John Horman and James Paice) and 317 Tory parliamentary candidates dissented from the official 'wait and see' policy on European monetary union, prompting Major to issue a desperate, public plea for unity (Butler and Kavanagh, 1997, p. 103).

Six weeks later, these divisions spilt into the 1997 leadership contest. Such was the dissonance among Tory MPs that, in the first ballot, not one of the five candidates gained even a third of his fellow MPs' support. The absence of any clear view about who should lead the party meant that, for the first time since leadership elections were introduced in 1965, a third ballot was necessary to produce a winner. Cowley (1998) has since shown that Hague's victory came not from any surge of enthusiasm among MPs as the campaign reached its close, but from a lack of real hostility. As with Lord Home (who 'emerged' in 1963), Hague became leader simply because he was the least unpopular candidate.

Hague quickly set about bridging these divisions in the parlia-mentary party, seeking a form of leader-based discipline compar-able to that developed in the Labour Party. He insisted that shadow ministers gave him weekly reports of their political activities, later requesting that backbenchers do the same on a three-monthly basis (*Daily Telegraph*, 20 September 1997).

Hague worked closely with his new vice-chairman Archie Nor-man, elected to Parliament in 1997 and a successful chairman of Asda supermarkets. Like Hague, Norman was a former employee of the McKinsey group of managerial consultants, and there was a feeling among MPs that the Hague/Norman axis would try to import McKinsey-style ethics into the conduct of Tory MPs. However, it soon became clear that the 'management science' favoured by Hague and Norman would not work until the party had a much clearer idea of what it believed in – 'corporate spirit' being the effect, rather than the cause, of coherent policy.

Hague's attempt to provide such a coherent policy on Europe, for example, remained fraught with difficulty. The 'wait and see' approach on the single currency was replaced by a policy of clear rejection at the next general election – in effect, ruling out Conservative support for the single currency over the next ten years. Although this may have clarified official Tory policy, it also exposed fresh Tory divisions, prompting the resignation from the shadow Cabinet of Ian Taylor and David Currie, and a flurry of criticism from pro-Europe 'grandees' like Michael Heseltine, Kenneth Clarke, Lord Howe and Lord Hurd.

A Moribund Party? The Grass Root Tories

Like Tony Benn in the Labour Party of the early 1980s, Hague as Tory leader was inclined to cite constituency members as the 'soul' of a political party – 'true blues' to whom MPs should pay more attention and be more accountable (*Daily Telegraph*, 24 September 1997). Yet Hague had no reason to suppose these members would give him automatic support. During the leadership contest, constituency chairs consistently opted for Kenneth Clarke, while a survey of 200 chairs a few months later found fewer than 40 per cent believing Hague's performance to be 'good' or 'very good' (*The Sunday Telegraph*, 21 September 1997).

This had not altered Hague's belief that the constituency membership should be revitalised and that, for this to happen, it needed to be empowered. Certainly, by 1997, the constituency parties ('associations') were in poor shape. The absence of any national membership list made it difficult to estimate how many members the Tories had, yet it seemed safe to bet that numbers had fallen dramatically since 1979; in the all-party ballot of autumn 1997 (to be discussed below), fewer than 177 000 voters were recorded. The members the party had retained were said to be inactive and elderly (Bethell, 1997), with membership of the Young Conservatives down from half a million in the 1950s to less than 5 000 by 1995 (Holroyd-

Doveton, 1996, pp. 239–43). Furthermore, owing to the subsequent fall-off in association revenue, the number of full-time constituency agents – vital to the existence of a healthy local party – had shrunk to less than 200. It should have come as no surprise that, during the 1997 election campaign, there were numerous accounts of 'moribund' associations in key marginal seats (Butler and Kavanagh, 1997, pp. 26–7); the party's reputation for having a grass-root organisation 'superior' to Labour's was clearly bankrupt.

For basic electoral reasons, these trends alarmed the new leadership. Recent studies had pointed to a link between constituency party spending and the strength of the Tory vote – and the Tories had always relied on constituency members to raise the bulk of their own funds (Whiteley, Seyd and Richardson, 1994, pp. 201–3). Although Labour's campaign seemed to vindicate central control (see above), the Tories own post-election analysis told a different story. ICM, the Tories' private pollsters, discovered a connection between the party's constituency vote and the intensity of its constituency campaigns, arguing that a 'low contact rate' may have cost up to 80 seats (*The Sunday Telegraph*, 5 October 1997).

Consulting the Party

At a meeting of party officers in July 1997, Hague proposed 'nothing less than a cultural revolution' inside the party, and a 'changed relationship' between leaders and members (*Daily Telegraph*, 24 July 1997). As part of this 'revolution', Hague sought the whole party's endorsement for his leadership and his 'six principles' of organisational reform. This was to involve an unprecedented ballot of all association members and the distribution of nearly 400 000 voting papers (given that only 44 per cent of these were returned, this proved a rather optimistic view of party membership).

Confident of success in the ballot, Hague instructed a trio of senior party figures, each representing one of the party's three 'wings', to put flesh on those six general principles: Lord Parkinson (recalled by Hague as Party Chairman and, *de facto*, head of Conservative Central Office and the professional extra-Parliamentary Party), Sir Archie Hamilton (newly-elected Chairman of the MPs' 1922 Committee) and Robin Hodgson (Chairman of the National Union of Conservative Associations) duly constructed a 'green paper' entitled *Blueprint for Change*, unveiling it in time for the 1997 Tory conference.

When drafting this green paper, it became clear that the three wings were not in total accord – especially on the thorny issue of leadership selection. Even before 1997, there had been numerous complaints within the party. The 1995 leadership contest aroused considerable unease, first because it had not enfranchised ordinary party members (the contrast with Labour's contest a year earlier was striking) and secondly because members' opinions – sought by MPs and officials in a variety of ways – were clearly not reflected in the voting pattern of MPs (Major won support from an estimated 92 per cent of associations but from only 66 per cent of MPs). In 1997 this democratic deficit was even more conspicuous, with the bulk of party members again excluded, and the views of constituency chairmen blatantly ignored.

There were few signs, however, that the 1922 Committee was amenable to radical reform of selection procedures. Its inquiry of 1996 had only tentatively advocated an electoral college, with MPs casting the lion's share of votes – a view restated by Hamilton during the 1997 inquiry. Furthermore Hodgson was also keen to protect association autonomy in the field of candidate selection, while Parkinson – mindful of the problems caused by some of the selections made before the general election (see below) – was eager to extend central control.

From Hague's point of view, the Tory conference of 1997 began well enough, with his 'back me or sack me' ballot, linked to endorsement of his 'six principles of reform', recording a vote of 142 299 in favour and 34 092 against. Yet the mood of the conference was not marked by an obvious determination to bury old differences and unite behind the new regime. Its mood was, in fact, redolent of the 1979 and 1980 Labour conferences. Accusations of 'betrayal' on the part of Tory MPs were loudly applauded, while Sir Archie Hamilton was actually booed when he argued that MPs should at least retain a majority vote when choosing Party leaders (*Daily Telegraph*, 9 October 1997).

The success of his 'back me or sack me' ballot, however, enabled Hague to develop further the ideas contained in *Blueprint for Change*, chiefly through a programme of intra-party consultation. Between October and November 1997, Lord Parkinson headed 26 'Party Roadshows' across the country, attended by over 3 000 Tory activists. At each of these Roadshows, the ideas behind *Blueprint for Change* were explained, while gauging the reaction of rank and file members. Each association was also sent a detailed questionnaire, inviting a formal response to the green paper's proposals.

Leaving aside leader and candidate selection, *Blueprint for Change* did offer a number of clear suggestions which members generally welcomed. These included a national membership database – giving new members the chance to join nationally, allowing officials to know for the first time how many members the party had, while tightening up the rules of enrolment and subscription renewal. It was also proposed that a new youth wing (Conservative Future) should merge the old Young Conservatives and the two higher education groups, while a Conservative Women's Network should be created to attract more would-be female candidates (only six women who were not already MPs were chosen to fight winnable seats in 1997, leaving the Tories with only thirteen women MPs after the general election).

The issue of candidate selection remained a sensitive one throughout the period of consultation. From the leadership's angle, the case for greater central control had been strengthened by a number of events during the 1992–97 Parliament.

First, it was felt that the damage caused by Euro-rebel MPs could have been contained had there been more central control over reselection. The nine MPs who were prepared to forfeit the Tory whip, and effectively act as 'alternative' Tories for almost a year, were naturally encouraged by the steadfast support of their associations and the guarantee of reselection this brought. Likewise, before the 1997 general election, the leadership was powerless to prevent the reselection of Neil Hamilton in Tatton and Piers Merchant in Beckenham, even though their candidatures strengthened the Tories' association with 'sleaze' and directly brought about the loss of one safe Tory seat (Hamilton's own).

During the Roadshows, it became clear that any serious erosion of this constituency autonomy was unacceptable as far as activists were concerned. However, activists were prepared to accept a slight amendment of rules for the choice of by-election candidates, enabling the new national sub-committee on candidate selection to insist upon certain 'fast track' candidates being shortlisted for winnable seats; the principle that all general election candidates be drawn from a national approved list (extant since 1988) was also reaffirmed.

In other ways too, Parkinson won some crucial victories affecting candidate selection – without activists being fully aware of it. In the wake of the Tatton fiasco, activists were persuaded of the need for a new Ethics and Integrity Committee, comprising senior party officials and able to suspend or expel members (including MPs) whenever 'the reputation of our Party is threatened' (Conservative Party, 1997, p. 32). Activists were aware that, had this Committee existed before the last election, it is almost certain that its powers would have been invoked to halt the reselection of Hamilton and Merchant. Yet 'disrepute' is such a loaded and ambiguous term that the Committee may also have had the power to suspend those Euro-rebel MPs whose dissent caused the party such problems – a point not really discussed at the Roadshows. As well as subtly eroding local automony in candidate selection, the new Committee could therefore provide the leadership with more leverage over troublesome backbenchers.

A Single Party

At the heart of both the green paper and the Roadshow discussions was the idea of a 'single party' organisation, uniting Central Office, the National Union and the parliamentary party. Ever since the extra-parliamentary party's inception in 1867, these three elements had been organisationally separate. In fact, 'The Conservative Party' did not even exist as a formal, legal entity.

To end this anomaly, *Blueprint for Change* proposed a single governing body which would override Central Office and supplant the National Union. This body would be known as 'The Board' (see Table 6.5), with its various subordinate bodies including the Ethics and Integrity Committee and the sub-committee on candidate selection. The Board would be ultimately responsible for all matters affecting Conservative business outside Parliament, although its members would include Tory MPs – thus providing a clear link with the parliamentary party. Its functions would be explained in, and underpinned by, another innovation – a Conservative Party Constitution, outlining the powers and responsibilities of all the new bodies (Table 6.5).

In early 1998 the leadership selection issue was also defused by developments at Westminster: Tory MPs, by a two-thirds majority, backed the principle of OMOV for future leadership elections – a major *volte-face* (seemingly prompted by the mood of the 1997 Tory conference) and an important concession, it seemed, to the

TABLE 6.5   *The Extra-Parliamentary Conservative Party, Revised Structures, March 1998*

The Board   The Board will normally meet once a month, and will have supreme responsibility for all aspects of party management outside West-minster – budgets, senior appointments, candidate recruitment, conference management and the new national membership scheme (delegating these tasks to sub-committees where appropriate). It will also oversee the new Ethics and Integrity Committee. Drawing from all three wings of the party, it will comprise 14 members, five of whom (including the Party Chairman) will be appointed by the leader. Five members will be activists drawn from the National Convention (see below), with the remaining four members coming from Wales, Scotland, the Association of Conservative Councillors and the 1922 Committee of MPs.

The National Convention   Replacing Central Council, and with a potential membership of almost 1,000, the Convention will meet twice a year and com-prise national, regional and area officials, officers of the constituency associa-tions and members of other affiliated bodies such as the youth and women's organisations. The Convention will be supported by a network of 11 regional councils and 42 area councils, including an area for Northern Ireland. It will channel to the leader grass-roots views concerning policy and electoral strat-egy and advise the Board on all aspects of extra-parliamentary organisation.

The National Convention Executive   Replacing the National Union Execu-tive Committee, the NCE will be much smaller than the Convention and meet more frequently. It will comprise the six senior officers of the National Convention (including its Chairman and Deputy Chairman), five of whom will be the Convention's representatives on the Board. It will have day-to-day responsibility for voluntary Tory activity and be accountable to the Board.

The Policy Forum   Superseding the Conservative Political Centre, the Forum will allow ordinary members to take 'a more active role' in policy development. Overseen by a Forum Council (chaired by the shadow min-ister specially responsible for policy development), the Forum will comprise 'regional policy congresses' which 'co-opt experts' and ensure 'regular interchange' between parliamentary spokesmen and the grass roots. Draw-ing upon these 'congresses', the Forum Council will then have a 'major input' into the Conservative Party's annual conference.

NB: Party members were asked to approve these structures in a party ballot, with the result announced at a 'Special Reform Convention' on 28 March 1998. Following the distribution of approximately 330,000 ballot papers, 116,185 (35%) were returned, with 110,165 members voting approv-ingly. This approval represented 96% of those who voted, yet only 33% of the party's estimated membership. Conservative critics of the reform – like the Charter Movement's Eric Chalker – thus contest the legitimacy of the reforms and believe they could overturn them in any legal wrangle.

Source: *The Fresh Future* (1998), CCO Publications. For a comparison with previous Tory structures, see *Politics Review*, vol. 4, no. 4, April 1995.

The Governing Parties

TABLE 6.6 *Challenging Conservative Leaders, Revised Rules, 1998*

1 Vote of no-confidence proposed by no fewer than 15% of Tory MPs.
2 Tory MPs vote on no-confidence motion. If defeated, no further confidence motions allowed for another 12 months.
3 If a no-confidence motion is carried, the leader must resign and take no part in subsequent contest. Formal leadership contest instigated, and nominations invited, by officers of 1922 Committee.
4 Candidates require backing of two other (named) MPs.
5 (a) If there are only two other candidates, a one-member-one-vote contest is convened, involving all those who have been members of the Conservative Party for 6 months prior to the vote of no-confidence.
   (b) If there are more than two other candidates, Tory MPs vote in first-past-the-post 'primary' elections until only two candidates remain (the bottom-placed candidate being eliminated after each ballot).

Source: 1922 Executive Committee Paper, March 1998.

'single party' idea. Henceforth, Tory leadership contests would be determined by a ballot which appeared more democratically 'pure' than that used by the Labour Party (Table 6.6).

Shortly after the MPs' decision, the green paper was formally revised, renamed *The Fresh Future* and published in February 1998. The new document was careful to both highlight and accommodate the views which emerged from activists during the October–November consultation period. It was therefore unsurprising that, in a subsequent ballot of all party members – the second since both 1997 and 1867 – there was overwhelming support for its proposals (albeit on another low turnout – see Table 6.5). The results were announced at a 'Special Reform Convention' on 28 March, which marked the end of the old National Union and its attendant bodies.

Plus ça Change...

The Convention was acclaimed by Hague as a watershed in Tory history. It marked, he claimed, the start of a new, unified party and a fresh, democratic approach to party affairs. As part of his 'ongoing cultural revolution', Hague also arranged (for autumn 1998) a third all-party ballot, this time in respect of his new 'sceptic' policy on the European single currency – one which gave him 84 per cent backing with 59 per cent of the 340 000 ballot papers being returned. A 'primary ballot' among London Tories, to determine the party's mayoral candidate for the new Greater London Authority, was also promised, as well as a further all-party ballot to endorse the next Conservative manifesto.

Yet a few cautionary notes are in order. First of all, the new structures offer only a limited extension of formal party democracy. For example, the new Convention and Executive (see Table 6.5) are strikingly similar to the two bodies they replaced (Central Council and National Union General Purposes Committee), both noted for their toothlessness vis-à-vis the parliamentary party.

Given Hague's stress upon democracy, it is noticeable that the reforms offer no precise details of *how* members will influence policy, and *how* such influence may be guaranteed. Similarly, there are no provisions which *compel* Tory leaders to heed the opinion of Tory members, be it expressed through conference or any of the new party organs. In other words, the membership's role remains purely 'advisory'. The arrangement mapped out by Disraeli in 1867 emerges relatively unscathed.

These harsh realities, plus the existence of new 'efficiency criteria' and an Ethics and Integrity Committee, create an impression that Tory members may have been given extra responsibilities without much extra power, while parliamentary leaders have been given extra power without much extra responsibility. It is noticeable that, while containing MPs, the new Board – which claims responsibility for the whole of the extra-parliamentary party – has no control over the conduct of the party at Westminster.

Even in respect of leader selection, Tory activists may not have gained as much as initially supposed. As Table 6.6 reveals, Tory MPs retain a strong element of 'quality control' in the selection process, with ordinary members only being allowed a choice of two candidates (Labour's electoral college system allows extra-parliamentary members a choice of up to eight candidates – see Kelly, 1995). Furthermore, any vote of confidence in the existing leader is still confined to MPs, with any defeated leader unable to take part in a subsequent leadership contest. As a result, a leader who has the overwhelming support of the party at large could still be deposed.

Cliquish *coups d'état*, of the sort which deposed Margaret Thatcher in 1990, are still possible.

Lessons from Labour

For students of party organisation, events inside the Conservative Party leave a strong sense of *déjà vu*. It will be recalled that in the Labour Party after 1983, and particularly during the Blair era, there were repeated attempts supposedly to empower ordinary members while actually strengthening central authority. The Tory high-command, notably Hague and Norman, seems impressed and influenced by Labour's precedent. Among some Tory MPs (such as Alan Clark and Nicholas Winterton) there was a growing feeling that Hague's reforms were little more than a 'subtle decoy', allowing him to gain a Blair-esque control of the party while the bulk of it is 'distracted by constitutional niceties' (*Daily Telegraph*, 20 September 1997).

As in the Labour Party, the 'democratisation' of leadership elections may also end up bolstering the power of the leader. Following the 'back me or sack me' ballot of 1997, Hague is already the first Tory leader able to claim a mandate from the whole party – a useful weapon when dealing with dissent, as recent Labour leaders have shown. It has also become harder for a leader to be overthrown. To begin with, any challenging ballot now requires support from 15 per cent of Tory MPs, as opposed to 10 per cent under the old rules, while to survive such a ballot a leader only needs a straightforward majority, instead of a majority plus a 15 per cent lead (a tough criterion which fatefully eluded Thatcher in 1990).

The Liberal Democrats

The 1988 constitution of the Liberal Democrats still accords supreme power to the party's twice yearly national conference. In practice, however, the conference's power is limited by the need for flexible, dynamic decision-making on the part of the parliamentary leadership. This has been made particularly clear by developments since the 1997 general election.

Since the creation of a Joint Consultative Committee with senior Labour MPs in 1996, to assess the possibilities of reform to Britain's constitution, the influence of the Lib Dems' own parliamentary wing has allegedly grown – in a way which has exposed the limitations of its extra-parliamentary wing. The possibility of regular influence within Blair's government – signposted by the Prime Minister's talk of 'inclusivity' and a new era of permanent 'progressive' government – has also focused further attention upon the locus of power within Britain's third party.

The Federal Policy Committee has continued to function as the Lib Dems' main policy-drafting body; the status of its 'green papers' and 'white papers' on constitutional reform has naturally been enhanced by the presence of Lib Dem MPs on the relevant Cabinet sub-committee set up by Blair after the 1997 general election. Yet the fact that the advancement of such proposals depends upon a compromise with Labour ministers gives Lib Dem MPs massive scope for interpretation and therefore considerable discretionary power. This was particularly evident during 1998 in respect of electoral reform.

Both the Committee and the conference insisted in early 1998 that the party should not accept the recommendations of the Jenkins Commission on electoral reform unless they supported proportional representation (*The Guardian*, 7 January). The Lib Dem leader, Paddy Ashdown, however, publicly renounced this idea, claiming it would tie his hands when trying to reach a mutually agreed formula with the Prime Minister. Indeed, the fact that Lord Jenkins himself, a senior Lib Dem in the Lords, should so obviously tailor the feelings of his own extra-parliamentary followers to the sensibilities of the Labour Party – on an issue as important to the Lib Dems as electoral reform – was itself revealing about the spread of power among Liberal Democrats.

Article 8 of the party's constitution gives the Lib Dem Federal Executive the power to poll the whole party on any issue it considers of 'vital importance' (Garner and Kelly, 1998, p. 176). Despite pressure from grass-root Lib Dems – anxious to make the extra-parliamentary party's views on electoral reform crystal clear to the Jenkins Commission – the Executive, sensitive to the position of the parliamentary leadership, did not yield such a referendum. Following the rather tame proposals of the Jenkins Report, and the government's subsequent failure to promise a foreseeable referendum on the subject (as hinted in Labour's manifesto), there was a widespread feeling among Lib Dem activists that they had been 'shafted' by Lib Dem MPs 'who were acting more like members of a Labour government than our Parliamentary spokesmen' (*The Guardian*, 4 November 1998).

The Lib Dems after 1997 provide an interesting example of a point made by R. T. McKenzie in his study of party organisation in 1955, namely, that even the most 'democratically' organised parties experience an accretion of power to their parliamentary leaders once those parties acquire, or come close to acquiring, governmental responsibilities – the imperatives of intra-party democracy being inevitably challenged by both the demands of wider public opinion and the imperatives of public administration (pp. 639–49). Indeed, the unofficial redistribution of power within the Lib Dems recalls the 'iron law of oligarchy' posited by Robert Michels as long ago as 1911 (McKenzie, 1955, pp. 629–30).

Of course, parties with a culture of internal democracy are likely to suffer a reaction to these uncomfortable 'realities', as the Labour Party conference showed from about 1918 until recently (Minkin, 1978). At the start of 1999 there were already signs that Lib Dem activists were preparing to fight for changes in the party's organisation, changes which would ensure that any regular influence in government did not lead to any further erosion of intra-party democracy. Paddy Ashdown's resignation as party leader, and the OMOV leadership contest which followed, gave a chance for the issue to be discussed more seriously by the bulk of party members.

Conclusion: New Structures, New Doctrines

It is wrong to look at party organisation in isolation from party ideology; certain types of structure are nearly always designed to produce certain types of policy. R. T. McKenzie argued as long ago as 1955 that 'oligarchic' party structures were the necessary prerquisite of moderate, centrist manifestos (pp. 635–49), while Tony Benn's 'Campaign for Labour Party Democracy' after 1979 had the opposite ideological purpose – the empowerment of Labour activists being considered vital to the adoption of a 'socialistic' Labour programme (Shaw, 1994, pp. 2–29).

In recent years, this connection has again been evident in respect of Britain's two governing parties, with both Tony Blair and William Hague embracing organisational reform as a conduit to policy revision. In the case of Labour, it must first be remembered that the party's traditional ideology has been an uneasy mix of trade unionism, doctrinaire socialism and liberalism (Elliott, 1993, pp. 22–66). Blair's ideological goal since 1994 has been to exalt Labour's liberal element and virtually eliminate the two others. This has involved two related tactics.

The first of these has been to make Labour more 'inclusive' of liberal-minded people outside the Labour Party – hence the cultivation of links with the Liberal Democrats, the absorption into government of 'progressive' businessmen like Lord Simon, the talk of 'patriotic alliances' with centrist Tories over Europe, the fanfare which greeted Tory defectors like Alan Howarth (1995) and Peter Temple-Morris (1998), and the movement towards a new electoral system which could cement such links while sidelining both Thatcherite Tories and Labour socialists.

The second tactic has been to change Labour's own organisation. As we have seen, this has involved greater central authority, the enfranchisement of 'ordinary' party members (thought to be passive, moderate and generally supportive of the leadership) and the weakening of leftist power bases inside the party (such as CLP committees, union block votes and the whole 'delegatory' system enshrined by Labour's annual conference). To date, this strategy has been vindicated by electoral success. It remains to be seen whether it will survive a period of electoral unpopularity.

In the case of Hague's reorganisation, the ideological goal has not been so conspicuous. Yet some valuable clues have emerged – clues which indicate that Hague, like Blair, is seeking to revise and refound his party's ideological position. On the crucial issue of Europe and the single currency, Hague has adopted a clear, 'sceptical' position – a much more 'sceptical' position than the one offered by his predecessor and, by implication, a much 'purer' version of laissez-faire economics. Yet Europe is not the only area where Hague's 'Fresh Conservatism' looks quite adventurous. After the Tory conference of 1997, there were signs that the leadership (supported by the absent Michael Portillo) was flirting with American-style libertarianism (Durham, 1997). There were hints of this in Hague's first conference speech as leader, one which refuted the 'moralising' and 'preachy' tone of New Labour, while defending 'unfettered individualism', 'cultural pluralism' and 'alternative life-styles' – including those of gay couples, ethnic minorities and unmarried cohabitants (such as Hague himself at the time of the conference).

At one level, Hague was simply trying to distinguish the Tories from the 'nanny state' tendencies he ascribed to Blair's government – illustrated, he claimed, by its 'restrictive' policies on handguns, fox-hunting and 'rights of access' to rural property. Yet at another, more interesting, level, he may have been 'flagging up' a type of laissez-faire morality which libertarians see as the natural concomit-ant of laissez-faire economics (Evans, 1996, pp. 129–37).

Hague's 'Fresh Conservatism' will not go unchallenged: neither Euro-scepticism nor libertarianism have overwhelming support inside the Conservative Party. Norton (1998) has revealed that, among Tory MPs elected in 1997, at least 21 per cent have clear 'pro-European' views. As far as libertarianism is concerned, White-ley, Seyd and Richardson's survey of grass-root Tories offered Hague little encouragement, with the bulk of constituency members seeming *authoritarian* rather than libertarian in their approach to social policy (Whiteley, Seyd and Richardson, 1994, pp. 54–9). This is scarcely surprising, given that Conservatism, somewhat paradoxically, has always proposed the restriction and containment of human behaviour as well as its liberation – *vide* its perennial enthusiasm for both law and order and economic laissez-faire (Evans and Taylor, 1996). It is unlikely that the Conservatives approached by Whiteley's team would have been greatly impressed by the principles of libertarianism which, according to Evans, include 'an acceptance of abortion, prostitution, surrogate mother-hood, homosexuality, lesbianism, ticket-touting and a failure to see why Sunday trading should have been illegal until recently' (p. 107).

However, other surveys of Tory members show that, among younger activists (often dubbed 'Thatcher's children') there is much more enthusiasm for this new and bold brand of right-wing politics. (Kelly, 1989, pp. 98–114; Evans, 1996, p. 103). If this generation of members can be multiplied, in the way Hague intends, and its voice amplified in a new regime of regular, all-party ballots, then these younger Tories could yet give Hague the support he needs in any new battle for the soul of Conservatism.

These possibilities are likely to refocus the study of party organisation in Britain. For the most part, students since 1979 have tended to concentrate on changes in the Labour Party. The first year of William Hague's leadership, however, suggests that it will be the Tories who deserve the most attention in the decade ahead. Perhaps this highlights another 'iron law' of British politics – that while electorally successful parties concentrate on how to govern the country, their unsuccessful rivals concentrate on how to govern themselves.

References

Anderson P. and Mann, N. (1997) *Safety First: The Making of New Labour* (London: Granta).

Acherson, N. (1994) 'Fuzzy democracy', *New Statesman*, 11 March.

Baggott, R. (1995) *Pressure Groups Today* (Manchester: Manchester University Press) pp. 220–31.

Bethell, J. (1997) *Blue Skies Ahead?* (London: Centre for Policy Studies).

Butler, D. and Kavanagh D. (1997) *The British General Election of 1997* (Basingstoke: Macmillan).

Conservative Party (1997) *Blueprint For Change* (London: CCO Publications).

Conservative Party (1998) *The Fresh Future* (London: CCO Publications).

Cowley, P. and Norton, P. (1996) *Blair's Bastards: Discontent within the Parliamentary Labour Party* (Hull: Hull University Publications).

Cowley, P. (1997) 'Men (and women) behaving badly? The Conservative Parliamentary Party since 1992', *Talking Politics*, 9(2).

Cowley, P. (1998) 'Just William?', *Talking Politics*, 10(1).

Draper, D. (1997) *Blair's Hundred Days* (London: Faber).

Durham, M. (1997) 'What future for the Tories?', *Talking Politics*, 10(1).

Elliott, G. (1993) *Labourism and the English Genius* (London: Verso).

Evans, B. and Taylor A. (1996) *From Salisbury To Major: Continuity and Change in Conservative Politics* (Manchester: Manchester University Press).

Evans, T. (1996) *Conservative Radicalism* (Oxford: Berghahn Press).

Garner, R. and Kelly, R. (1998) *British Political Parties Today*, 2nd edn (Manchester: Manchester University Press).

Gummett, P. (ed.) (1996) *Globalisation and Public Policy* (Cheltenham, Edward Elgar).

Hall, S. and Jacques, M. (1988) *New Times* (London: Lawrence & Wishart).

Holroyd-Doveton, J. (1996) *Young Conservatives* (Durham: Pentland Press).

Hughes, C. and Wintour, P. (1990) *Labour Rebuilt* (London: Fourth Estate).

Jones, N. (1997) *Campaign 97* (London: Indigo).

Kelly, R. (1989) *Conservative Party Conferences* (Manchester: Manchester University Press).

Kelly, R. (1995) 'Labour's leadership contest and internal organisation', *Politics Review*, 4(3).

Kelly, R. (1996) 'Selecting parliamentary candidates', *Talking Politics*, 9(1).

Kelly, R. (1997) 'The Tory way is the better way', *Political Quarterly*, 68.

Kelly, R. (1999) 'Does Party Policy Matter?' in Kelly, R. (ed.), *Changing Party Policy in Britain* (Oxford: Blackwell).

Kelly, R. and Foster S. (1991) 'Power in the Labour Party', *Politics Review*, 1(1).

Labour Party (1995) *Labour News*, March.

Mandelson, P. and Liddle, R. (1995) *The Blair Revolution* (London: Faber).

Marr A. (1995) *Ruling Britannia* (London: Penguin).

McKenzie, R. T. (1955) *British Political Parties* (London: Heinemann).

Minkin, L. (1978) *The Labour Party Conference* (London: Allen Lane).

Norton, P. (1998) 'Electing the leader', *Politics Review*, 7(4).

Rentoul, J. (1995) *Tony Blair* (London: Little, Brown).

Seyd, P. (1987) *The Rise and Fall of the Labour Left* (Basingstoke: Macmillan).

Shaw, E. (1988) *Discipline and Discord in the Labour Party* (Manchester: Manchester University Press).

Shaw, E. (1994) *The Labour Party Since 1979* (London: Routledge).

Williams, J. (1997) *Victory: With Blair on the Road to a Landslide* (London: Bookman).

Whiteley, P., Seyd P. and Richardson, J. (1994) *True Blues* (Oxford: Oxford University Press).

7

The Media and Government

BILL JONES

This chapter analyses developments in the relationship between politics and the media since the start of Conservative rule in 1979. The first section examines the period 1979–97; the second the 1997 election; and the third, Labour's subsequent period in power.

Spinning and Weaving: 1979–97

This period marks the growth of modern campaigning techniques, mostly pioneered by the Conservatives. It was from this crucible – a flattened Labour party combating triumphant Thatcherism – that the new media politics of the 1990s, was fashioned.

Spin Doctors

These specialist media advisers and experts in persuading the media to interpret political messages in the desired fashion were originally introduced by the Conservatives. Sir Gordon Reece and Tim Bell became Mrs Thatcher's media gurus and they did much to import American-style techniques across the Atlantic. Sir Bernard Ingham, her gruff Yorkshire Press Secretary, became virtually her Minister for Information, centralising control of the government's interfaces with the media. He dominated the dissemination of information at the daily press conferences with political correspondents of the main newspapers, though always maintaining the 'lobby' fiction that such briefings did not occur and were not attributable to Number Ten.

Michael Foot was something of an innocent regarding the media and it took Neil Kinnock in 1985 to appoint Labour's first spin doctor, the redoubtable Peter Mandelson. As the party's Director of Campaigns and Communications, he personally transformed Labour's media relations and brought them up to speed with, if not exceeding, the professionalism of the Tories. Crucially there emerged in the mid-1980s the Shadow Communications Agency – a network of voluntary Labour supporters from advertising and marketing who did much to plot the overthrow of the Tory hegemony (Wring, 1998, p. 201). The emergence of Labour's spin doctors (see below) marked the party's realisation that it was the media which were likely to be its conduit to power. It was almost certainly the case that Tony Blair was crucially preferred by many Labour MPs and members to Gordon Brown (despite the latter's somewhat frenetic efforts to prove otherwise (Jones, 1996)) because he was more fluent, sympathetic and convincing on television. The cleverest member of the Shadow Cabinet, Robin Cook was widely, though cruelly, judged by the media experts, in televisual terms, to be a non-runner because of his allegedly 'garden gnome' appearance. With television taking political leaders into everyone's front room Labour realised the relationship between politicians and the public had been transformed into one in which voters felt they 'knew' their leaders through their exposure over the airwaves. The skills now required are more akin to the actor or even the therapist than those of the pre-television politician. Media advisers have burgeoned with a host of new actors sidling onto the political stage, including speech writers and others specialising in 'one liners' for set piece speeches (Jones, 1996, p. 10).

Tabloids

The rise of the tabloids with their penchant for sensationalism and focus on personalities (easy to understand and spicy) rather than policies (difficult and boring) was a feature of the Tory years. Precisely why they chose to become so aggressive to politicians and other public figures is partly to do with the decline of deference: the sentiment which led journalists not to write about the affair between Harold Macmillan's wife and his fellow MP Bob Boothby.

Pippa Norris suggests (Norris, 1998, p. 123) that the change in styles of reporting was also to do with increased competition for readers. Between 1979 and 1995 newspaper readership fell from 72 to 62 per cent for men and from 68 to 54 per cent for women. The tabloids tried every ploy to capture a larger share of this diminishing pool of readers; bingo, spot the ball, page three girls and a new brash editorial style regarding the private life of public figures, associated most closely with *The Sun*'s legendary 1980s' editor, Kelvin Mackenzie. (Ironically Mackenzie moved to the *Daily Mirror* in 1998 and whilst briefly there endeavoured to move it upmarket to win more educated readers. *The Sun*'s new editor in June 1998, David Yelland, adopted a similar strategy.)

During the 1980s the tabloids tended to influence the political agenda by the back door; television and the broadsheets tried sniffly to ignore the tabloid campaigns but eventually could not resist the topics everyone else was talking about. The rest of the news tended to follow suit. *The Economist* noted the paradox that in a globalised world *The Times*, on a particular day, carried only one foreign news story – the fact that Leonardo DiCaprio had a new girlfriend – compared to the nineteen columns of international news the same paper carried on a typical day back in 1898 (*The Economist*, 4 July 1998). The laissez-faire approach of the Conservative government enabled newspaper owners to move into television and radio, making these agencies 'subject to the same kind of competitive forces which took the popular press even further down market' (*The Economist*, 4 July 1998). Now news programmes competed with each other head-on, as well as with the press, they tended to dip into the bag of 'down market' populist ricks used by the tabloids to attract readers.

Logistics and Output

In the 1980s, newspapers began to devote less space to political reporting – speeches, parliament, even routine events – because editors knew television was doing this more immediately and effectively. Nicholas Jones, in his perceptive and entertaining *Soundbites and Spin Doctors* (1996), relates how he joined *The Times* as a parliamentary reporter in 1968 to take shorthand notes of proceedings. The 'serious time disadvantage' of print journalism led the paper to reduce its coverage as television journalists, the ranks of

Figure 7.1   Press reporting of Parliament (*Times* and *Guardian* averages on typical days)

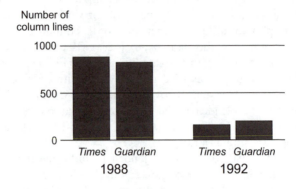

which Jones then joined, burgeoned to rival or exceed those of newspaper colleagues. The latter now only observe proceedings during Prime Minister's Questions (PMQs) or front bench speeches and many journalists watch not in the chamber but via the small screens built into their desks in the Millbank Tower and write their stories on desk-top computer terminals. Journalists now tend to write analytical articles rather than the straight reporting which once led *The Times* to sub-edit the massive copy produced within Westminster itself (see Figure 7.1).

Some commentators have seen the decline of political reporting as a casualty of the general decline in newspaper sales. Winston Fletcher, writing in the *The Guardian* (30 January 1998) pointed out that sales of daily papers have declined from 15 million in 1990 to 13 million in 1998; the Sundays have fallen from 17 million to 15 million over the same period. Fletcher explained why this competition had produced more emphasis on lightweight stories and sleaze: 'Publishers and editors know what is selling their newspapers with greater precision than ever before. And the figures show it is scandals, misfortunes and disasters'. Meanwhile the media's broadcast output has been increasing. *The Economist* noted that NBC's output of news between 1996 and 1998 had increased from 3 hours to 27 per day, not to mention a constantly updated website. And all this with only a few more reporters. In the old days a reporter might spend a day compiling and improving his report but the TWA crash in July 1996 was on the screen almost as soon as it happened.

MSNBC was delighted to beat CNN to the punch by a full eight minutes. News gathering agencies have also had to adapt to changing viewing patterns. In 1993 30 per cent of Americans watched only the evening news programmes; by 1998 it was 15 per cent. In 1995 4 per cent of Americans used a website; in 1998 it was 20 per cent. News making is moreover now cheaper. In 1993 it cost over £1000 to buy satellite time from Australia; in 1998 it was only £300. In the old days there was a huge retinue of technicians to help report the news; now presenters do much of the job themselves and use light hand-held cameras plus a lap-top editing machine. Some media experts reckon there is too much on-the-spot reporting now that it has become cheaper than crafting balanced quality analyses. (Figures in this paragraph from *The Economist*, 4 July 1998.)

Interviewing Politicians and Presenter Power

TV entered the House of Commons in November 1989 but the restrictions on picture coverage allowed made much coverage less than compelling and ratings for parliamentary programmes were abysmal. To compensate, producers took to supplementing coverage with interviews, mostly taken on College Green outside the Houses of Parliament. This meant that many MPs eschewed the chamber for the TV interview, so much more personal and likely to be picked up by constituents not to mention whips looking for new talent. Despite this tendency a Hansard Society report in 1990 recorded an 80 per cent increase in Commons reporting on national television news during the first three months of the television experiment (*The Economist*, 4 July 1998). Some commentators have noted how power has shifted markedly to presenters.

Jones noted how current affairs reporting in the 1980s moved away from prerecorded material and the use of specialist correspondents to direct intervention by presenters (Jones, 1996, pp. 18–19). These highly paid celebrity figures now interview important players live on their programmes. This possibility has enhanced the power and remuneration of presenters but has also strengthened the hand of politicians who can now exploit a seller's market and dictate terms before agreeing to be interviewed.

Mrs Thatcher had a blacklist of presenters by whom she did not wish to be interviewed. Those who were allowed were forced to accept conditions regarding such aspects as questions to be asked, length of interview and so forth. Politicians prefer to be interviewed live, which gives them more control, and like to select the time at which they appear; Tony Benn, for example, always like to be interviewed at 8.10 on the *Today* programme. Ingham was ruthless in demanding such conditions for his boss and would punish recalcitrants, like *Today*'s Brian Redhead, with future exclusion from access to the highest sources.

But the pressure exerted by the media brought its own problems too. Jones records that Douglas Hurd, in a speech to the Travellers Club in 1993, described how, when made Home Secretary in 1987, he found

> that the staff in his private office were catching trains almost exactly an hour later than when they had five years earlier when Whitelaw was doing the job... the additional workload being due entirely to the need to communicate: more time was having to be spent dealing with the news media, preparing for television and radio interviews, issuing statements and answering parliamentary questions... [he] acknowledged that openness and the need to take account of public opinion had become almost as vital to the success of any policy as the sensible construction of that policy in the first place. (Jones, 1996, p. 25)

Furthermore, in telling the public about its new ventures, especially privatisation, the government blurred the distinction between public information and propaganda. Expenditure on advertising rose from £60 million in 1982 to £200 million in 1989–90 (Jones, 1991, p. 206).

Soundbites

Finally, politicians have been forced to shorten their messages to take account of the shortened attention span of their audiences, in order to compete with multifarious other media and leisure attractions. The tendency for politicians to use short pithy formulations of complex ideas has long been a feature of modern political communications. Its provenance lies in the extremely short attention span of the average viewer and the consequent tendency of news editors to use only that part of a televised speech which is at once memorable and encapsulating. Politicians soon realised that if they did not invent such 'soundbites' and place them in their speeches they would be ignored. Walter Cronkite observed in his memoirs that the average length of time of presidential candidates' televised speeches fell from 42.3 seconds to 8.2 in 1992 (*The Guardian*, 27 January 1997). Alastair Campbell, Blair's press secretary, had a background in tabloid journalism and was consequently good at hatching headline soundbites. Blair's apparently spontaneous speech in the wake of Princess Diana's death was illuminated by the phrase 'The People's Princess'; clearly the product of the tabloid journalist Campbell and not his boss.

Blair's appearances at PMQs were so studded with soundbites that John Major used to make fun of them. Such excess can be counter-productive. Gordon Brown could display a rare talent for soundbitery but often prefaced them with too much information e.g. 'With three million people out of work . . .' He was also criticised (Jones, 1996, p. 48) perhaps unfairly, on other occasions for using incomprehensible economic jargon as in 'post neo-classical endogenous growth theory' (Jones, 1996, p. 48). Soundbites to some extent, however, in the form of political slogans have been around for some time; as Ken Livingstone remarked, 'I watched everything that was on [television] from 1956 when I was 11 until joining the Labour party and being out of an evening. I *think* in soundbites' (Norris, 1998, p. 130).

The Harvest is Gathered: The 1997 Election Campaign

The campaign opened with the usual row over debates: between party leaders, on television; but this time the difference was the potential participants wishing to take part. Surprisingly Margaret Thatcher had been advised by her media guru Gordon Reece in the 1983 election to debate with Michael Foot live on television. 'British Prime Ministers have never accepted challenges to election debates of this kind,' she commented in her memoirs, adding that she rejected the the idea as she 'disliked the way elections are being turned into media circuses'. Unsurprisingly she neglected to acknowledge the major contributions she herself made to such circuses. In 1992 Kinnock challenged Major to a debate and was put down with 'every party politician that expects to lose tries that trick; every politician who expects to win says no'. However, Major's reluctance melted away when his own poll rating was 26 points behind his challenger in March 1997. From dismissing a TV debate as a 'stupid PR stunt' he now eagerly sought one and soon accused Blair of 'running scared' when the negotiations ran into trouble and were then abandoned. The role of the Liberal Democrats was the sticking point; Blair and Major wanted to dominate the airtime whilst Ashdown, with near equal time for party political broadcasts, felt he should be more than a sideshow to the main protagonists. A Gallup Poll showed 82 per cent of respondents in favour of a debate between all three leaders and the discussion commanded 10 per cent of press coverage. But it was not to be.

The Economist (22 March 1997) questioned the utility of such devices throughout the world citing a report by the Hansard Society which found they 'at best strengthened voting intentions among the weakly committed' but only in a closely fought election. The journal cited 'other studies' which have found that even influences on how candidates were regarded were 'small and brief' and that the media reporting served to affect those who did not see the debates as much as those who had. Writing in his *Guardian* column, however, Jonathan Freedland begged to disagree: 'television has a knack of peering into places the naked eye can miss'. The US presidential debates, he claimed, served to reveal important truths about the candidates: Nixon was indeed untrustworthy; Dukakis was an 'introvert and depressive utterly unsuited to the father of the nation duties of the president'; and Bush was 'disengaged with the day to day task of domestic leadership'. He also cited the time when Mrs Thatcher could not escape the 'beady eye of television' and expressed her contempt to David Dimbleby for those who ' "drool and drivel" that they care'. 'If it's good enough for the Americans,' he concluded, 'then it should be good enough for us', calling for a full 90-minute debate at the next election (*The Guardian*, 13 August 1997).

The Earth Moves: Labour wins the Tory Press

The most dramatic aspect of the 1997 election was what Pippa Norris calls the 'partisan dealignment' of the press (Norris, 1998, p. 117). In 1945 the balance of readership of Conservative-to Labour-supporting newspapers was 6.7 million to 4.4 million respectively. There was a further shift to the right in the 1970s when the *Daily Herald* was reincarnated as *The Sun* and Murdoch brought his Thatcherite agenda to *The Times*. This shift was such that by 1992 the readership figures were 8.7 million to 3.3 million respectively (Norris, 1998, p. 122). But the shift of support had taken place before the 1997 campaign started. By the end six of the ten national dailies had opted for Blair and five of the nine Sundays; 3.43 million readers to Conservatives and 8.6 million to Labour. A historic shift of allegiance had taken place. Why? The reasons were several.

First, press disillusion with the Conservative Party began in the late 1980s when a deep recession coincided with the beginning of the Prime Minister's more 'manic' phase of political leadership. This followed the Westland crisis in 1986 and was perhaps best reflected in her stubborn determination to ignore all arguments to the contrary and force through the poll tax legislation. Journalists, even on Tory papers, were fed up with her imperiousness and the crisis in November 1990 was to a large extent encouraged by a lukewarm press and falling poll ratings. Major's accession improved the Conservative case for a while and the new man seemed to many less than well informed voters to be heading a 'different' government. But it was not to last.

Second, the 'Major effect' was washed away by the extraordinary events of 'Black Wednesday'. On 16 September 1992, Britain was ejected from the European Exchange Rate Mechanism (ERM) when speculators exploited the fact that Britain had joined at an unsustainably high rate for the pound. Staunch Tory papers were scathing; 'Now we've all been screwed by the government' was *The Sun*'s headline comment on the government's loss of £9 billion to currency speculators.

Third, if the poll tax caused lacerations on the Conservative body politic, then Europe caused numerous and near fatal haemorrhages. Mrs Thatcher soon regretted that she had signed the 1986 Single European Act, which had accelerated the integration process, and became a fierce critic of policies her own government had endorsed. Maastricht, in 1991, was even more reviled by those Conservatives, like Nicholas Ridley, who had come to see Europe as a plot to erode sovereignty, and to satisfy the long unsatisfied German appetite to dominate the continent. In May 1992, 65 per cent of respondents to a Gallup poll perceived the Conservatives as united; by March 1997 80 per cent perceived the party as divided (Denver, 1998, p. 27). The press reflected the consequent loss of respect.

Fourth, Major was increasingly perceived as a weak leader. Whilst his likeability earned him a plus 20 rating his 'effectiveness' rating was minus 46; his 'toughness' rating minus 49; and his 'firmly in charge' rating a catastrophic minus 60 rating, exceeded only by his minus 67 rating on 'likelihood to unite country' (Denver, 1998, p. 42). The Conservative press began to criticise Major and his attempts to control his party were seen as pathetic. This was almost certainly unfair – that shrewd judge John Biffen saw him as 'a very good leader but with an impossible task' (personal communication) – but this was not the line the press, Labour and Conservative, purveyed to their readers.

Fifth, the Conservative Party was submerged in a deluge of sleaze stories; nine sexual scandals involving MPs and one in which an MP died as a result of a bizarre sexual practice. That was bad enough but the British public, as Denver note (Denver, 1998, p. 29), quite enjoys such tabloid delicacies; it only becomes truly indignant when it appears a politician has used a position of trust for personal financial advantage. From 1993 to the election there was a non-stop succession of such stories, the most harmful of which concerned the suggestion that Conservative MPs were prepared to take money in exchange for performing their duties in Parliament, especially asking questions. Neil Hamilton, MP for Tatton was accused by *The Guardian* of taking cash and favours from the owner of Harrods, Mohamed al Fayed, in exchange for acting on behalf of his interests in Parliament. Hamilton resigned and sued the newpaper but then abandoned his action in September 1996, prompting *The Guardian* to run a front page featuring a photograph of the MP and the vengeful banner: 'A Liar and a Cheat'. Gallup polls in 1997 revealed the public divided about two to one in favour of the statement that the Conservatives appeared to be 'very sleazy and disreputable' (Denver, 1998, p. 37). During the election campaign the challenging parties withdrew from the Tatton contest and Martin Bell, respected BBC foreign correspondent, decided to enter the fray as an anti-sleaze candidate. Major had chosen to fight an unusually long six-week campaign and the press had trouble filling their pages. The gladiatorial contest between an arrogant ideologue with an apparently termagent wife and the honest, trusted newcomer in his trademark white suit was irresistible for the press, especially as Bell attracted much high-profile neutral support, like that of American TV star and singer, David Soul. Bell won by an astonishing 11 000 majority.

Sixth, in July 1995 Major decided on a bold and unexpected course of action to reassert his control over his party: he resigned and challenged anyone to stand against him; to 'put up or shut up'. It seemed at first as if he had 'fixed' all potential opponents but John Redwood eventually put himself forward and such was Major's unpopularity, even the former Welsh Secretary received considerable support from the Tory press, especially the *Daily Mail*; only the *Daily Express* remained wholly loyal to the Prime Minister. 'Major is a Loser and He Must Go' wrote Andrew Neil in *The Sunday Times* and the *Mail*, *Sun*, *Times* and *Telegraph* were scarcely more supportive. Major won comfortably according to the strict rules but Redwood gained a worryingly high degree of support and it took some valiant 'spinning' by Jeffrey Archer and other Major loyalists before he was pronounced a clear winner. But the contest designed to display strength had only served to highlight his political frailty and the press criticism, this time even more merciless, soon re-emerged.

Seventh, by election time the readerships of many newspapers had already deserted the Tory ship, putting huge pressure on editors to reflect this fact in their coverage and editorial opinions. Between the 1992 election and March 1997 the percentage shift to Labour amoungst Conservative newspaper readers was: *Express*, 17 per cent; *Mail*, 19 per cent; *Telegraph*, 16 per cent; *Sun* 23 per cent and *The Times*, 22 per cent. The volte-face of *The Sun* caused a sensation at the time; this was the publication which, after attacking Kinnock throughout the 1992 campaign, gloatingly claimed credit for the Major victory. But the conversion of so many of its readers to Labour by March 1997 offers an alternative explanation: the editor was merely following sound Fleet Street practice and bringing his editorial opinions into line with those of his readers.

Academic opinion differs on whether the tabloids are a major electoral force. Curtice and Semetko found little effect; another, by journalist Martin Linton, calculated *The Sun* swung 8 per cent more to the Tories than Mirror readers. A further study in March 1997 by Curtice used the British Election Panel Study of voters to examine the possible effects. *The Economist* (22 March 1997) summarised its findings: 'Curtice finds no evidence that the rebel Tory papers, including *The Sun* took their readers with them. Partisan newspapers of any shade have little effect on their readers' perceptions of parties or leaders, and the overall swing to Labour among those who read such papers is no different from those who don't.'

Finally, Tony Blair visited Rupert Murdoch in 1995 and, so the story goes, so impressed the media mogul, that he won the support of the Murdoch tabloids. It is hard to say if Blair did a deal but it was the case that Labour confirmed before the election that on cross-media ownership, a cause close to Murdoch's heart, it would not impose new restrictions.

Some other points need to be made about the media and the 1997 election. It is clear from all available sources that Labour won the battle for the agenda handsomely. The Conservatives fought to focus on the successful economy but 'simply failed to set the media agenda' being submerged in stories about sleaze, and their own record on unemployment and inflation. Labour, for its part, managed to direct media attention towards its priorities of education, the health service, pensions and crime (Norris, 1998, pp. 129–36). Further, the press provided detailed poll-based information for the first time of those constituencies where tactical voting might unseat the Conservative tenant. *The Observer* claimed credit for unseating a number of MPs in this way, including Michael Portillo. Moreover, there was good reason to suppose media coverage of the election was excessive in the views of most voters. Television news broadcasts suffered dramatic falls in viewers as the campaign progressed. According to the survey undertaken for the Independent Television Commission, up to two-thirds of viewers felt the television channels devoted 'far too much coverage' to the election and only the new Channel 5 received a majority verdict of 'about right' (Norris, 1998, p. 140).

Labour won an astounding success in May 1997, substantially through the short comings in office of the Conservatives but also through its mastery of media techniques. Labour spin doctor Dave Hill responded to the victory by saying the new priority was victory for a second term. Already Labour was planning to apply the same winning formula to government as it had to opposition. Writing in the *New Statesman* (18 June 1998) Ivor Gaber reported a 'senior Labour media manager' as saying, revealingly: 'Communications is not an after-thought of our policy. It's central to the whole mission of New Labour'. And so it has come to pass. Bob Franklyn (Franklyn, 1994, p. 8) reports how background briefings for MPs are distributed to constituency offices by Number Ten marked 'From the Head of Attack', an eloquent indication of opposition-mindedness even though the party is now in government.

Labour in Power

This third section examines relations between government and the media since New Labour have been in power.

Much attention has focused on the impact that Labour's media management has had on the nature of government and governing. In particular it has been argued that under Blair's leadership, government is prepared to pursue radical and sometimes high risk policies with the conviction that any resulting adverse consequences can be eliminated by the machinery of spin. In other words, government becomes as much concerned with the positive presentation of policy as with the actuality of policy. The government is willing to 'let the genie out of the bottle' across a range of policies – from devolution, genetically-modified crop production, to the conflict in Kosovo – without attempting either a full appraisal of policy implementation or the necessary options for modification in the event of policy failure. Rather there is a faith in the efficacy of careful presentation and agenda control being able to ease government through any resulting policy messes. Below the process is examined in terms of the most significant *dramatis personnae*: The 'Prince of Darkness', 'the Enforcer' and 'the Serial Killer'.

Peter Mandelson

Foremost among the new controllers of the Labour message was Peter Mandelson, made Minister without Portfolio in May 1997 in charge of policy coordination and the presentation of government policies. Much has been written about Mandelson and his mastery of the black arts of media manipulation, as his nickname, the Prince of Darkness, attests. Nicholas Jones writes of his *modus operandi* in some detail. Though friendly with both fellow 'modernisers' Brown and Blair he opted to support Blair when Smith died. In 1994 he was a close member of Blair's team but wished to remain anonymous (consequently codenamed 'Bobby' as known involvement might have alienated some Labour support). He has always been more than an expert on presentation and has been keen to feed ideas into policy content, invariably shifting the ship away from the left and steering it towards the centre/right. Blair's early opposition keynote speeches probably bore Mandelson's stamp. They certainly bore his summaries and markings indicating the key themes when they were distributed to journalists who were then often contacted by phone for discreet elaborations. He was insistent during that campaign that his role should be kept wholly secret and he frostily told Jones that the connection would not be mentioned 'either by you or by anyone else' (Jones *et al.*, 1998). Mandelson was extraordinarily assiduous in contacting the key reporters by pager and attempting to steer them in the desired direction. Jones records that even though Blair was assured of victory in the 1994 leadership contest, he was keen to appear neutral in relation to the contest for Deputy. Jones had hinted in an early broadcast that some Blairites were keen on Beckett but Mandelson harried him relentlessly all day until he issued the desired 'neutral' message in his evening bulletin. Mandelson, by all accounts has the silken charm of a cat – smooth words issuing forward reassuringly; but, like a cat, he can turn in an instant to being cold, commanding, vengeful and predatory.

Such a manner creates enemies and this substantial minority must have toasted his demise in *schadenfreude* in December 1998.

Alastair Campbell

Campbell has some similarities to Mandelson but is a different character. He is a product of print journalism and was a typical hack with a colourful past and a strong streak of aggression. Once a *Mirror* journalist – where he served Maxwell loyally – he moved to *Today* as a columnist and then to Blair's office.

There he has become the accepted mouthpiece of his master, criticised by Tories and Labour alike, though widely respected as a tough uncompromising operator in the Sir Bernard Ingham mould. Adam Boulton of *Sky News* says of him: 'To travel abroad with Alastair and Blair is amazing. No one else has such an intuitive understanding of the needs of journalists, the deadlines. Alastair will have a word, give each enough to get on the front page, and get ahead of the reporter who might be covering the same story back home.' But Campbell, according to Boulton, only gives when there is something to receive in return; for example, 'Alastair makes it plain the government will only do interviews when it's to their advantage'. As Kevin Toolis wrote in his *Guardian* piece in September 1997, 'Campbell's formative years were spent in the Eighties when sections of the press – led by the *Mail* and the *Sun* – acted as semi-official attack dogs for the Thatcher government and electorally destroyed Neil Kinnock. Now the boot is on the other foot – and he is the one doing the kicking, and petting. Campbell is unlikely to voluntarily relinquish that power, or loosen the leash' (*The Guardian*, 24 April 1998).

Campbell's manner can be alarming: he is a big man not afraid to use his size to intimidate journalists he wishes to berate and put down. On one famous occasion in public he punched Michael White from *The Guardian* for making a joke about Robert Maxwell's death. Campbell is nothing if not loyal to his masters. Writing in *The Times* Stephen Glover saw him as 'potentially dangerous ... an aggressive man who cannot always control his aggression' (*The Times*, 24 April 1998).

According to Clare Short in an article by Roy Hattersley, Blair and Campbell play 'good cop and bad cop'. When called in to discuss her suggestion that the rich might pay more tax, 'Blair, she told her friends, gave his emollient smile while Campbell, with the Prime Minister's approval, did the dirty work' (*The Observer*, 22 February 1998). Toolis's tag of 'The Enforcer' seems well earned (though it was usurped by Fleet Street to typify Jack Cunningham's Policy role).

Campbell biffs his critics
Tony Blair's Press Secretary, Alastair Campbell met the Public Administration Committee in June 1998 and responded to a number of widely voiced criticisms of his way of working. *The Economist* commented:

> Any unelected official who comes to be described as the second most powerful man in Britain is riding for a fall. The power of Alastair Campbell, Tony Blair's towering press spokesman, is especially resented by backbench members of parliament, who find that being elected has conferred on them vitually no power whatsoever. Courted by the press, forever at the side of the Prime Minister, present at every meeting of the Cabinet, the former Mirror journalist has become everything that the average MP wants to be but is not. No wonder many of them would like to see him cut down to size. If that was the aim of the Public Administration Committee when it summoned Mr Campbell to committee room eight of the House of Commons this week, the effort has been a flop.

The journal judged Mr Campbell to be a 'class act' who made 'short work' of their questions:

(1) He was merely acting as the prime minster's emissary when he wrote to Harriet Harman and Frank Field about leaks to journalists.

(2) Were he and his colleagues using leaks to bypass Parliament, as the Speaker, Betty Boothroyd, had complained. Was this true, asked the committee? No, answered the Press Secretary, adding that the committee could hardly accuse him both of leaking too much and (in the case of Harmon and Mr Field) also doing too much to suppress such escaped information.

(3) In reply to the question of whether during an argument between numbers 10 and 11, that Gordon Brown, was 'psychologically flawed', Campbell assured the committee he never briefed against ministers and did not know who this had badmouthed Mr Brown.

(4) The committee asked whether being a political appointee undermined the neutrality of the civil service? No, Campbell confidently answered. Although he had a special contract which enabled him to operate 'in a political context', he did so with the utmost care.

(5) Had he lied, asked the committee, when he described as 'crap' a story that Mr Blair had sided with Rupert Murdoch in relation to Romano Prodi, the prime minister of Italy? By no means, was the reply. He had only said that it was Mr Prodi who had phoned Mr Blair, not vice versa, and not in any case specifically to discuss the media mogul.

Charlie Whelan

According to Jones, Gordon Brown appointed Whelan as his press adviser at a time, January 1994, when he was trying desperately to lift his own profile in the leadership stakes. Whelan began life as a foreign exchange dealer in the City and went on to become an official for the AUEW, the engineering union. Politically he was then a member of the Communist Party but left in 1990. Mandelson recruited Whelan to Labour in 1992. He immediately improved Brown's public output. Subsequently, with Brown as Chancellor, Whelan assumed a profile similar to that of Campbell both in terms of loyalty to his boss and feared effectiveness in his job.

'Politics is a dirty business,' commented 'a senior Labour source' (code usually for the Prime Minister's press secretary) in a profile of Whelan in *The Sunday Times* (26 October 1997) 'and all politicians have a sort of dark or sinister side. You need someone to do your dirty work, and that is what Charlie does for Gordon.' Another source cited in the same profile described him as a 'serial killer'. It is worth noting, in passing, how the person charged with a senior politician's media relations seems, in the modern era, to have become known for ruthless behaviour in the cause of his boss, though it emphasises yet again the centrally crucial role the media now plays in the career of every modern politician. Whelan appeared in two documentaries broadcast in September 1997 called *Out of the Shadows* and *We are the Treasury* charting Brown's political rise to the next but one top job. In these revealing programmes it was obvious Whelan exercised a degree of power most unusual in a press adviser. At times it was Whelan who appeared to be making policy rather than Brown and he clearly took mischievous pleasure in conning journalists with false trails. In October his role hit the headlines when it transpired that he had purveyed a much more sceptical line on the single currency than Brown had been prepared to, causing financial doubt and confusion.

Later in the year political journalist, Paul Routledge, published a biography of Brown which contradicted the received wisdom that Brown had willingly stood aside for his friend Tony Blair alone to go for the leadership in the wake of Smith's death in 1994. Neither Brown nor his staff contradicted this version, stimulating much gossip that the Chancellor still hankered after the top job. In reply in a vicious briefing war, journalists claimed they were told by Campbell – though he subsequently denied it – that Brown had 'psychological flaws'.

The Plot Unravels

Both Whelan and Campbell were criticised in December 1997 for arrogant rudeness to foreign correspondents. During a press conference in Luxembourg, Campbell behaved with impatient lack of courtesy to those present prompting angry reactions. The correspondent for *Die Zeit* said 'They've got used to owning their country. They've started to think they own Europe as well'. Whelan, for his part was alleged to have described a group of correspondents as 'that lot' who purvey 'Euro-crap and Euro-bollocks' (*The Times*, 19 December 1997). Press secretaries can overdo things and sometimes seek to exercise in their own persons authority which belongs to their political masters.

Criticism of the 'spinners' also came from another more lofty domestic source. According to Michael White in *The Guardian* the Speaker, Betty Boothroyd,

> implied Labour is taking the skills it learned in 18 years of opposition to new lengths in order to control the media agenda. 'All governments have done this ... it's been rather blatant in the last six months ... there are too many of what I call apparatchiks who are working in government departments and who have been accustomed, when a party was in opposition, to want to get the maximum publicity ... Now in government they have to be harnessed a little more. (*The Guardian*, 8 April 1998)

The Conservatives regularly felt the BBC was somehow a repository of leftish consensual sentiments; to some extent, as Ralph Negrine maintained, distrust of the corporation became a litmus test of Thatcherite othodoxy. Conference cheers were guaranteed by attacks on the Beeb and few Tory ministers could resist. In the run-up to the 1987 election Norman Tebbit led a series of attacks on the alleged leftward bias of BBC journalists in an attempt to intimidate them before the fight was enjoined accusing, Kate Adie of being an agent of Gaddafi following her coverage of the American attack on Tripoli in April 1986. Brian Redhead, anchor of Radio Four's *Today* programme, was regularly pilloried and once accused by Lawson of being a Labour voter (actually he voted for the Conservative Nicholas Winterton whom he regarded as a good constituency member). When Labour came into power there was a naive belief in some quarters that they would never stoop to such petty partisanship. Not so. On 12 December 1997 senior spin doctor David Hill wrote a letter to the BBC complaining that an interview by John Humphrys had exceeded the bounds of propriety: 'The Humphrys problem has assumed new proportions,' it said, 'This can't go on.' The clear implication was made that Labour would consider denying ministerial interviews to the programme.

The dispute centred on questions asked of Harriet Harman about the cuts in benefit to single mothers. Harman refused to answer questions thirteen times according to *The Guardian* (13 December 1997) though to the author of this chapter it sounded like a typical attempt by a skilled broadcaster to extract answers from a minister who sounded as if she had something to hide. *The Guardian* editorial commented on Hill's 'confusion of party and government... It is not for a political party to decide how the Government is held to account. That Millbank even tried suggests arrogance of power is fast becoming a Labour disease'. However Labour did try to make the lobby system more transparent. The Westminster lobby has existed for decades as a kind of unacknowledged contract between ministers and the press; privileged information was given in exchange for secrecy about its source. Even the room in which it was given officially did not exist. Some papers, notably *The Guardian*, *The Independent* and *The Scotsman* disagreed with the system, which, they claimed, enabled Bernard Ingham to control the news agenda and they boycotted it. Yet on 27 November 1997 Alastair Campbell agreed to give on the record briefings to remove the secrecy. He also agreed to be identified as 'The Prime Minister's official spokesman', though insisted he wished to remain in the background as 'The important person in the equation is the Prime Minister... This is not a presidential system' (*The Guardian*, 28 November 1997). However television cameras were not to be allowed in and Campbell reserved the right to go off record in which case he would become merely 'a Labour source'.

Franklin showed beyond any doubt that New Labour has maintained its tight control of political communication in government (Franklyn, 1998, pp. 9–10). A Strategic Communications Unit has been set up in Number Ten comprising six civil servants answerable to Campbell, with a brief of ensuring 'key government messages' are being coordinated across the whole gamut of government. Furthermore, every day there is a 9 a.m. meeting of communications staff from the offices of Blair, Prescott, Brown, Cook and the Chief Whip's office, formerly chaired by Mandelson. It deals with urgent current problems. Effects of this central control – 'control freakery' according to its critics – have been easy to discern. Before the August break in 1997 the Chief Whip wrote to all Labour MPs reminding them of Rule 2a. 8 which states that 'no member shall engage in a sustained course of conduct prejudicial, or detrimental to the party'. Famously all MPs are now equipped with pagers to keep them 'on message' at all times. This can affect ministers, too. Tony Banks has long been something of a maverick, even as sports minister. His appearances on an LBC radio show were curtailed on the grounds that 'we don't want the airwaves clogged with too many opinions' (*The Guardian*, 12 May 1997). In January 1998 Campbell sent Frank Field and Harriet Harman a fax which astonishingly said 'I see from today's papers that no matter how much we urge silence, congenital briefing goes on about who is responsible for what. It is time facts took over from personalities.'

Campbell also demanded to know why Harman interviews with *The Guardian* and *The World at One* were 'not cleared through this office'. Franklin (1998, p. 9) rightly pointed out the worrying fact that a civil servant, of highly political provenance, was here giving orders to elected ministers. Such behaviour was surprising even by the robust standards of Bernard Ingham himself. Journalists with the temerity to take anti-Labour lines came under attack. Franklyn recorded how Kevin Marsh, editor of *The World at One*, and up for the *Today* job, was attacked by Campbell in a letter to *The Guardian* and a five-page letter to the head of BBC news programmes. Paul Routledge, about to take up the political editorship of the *Daily Express*, was suddenly told he had not got the job. It was an open secret that this resulted from negative pressure from Number Ten. In *The Times* that wise and highly respected commentator Peter Riddell saw these centralising developments as issuing from the very heart of New Labour:

> a closed style of policymaking in which decisions were taken by a tight circle around the offices of Tony Blair and Gordon Brown . . . New policy initiatives were leaked/floated, often on an unattributable and thus deniable basis, without any real collective discussion. These habits have been transferred to office. The culture of government is different, relying on deliberation, consultation and acceptance that Parliament should be informed first. (*The Times*, 17 October 1997).

The Government Information Service (GIS) now employs over a thousand civil servants who are in theory wholly impartial and not the instruments of ministers ambitious for self or party. However, Labour was quick to criticise the 'defensive' attitude of the GIS and encouraged it to be more pro-active regarding positive stories. Admittedly the line between legitimately publicising government activity and illicitly advancing party causes is a fine one, but Franklyn identified several reasons why GIS civil servants believe their organisation is being 'politicised' Firstly, the appointment of 60 ministerial advisers – usually former political aides now paid out of taxpayers' money – compared with Major's 32; secondly, the emergence of a 'two-tier' system whereby the advisers have become dominant over the career civil servants. Jill Rutter, who featured in the documentary made about Gordon Brown, complained that Charlie Whelan had 'taken over three-quarters of her job'. Thirdly, Campbell has urged GIS civil servants to take a tougher, more 'heavy handed' attitude to the media. Fourthly, the GIS has been exhorted by Campbell to stay 'on message', comprising four elements: Labour is a 'modernising' government; for 'all the people'; which is 'delivering on its promises' with 'mainstream policies' providing new directions for the country. Fifthly, the centralised control of government communication makes accountability more difficult and creates an atmosphere in which the GIS feels it is being watched critically; and finally the chief spinners no longer pretend they are doing anything but managing the news: 'You have to be economical with the truth sometimes,' says Whelan, 'you should never lie . . . but it's very difficult' (Franklyn, 1998, pp. 11–13).

It was perhaps inevitable that those already tasked with the job of handling government communications should object to the influx of new personnel and unwelcome new guidelines. Almost as soon as the new party took office, clashes ocurred between ministers and their press officers; the latter felt they were just doing the job they had done under the previous government, whilst the former wanted an approach which maximised good news and minimised the bad. Heads of information at the Northern Ireland and Scottish Offices soon packed their bags followed by others including Defence, Trade and John Major's former press secretary Jonathan Haslam at Education (see *The Times*, 17 October 1998). In September 1997 Campbell had issued a memo to information heads lambasting their failure to put the government's case across. Riddell commented in *The Times*, 'The job of civil servants is to ensure that the government is successful, not that Labour is re-elected'. The paper's editorial that day commented: 'Chief information officers have at least traditionally been trusted not to lie; and if Downing Street instructs them to deny stories that are true but inconvenient, this will diminish their credibility. Trust is hard earned and easily lost' (*The Times* 11 February 1998). But Mandelson, unabashed 'insisted that fears about the "politicisation" of the information service are groundless.'

Labour has also promised to reform the traditionally bipartisan practice of party political broadcasts. The first election broadcast speech occured in 1924 and was made by Ramsay Macdonald during the campaign of that year. In 1947 the Committee on Political Broadcasting was formed, made up of MPs and broadcasters, which made time allocations. These were made on the basis of votes cast for each party together with their seats won and candidates fielded. On this basis the time allocated in 1997 was, according to the ration, 5:5:4 with Labour and Conservatives getting the fives. During 1997 the big parties made ten broadcasts each – five party political and five election broadcasts; the Lib Dems made seven. However, broadcasters have noted how effectively such broadcasts turn off viewers despite the millions which parties pour into them. Moreover with European elections in 1999 and elections for the Scottish and Welsh assemblies, there could be up to thirty broadcasts under present rules. A discussion paper in spring 1998 proposed an end to: the 5–10 minute broadcasts between elections, scheduled five minutes before main evening news bulletins; the post-budget broadcasts; and that election broadcasts should be no more than three to four minutes instead of five to ten.

As far as most commentators are concerned, party political broadcasts are small beer compared with the favourable coverage parties can command in the press, especially the Murdoch owned press which includes tabloids as well as broadsheets.

Murdoch's Role

A Marxist at Oxford, Rupert Murdoch made some good friends in the Labour Party, like Gerald Kaufman. However, in the 1970s, already a media magnate, he showed how much he had become the champion of the system Marx wished to destroy. His *Sun* and *Times* assiduously argued the Conservative case and in the 1980s the former's raucous, chauvinistic brand of support became one of the defining characteristics of Thatcherism. Its assaults on Kinnock in the 1992 election set new lows in scurrilous journalism and earned the hate of Labour supporters. On election day it suggested that if Kinnock won, the last person leaving the country should turn out the lights, later claiming 'It's the *Sun* wot won it!' However, Murdoch is nothing if not pragmatic in the promotion of his business interests: he adopted American citizenship in order to buy a television station; and he dropped the BBC news channel from his satellite service to China because it regularly carried reports of human rights violations unacceptable to the Chinese government.

In 1994 he began a price cutting war which many commentators saw as aimed at removing *The Independent* and the *Daily Telegraph* as rivals to *The Times*. His campaign was denounced by Robin Cook, Alastair Darling, Chris Smith, Nigel Griffiths (the future Competition minister) and Mo Mowlam. In the same year however Blair met Murdoch who was impressed by his 'youthful company lawyer image' (*The Guardian*, 28 March 1998). When he was elected leader, Murdoch spoke of possibly supporting the new man; the progress of Major's Conservatives at this time of course, scarcely inspired confidence. In July 1995, while Major was reapplying for his job as party leader, Blair was invited to lecture to News Corporation staff on Hayman Island, Australia. The tycoon introduced him thus: 'If the British press is to be believed, today is all part of a Blair–Murdoch flirtation. If that flirtation is ever to be consumated, Tony, I suspect we will end up making love like porcupines – very carefully.' Some claim that is exactly what they subsequently proceeded to do.

In March 1997 the political world was stunned when in the wake of several visits by Blair to Murdoch's London home (*The Observer*, 14 June 1998), *The Sun* came out for Blair and campaigned furiously for him, assisted by sister paper *News of the World*, but not *The Times*. For his part Blair did not alter Conservative rules on cross-media ownership as many, concerned at the power of the proprietor, had demanded. In February an amendment was passed in the Lords to the Competition Bill seeking to outlaw the kind of 'predatory pricing' Murdoch was still practising in his stuggle with rival broadsheets. On 10 February Number Ten launched a passionate attack on the the movers of the amendment and vowed to overrule it in the Commons. Another clear sign of Labour's closeness to Murdoch came in March 1998 when it was claimed that Murdoch had used information derived from a conversation between Blair and Romano Prodi, the Italian Prime Minister, in deciding not to bid for Mediaset, the Milan based Berlusconi TV holding company. Should anyone be worried about this closeness? After all, tabloid support, whilst experts cannot agree on its efficacy, is better to have on your side rather than against you. Was Blair not just doing his best to win important political support for his party? No doubt this is true but it is the favours given in return which cause the concern. Murdoch is the cleverest of operators and there are fears that he only 'sells' his newspapers' support in exchange for business favours. There is some evidence however to suggest he influences, albeit negatively, a crucially vital area of economic policy: he is said to be very hostile to the EU – why is not wholly clear but business probably explains – and opposed to UK joining the single currency. In a Channel 4 documentary on *Blair's Year* on 19 April 1998, Mandelson suggested, 'Blair feels he has to convert Murdoch before he calls a referendum on the issue'. Apparently Blair ruled out entry before the next election as it would have cost the support of the Murdoch's newspapers. Cook revealed in the same programme the Cabinet was never consulted over this and that the decision was made by only himself, Prescott, Brown and Blair.

Whilst the majority of the EU queued up to join the Euro, Britain is left uncomfortably on the sidelines and some worry Murdoch's influence is proving harmful to national interests. A senior Treasury official told a meeting in Brussels that UK entry date might be 'as late as 2005 or 2006'. *The Observer* commented 'Mr Blair has not the courage to tackle Rupert Murdoch before then or spend political capital in defending preparations for the euro' (14 June 1998). The matter achieved higher profile when *The Sun* decided to attack Blair over Europe in late June 1998. A banner headline over the face of the Prime Minister asked 'Is this the most dangerous man in Britain?' Inside the editorial threatened the paper would become a 'determined opponent' if Blair continued to drift towards a more flexible attitude on monetary union.

Mandelson's Fall

It could be maintained that the popularity of the Blair government – at the end of 1998 still 30 points ahead of the Conservatives after 18 months in office – was the result of the tight media control exerted by Labour's spin doctors. However, in December 1998 the government was impaled upon the most embarrassing crisis it had encountered up until then through an apparent disaster in communication control. The crisis broke with *The Guardian*'s revelation that Peter Mandelson had been able to move from his modest flat in Clerkenwell to an elegant town house in Notting Hill courtesy of a loan from Labour's millionaire MP and fellow minister, Geoffrey Robinson. In itself this would not have been reprehensible, but Robinson's business affairs had already been under the Conservative microscope when it transpired he had millions held in off-shore tax havens, a practice deplored by Labour and one which Robinson was himself investigating as a Treasury minister. As a result of such pressures the Department of Trade and Industry was investigating Robinson's finances when Mandelson was put in charge of it in July 1998. There was a clear conflict of interest now which the minster should have confided to his permanent secretary as well as the Prime Minister. He failed to do so. When the news of the loan came out Mandelson sought to brazen it out in a flurry of media interviews but the next day he resigned and Robinson reluctantly followed. Blair's political alter ego had gone, through a lapse of judgement worthy of a political novice. The media, whilst acknowledging his proven skills as a minister, attributed his fall to the hubris which drove him to acquire the kind of house and furnishings common to the social circles in which he now famously enjoyed moving. But the story had another twist. Many believed the news of the loan had been passed on by the Chancellor's spin doctor, Charlie Whelan, as part of the alleged feud between Blair and Brown and their spin doctor proxies. Whelan was known to be distrusted by many ministers and the rumour that he was the agent of Mandelson's downfall gained currency. His closeness to Paul Routledge, author of a forthcoming hostile biography of Mandelson which contained the loan story, did nothing to quieten speculation. Finally Whelan succumbed to the pressure and in January declared it was no longer possible to do his job: he resigned. Labour's obsession with the media had bitten back viciously and harmed the party which it had helped to enthrone with such unprecedented power.

Conclusions

From this review of developments in media–government relations a number of things can be asserted. Firstly, the increased competition caused by cross-media ownership and by the plethora of new media outlets has tended to drag output downmarket (though demographic factors seem to be pushing tabloids back upmarket). Secondly, Labour won the battle for the 1997 election agenda handsomely. Thirdly, the shift of large sections of the Conservative press to Labour had its origins in the 1980s and the poor governing record of the Major administration. Fourthly, Labour in power has continued conducting media politics as if still in opposition; centralised control of the media to the extent that it threatens democracy; arguably politicised the Government Information Service in an unconstitutional fashion; and displayed a worrying tendency to listen to Rupert Murdoch, especially over the key question of a single currency.

It may be that there is so much information emanating out of government that the public switch off and are none the wiser for it. In his excellent analysis on *Packaging Politics*, Franklin illustrates this possibility by repeating a story from a congressional hearing in which a government official is said to have remarked 'The Russians keep their people in the dark by telling them nothing. We do the same by telling them everything' (Franklin, 1998, pp. 20–2). Franklyn recommends televising Prime Minister's press briefings; bringing special advisers under the same code of professional practice as civil servants; the establishment of an Independent Press Authority to strengthen journalistic dealings with government; and regulation of cross-media ownership and predatory pricing which threatens diversity of the news media.

Jonathan Freedland in *The Guardian* (17 December 1997) pointed out that in the absence of a credible opposition, and the poor poll showings of the Conservatives suggested this was the case, the media *were* the current opposition: left-leaning newspapers, John Humphrys and Jeremy Paxman, together with a few Labour rebels and Rory Bremner. Labour have enjoyed a period of extraordinary popularity, partly because the Tories remained so catastrophically unpopular and possibly also through the media manipulation of that grimly named triumvirate described above: the 'Enforcer', the 'Serial Killer' and, returned to the Cabinet in autumn 1999, the former 'Prince of Darkness'.

References

Denver, D. (1998) 'The Government that could do no right' in King, A. (ed.) *New Labour Triumphs at the Polls* (London: Chatham Mouse).

Franklin, B. (1994) *Packaging Politics: Political Communication in Britain's Media Democracy* (London: Edward Arnold).

Franklin, B. (1998) 'Tough on soundbites, tough on the causes of Soundbites', London: Catalyst Paper (3).

Jones, B. (1991) *Politics UK* (Hemel Hempstead: Philip Allan), p. 206.

Jones, N. (1996) *Soundbites and* Spin *Doctors* (London: Indigo).

Norris, P. (1998) 'The battle for the campaign agenda' in King, A. (ed.) *New Labour Triumphs at the Polls* (London: Chatham Mouse).

Wring, D. (1998) 'Political communication', *Talking Politics*, 10(3), pp. 197–203.

8

The European Union and UK Governance

NEILL NUGENT

Britain's membership of the European Union impacts on British government and politics in many ways. Four of these ways are especially important.

First, the importance of EU membership is such that issues relating to it inevitably require and attract extensive attention from Britain's decision-makers. Relations with, and policies to be pursued within, the EU have to be very much to the fore of elite thinking and strategy.

Second, the importance of EU membership also means that EU-related issues are the focus of much domestic political debate. Over the years this debate has been the subject of intense exchanges between the main political parties and has also been a significant source of internal division within them.

Third, EU membership has greatly curtailed the independent decision-making capacity of British decision-makers. The responsibility for making many of the laws that apply in Britain no longer lies with the British government and Parliament but rather has been transferred to EU institutions. Britain is represented in these institutions, but since many EU decisions are taken by majority vote the British representatives are not necessarily in a position to determine or control what decisions are taken. In consequence, those who are elected to power in British general elections are, on the one hand, unable to introduce and apply all the laws they would like to see on the statute book, whilst on the other hand they are obliged to accept and apply some laws that they do not favour.

Fourth, EU membership has promoted, and in some respects has necessitated, important organisational changes in the structure and institutions of British governance. These changes have been wide-ranging in their extent and effect with, for example, all of the main institutions of central government having to be adapted so as to enable Britain to meet its European commitments and to be an effective performer in European arenas.

This chapter considers these different dimensions of the impact of EU membership on British government and politics. The first two dimensions are considered alongside one another via analyses of the policies and practices, in office and in opposition, of the two parties of government, Conservative and Labour. The third and fourth dimensions are considered separately in their own sections.

The Conservatives: Increasingly Euro-sceptical and Increasingly 'Awkward'

It was the Conservative government of Edward Heath that took Britain into the European Community (EC) in 1973 and it was the Conservative Party which was by far the most pro-European of the two main British political parties in the early years of Britain's Community membership. Although, however, the Conservatives were more pro-EC than Labour in the early years, their attitude became increasingly wary and suspicious from the mid-1980s. Growing concerns about the direction in which the EC (EU from 1993) was moving resulted in the Conservative Party becoming increasingly Euro-sceptical in its attitudes and approach and the Conservative government becoming an increasingly awkward part-ner for the other member states of the EC/EU.

Euro-scepticism

Increasing *euro-scepticism* was based essentially on what was seen to be a growing gap between Conservative ideology and values on the one hand and what the EC/EU was doing and was becoming on the other. The steady expansion of EC/EU policy interests and the increasingly supranational nature of much EC/EU decision-making were mostly not wanted by an increasingly uneasy government and parliamentary party. The Conservative vision of the EC/EU was minimalist in nature: promoting and creating the framework for an effective and efficient European market, and engaging in limited and loose inter-state cooperation in policy areas where joint activities could be beneficial. Above all, outside the internal market 'core' the EC/EU should not be challenging or threatening the powers of national governments to take decisions they believed to be in the interests of their citizens. As Mrs Thatcher declared in a famous speech she delivered in Bruges in 1988: 'My first guideline [for the future of Europe] is this: willing and active co-operation between independent sovereign states is the best way to build a successful European Community. To try to suppress nationhood and concentrate power at the centre of a European conglomerate would be highly damaging and would jeopardise the objectives we seek to achieve' (Thatcher, 1988).

This was somewhat inflammatory language – no European leaders, after all, were proposing to suppress nationhood – but it encapsulated the concerns that developed rapidly in the Conservative Party from the late 1980s over the extent and pace of the integration process. These concerns were such that during the 1992–97 Parliament 'Europe' became the major issue for many Conservative MPs, with europhiles very much on the defensive and with eurosceptical views of varying intensities increasingly heard and increasingly in the ascendant. This euroscepticism was reflected in a hardening sceptical stance by Mr Major: a stance which, as Ludlam has observed on the basis of detailed survey work, was not 'to satisfy a minority of die-hard anti-marketeers, but [was] consistent both with his own attitudes and with majority opinion in his parliamentary party' (1998, p. 55).

By the time Major resigned the Conservative leadership after the 1997 election defeat his party had become solidly entrenched in a firmly eurosceptical position. That this was so was no more clearly demonstrated than by the decision of Conservative MPs to replace Major not with the formidable and experienced Kenneth Clarke but rather with the relatively untried William Hague. There were a number of reasons why Hague was preferred, but probably the most important was that Clarke's well-attested pro-Europeanism was not supported by most Conservative MPs and was seen as being likely to greatly exacerbate existing internal divisions over Europe –

especially on the single currency, to which Clarke was known to be sympathetic.

On being elected Conservative leader, Hague wasted little time in confirming his euroscepticism: he ruled out any possibility of the Conservatives supporting membership of the single currency during the current parliament or the next – that is, for a period of at least ten or so years.

An awkward partner

Britain's position as an awkward partner can, as Stephen George – the best known proponent of the awkward partner thesis – has pointed out (1998), be traced back to soon after Britain became an EC member, when the then Labour government sought to renegotiate the accession terms. The reputation was consolidated after Mrs Thatcher became Prime Minister in 1979, notably via political battles in the early 1980s to reduce Britain's contributions to the Community budget, and sharp differences with the governments of the other member states over the contents of the 1986 Single European Act (SEA) – which, amongst other things, amended the founding treaties in various ways. (The British Government wanted a modest SEA, with only very limited extensions to Community policy-making competences and supranational decision-making processes.)

The awkwardness – in the sense of being out of step with other member states – increased in scope and intensity from the late 1980s, with the British government becoming extremely defensive, some would say negative, in its attitude towards many key Community/Union issues. Particularly troublesome, and for other member states particularly annoying, issues included the following:

- In 1989 the UK was the only member state to resist and refuse to sign the Community Social Charter.
- In the 1991 intergovernmental conference (IGC) that prepared the Treaty on European Union (TEU) – also known as the Maastricht Treaty – the UK government consistently adopted a minimalist position in respect of further integration on virtually all fronts. The government succeeded in making the final version of the treaty weaker than the other national governments wanted, but even then was only prepared to sign the treaty after being given opt-outs from the Social Chapter and from the

commitment that other governments gave to enter the single currency phase of Economic and Monetary Union (EMU).

- In response to what it claimed to be the lack of progress in lifting the ban on British beef products that had been imposed by the EU in March 1996 because of the possible link between the cattle disease Bovine Spongiform Encephalopathy (BSE) and the human disease Creutzfeldt-Jacob Disease (CJD), Mr Major in May 1996 announced a policy of non-cooperation with the EU. This involved not agreeing to decisions being made where unanimity was required. Over 100 decisions were so blocked before the strategy was dropped – without any significant concession on the EU side – in June 1996.

- In the preparations for what became the 1997 Amsterdam Treaty, which revised the TEU, the Conservative government adopted its customary minimalist position. In, for example, the Report of the 1995 Reflection Group, which was charged with identifying issues for the impending IGC, the positions of individual states were not identified but there was never much doubt as to which state was normally being referred to in the many phrases such as 'one of us believes...' and 'one of us is opposed to...' (*Reflection Group's Report*, 1995). In the IGC itself the pattern was repeated, with the consequence that most of the difficult issues were left aside until after the British general election when, it was hoped, a new government might be less intransigent and more 'helpful'.

Jim Buller (1995) has argued that the awkward partner thesis should not be overstated. He notes that even after Mrs Thatcher became Prime Minister Britain was not always the only awkward partner, British negotiators were constructive rather than awkward on some policy issues, and much of the perceived British awkwardness was a matter of style rather than substance. There is something in this view with, for example, Britain under both Thatcher and Major having indeed been constructive in its approaches to such important policy issues as the completion of the internal market, the reform of the Common Agricultural Policy, and the enlargement of the Union. However, as Stephen George has observed in replying to Buller, while Conservative Governments certainly did exercise a major role in promoting some EC/EU initiatives, Britain under the Conservatives was in general much less integrationist in its approach to policy development and far more persistent in its awkwardness than any other member state. Furthermore, style and substance are in practice not always as easily disentangled as Buller implies (George, 1995).

But however the merits of the 'awkwardness case' may be viewed by observers and commentators, the fact is that the governments of other EU member states most certainly did perceive Britain under the Conservatives as being an awkward partner. It is symptomatic of the way the Conservative government was viewed in the national capitals of other member states that its 1997 election defeat was generally welcomed by other EU governments, including those composed of what might be assumed to be the Conservative's natural allies on the right and centre-right. The BSE non-cooperation strategy and the minimalist position on treaty reform were seen by other member states as being all too symptomatic of the UK government's attitudes and stances towards the EU: unwilling to accept even limited integrationist advances; unwilling to play fully by the spirit of the EU's – often informal and unwritten – ways of working; but all too willing to use the EU for domestic political purposes – as evidenced by the frequent proclamation by UK ministers during the period of non-cooperation that 'we will defend Britain's interests whatever the cost' and 'we are not afraid to be isolated in Europe'.

It was thus not surprising that for a long time before the 1997 election most EU decision-makers were hoping, and waiting, for Labour.

Labour: New Labour, New Views and New Partner?

Following its defeat in the 1979 general election the Labour Party moved rapidly to the left. As part of this movement it committed itself for a while – most particularly at the 1983 general election – to withdrawal from the EC. This strongly anti-EC position was, however, soon modified as, from the mid-1980s, the party's stance was gradually transformed: so much so that by the early 1990s Labour was the more pro-European of the two main British political parties in so far as it took a broader view than the Conservatives of what the EU could and should be doing, and as part of this broader view it was more willing to accept integrationist advances.

What brought about this transformation and what have been the implications of it for Britain's relations with the EU now that Labour is in government?

There were three main reasons for the transformation:

- Following the disastrous 1983 election – which saw the Conservative Party greatly increase its majority in Parliament – Labour sought to establish a new realism in its policies, designed to make it once again electable. It proved to be a long and difficult process, but the policy path travelled under the leadership of Neil Kinnock, John Smith, and Tony Blair was consistent: on the one hand the party removed, or at least modified, policies that were unpopular, and on the other hand it renewed and revitalised its overall policy portfolio. As part of this overhaul of policies, the commitment to withdraw from the EC was quickly dropped and a more positive pro-European policy was gradually put in place.

- The EC is often described as having been 'relaunched' in the mid-1980s, with the 1985 Single European Market (SEM) programme (which was designed to 'complete' the internal market by 1992), the SEA, and the increasing appearance on the agenda of policies that had hitherto been little developed at EC level. Whilst the Conservatives were strongly supportive of the SEM programme, other aspects of the relaunch, especially the development of a social dimension, made them extremely uneasy. For Labour, by contrast, the development of the social dimension and related policies did much to dispel the negative image that was widely held in the party of the EC as a rather hostile capitalists' club. From having been something of an ideological foe, the EC came to be seen more as an ideological ally.

- In a somewhat similar fashion to the impact of the social dimension, the political persuasions of EC decision-makers helped in the late 1980s and early 1990s to 'warm' Labour attitudes and 'chill' Conservative attitudes. Throughout the eighteen years of Conservative government the balance of political opinion at EU decision-making levels was consistently to the left of the UK government: from the late 1980s there was just about a centre-left majority in the Council of Ministers, the College of Commissioners, and the European Parliament. Perhaps most importantly of all in this regard, Jacques Delors, the former

French Socialist Finance Minister and Commission President between 1985–94, helped, via his championing of EC/EU social and economic policies, to create and confirm a more positive impression of the EC/EU in Labour eyes but a more unfavourable impression in Conservative eyes.

The transformation in Labour's perspective meant that it came to office in May 1997 with a generally positive attitude towards the role it proposed to play in the EU. Its ambitions were essentially threefold: to 'normalise' relations with the EU; to exercise a leadership role within the EU; and to mobilise EU support behind its 'third way' strategy of combining market-based economic dynamism with social justice.

The effects of this more positive approach were seen almost immediately since the new government was plunged straight into the closing stages of the IGC. As it had promised to do in its election manifesto – *Because Britain Deserves Better* (Labour Party, 1997) – it announced that the Social Chapter opt-out of the Maastricht Treaty would be removed and it agreed to the extension of qualified majority voting in the Council of Ministers in a limited number of policy areas. There were some difficulties with justice and home affairs policies – where, amongst other things, the government insisted on remaining outside the Schengen system (which involves the removal of all border controls) – but on most of the issues that the IGC had put on hold until after the British election, agreement was reached without too much difficulty. In consequence, the final stage of the IGC – the June 1997 Amsterdam summit – was not dominated, as so many summits had been in the past, by wrestling with British demands and threats.

In addition to the IGC, two other EU matters of major importance demanded the government's early attention. The first was EMU and whether Britain should join the single currency – the euro – which was scheduled to start in January 1999 and membership of which was scheduled to be determined in the spring of 1998. In its manifesto Labour, like the Conservatives, had equivocated on the issue, adopting a policy of 'wait and see', backed up by a commitment that any decision to join would require the approval of the Cabinet, Parliament, and the people in a referendum (Labour Party, 1997, pp. 37–8). In office the tone became rather more positive, though both the Prime Minister and the Chancellor of the Exchequer, Gordon Brown, were careful to emphasise the finely balanced nature of the relevant arguments and calculations concerning single currency membership. With the deadline for a final decision fast approaching, the Chancellor announced the government's position to Parliament in October 1998 (House of Commons, 1997a). The central points were: the Government favoured membership of the single currency in principle, but only if the economic benefits were clear and unambiguous; the assessment of the economic benefits – made on the basis of five tests – led the Government to believe that it was not in the country's economic interests for Britain to be a member of the first wave of the single currency; the main economic problem was that the British economic cycle was not sufficiently converged with the economic cycles of other member states; there was no constitutional bar to Britain's membership of the single currency – 'The constitutional issue is a factor in the decision, but it is not an overriding one' (House of Commons, 1997a, col. 588); the Government would prepare for single currency membership and would make a decision at a later stage – probably early in the next Parliament – as to whether the British economy had sufficiently converged with the economies of single currency countries and whether the economic tests had been sufficiently met as to merit Britain joining the euro. In summary, the position was that 'if, in the end, the single currency is successful and the economic case is clear and unambiguous, the Government believes that Britain should be part of it' (House of Commons, 1997a, col. 584). An unspoken hope was clearly that if the government won the next election and judged entry to be in Britain's interests, public opinion would be supportive of membership.

The second matter was the UK Presidency of the Council from January–June 1998. Rotating between the EU member states every six months, the Presidency can be thought of as the chair of the Council. The position does not involve the exercise of any great independent power, but offers some opportunities for influencing the pace and direction of EU activities and requires that appropriate actions are taken to ensure that EU business is conducted smoothly and efficiently. No member state wishes to be seen to run a poor Presidency in the sense that either significant misjudgements or mistakes are made on its watch or that progress on pressing and/ or anticipated policy developments is disappointing. In the event, the report on the 1998 UK Presidency was marked, as indeed the previous UK Presidency in 1992 had been marked, by most observers as being generally satisfactory: there were a few minor problems, but the main challenges of the Presidency – overseeing the launch of EU enlargement negotiations and ensuring that important decisions were taken on the single currency – were successfully met.

There is no doubt that Britain's relations with the EU have greatly improved since Labour was elected to office in May 1997. Whilst Britain is still outside the European 'fast stream' – as the self-exclusion from the single currency and from the Schengen system bear testimony – the awkward partner label of the Conservative years in government no longer applies.

One aspect of the improved relations is the generally upbeat tone and mood that the Labour government has struck in its conduct within the EU. Another aspect is that most of the issues which under the Conservatives divided Britain from its EU partners – such as the social dimension and increased powers for the Council of Ministers and the European Parliament – have not been so problematical for Labour. This has been so partly for socio-economic ideological reasons and partly because Labour has not been as obsessed as the Conservatives with preserving (often largely fictitious) sovereignty. (For an analysis of the positions of the parties on the sovereignty issue and EU membership see Nugent, 1996.)

That the Labour government is comfortable with EU membership and is viewed as a positive player by other EU actors is testimony to how far Labour's ideological position has been transformed since the early 1980s. Whereas at that time the EC was widely portrayed in Labour circles as an organisation whose laws were incompatible with Labour's interventionist policies, the position is now such that most EU policies are seen as being almost wholly compatible with, and complementary to, Labour policies. Indeed, evidence of how far Labour has travelled ideologically is seen in Mr Blair regarding the EU as being, if anything, just a little too interventionist in some of its socio-economic policies: so whilst he has, for example, generally supported the EU's attempts to tackle high levels of unemployment, he has been anxious to assert that EU social policies should not weaken labour market flexibility, which he regards as central to reducing unemployment levels.

Decision-Making Capacity

The EU is sometimes portrayed, not least by politicians who are distrustful of it, as an organisation that has uniquely undermined the sovereignty and independence of its member states. It should, however, be recognised that no state in the modern world is truly sovereign or independent in that its decision-makers can take whatever decisions they judge to be in the national interests without any reference to external constraints or restrictions. Global interdependence in its various forms means that national decision-makers must take account of all sorts of realities of the international system: if they do not, they risk taking decisions that could be extremely damaging for their countries in economic, political, security, and other terms.

This inability to avoid the impact of global interdependence needs to be borne in mind when examining and evaluating the restrictions the EU places on British decision-makers. That there are such restrictions is quite clear, but the suggestion of many eurosceptics that Britain would be virtually independent and sovereign if it were not subject to EU rules is just not so, except in a wholly unrealistic theoretical sense. Indeed, it is pertinent to note that in Western Europe the effects of interdependence, especially economic interdependence, are so intense that those few countries which are not EU members – notably Norway and Switzerland – have adopted and are applying many of the EU's policies and laws.

What then are the restrictions that EU membership imposes on British decision-makers? They arise from three closely interrelated factors:

EU policy responsibilities are extensive. In many policy spheres some, or in a few cases virtually all, decision-making capacity no longer lies with the EU's member states but rather lies with the EU itself. The policy spheres in which the most extensive transfers of policy responsibility have occurred relate mostly to the functioning of the internal market: the rules governing the movement and selling of goods, services and capital; competition policy; commercial policy (external trade); and agricultural policy. The policy spheres in which there have been fewest transfers of policy responsibility are mostly those which are seen as not having direct implications for the operation of the market – such as domestic criminal and civil law issues – and/or involving heavy budgetary expenditure – most notably education, health, social security, and defence. In between these two poles of heavy and limited EU policy involvement are ranged many policies in which the EU is involved to some degree and in which policy responsibilities are therefore shared between the EU and the governments of its member states. Amongst these 'mixed' policy spheres are regional policy, environmental policy, energy policy, and foreign policy.

The EU makes laws. Of the many features that distinguishes the EU from other international organisations, arguably the most important is that it makes laws. It is not able to make laws in all of the policy areas in which it is involved – pillars two (common foreign and security policy) and three (police and judicial coopera-tion in criminal matters) of the TEU are restricted to intergovern-mental cooperation – but in most policy areas law-making is permissible. In an average year around 80 directives (framework laws) and over 2 000 regulations and decisions (administrative laws) are passed. As an indication of the sheer volume of EU legislation that is in place, it is instructive to note that there are well over 200 EU environmental laws, covering matters as varied as air and water quality standards, the disposal of waste material, and the protection of endangered species.

An absolutely crucial feature of EU law is that it takes precedence over any national laws that conflict or clash with it. This has to be so for the EU to be able to function as an integrated system with common laws. Consequences of this principle of the primacy of EU law are that member states should not introduce national laws that conflict with EU laws and should not attempt to apply laws that conflict with EU laws. In the event of them trying to do so, they are likely to be subject to legal proceedings. So, to cite a celebrated and much publicised case in Britain, in 1990 the House of Lords ruled that the 1988 UK Merchant Shipping Act – which prevented non-UK boats from acquiring part of the UK's fishing quota under the EC's Common Fisheries Policy – invalidated EC law because it discriminated on the grounds of nationality. In 1991 the European Court of Justice (ECJ) – the highest judicial body in respect of EC law – confirmed the House of Lords' view, and in 1995 further ruled that owners of Spanish fishing boats could claim compensation for losses incurred in the period between the passage of the Act and its suspension by the House of Lords.

Much EU decision-making is supranational in character. There are many EU decision-making procedures, with the procedure to be applied in particular circumstances being specified in the treaties. The procedures vary in a number of ways, the most important of which are: the number of stages (EU legislation can be subject to a one, two, or three reading procedure); the powers allocated to the EU institutions (especially the Commission, the Council, and the European Parliament); and the intergovernmental/supranational balance. (For further information on EU decision-making procedures, see Nugent 1999a and b.) It is the last of these varying ways that is of most significance for the decision-making capacity of British decision-makers. This is because if procedures are essentially intergovernmental in character British decision-makers, and more especially the British government, can be said to retain an important control over EU decision-making, whereas if they are essentially supranational then control is difficult.

There are several dimensions to intergovernmentalism and supranationalism, but the key one in terms of the implications for national decision-making capacity is whether or not decisions in the Council of Ministers – the EU's single most important decision-making body, which brings together representatives of the governments of the member states – require unanimity or can be taken by majority vote. If they require unanimity, that is, if the procedure is intergovernmental, national governmental control can be said to exist in the sense that no government can be forced to agree to a decision to which it is opposed. If, however, decisions can be taken by majority vote or, more usually, qualified majority vote, that is, if the procedure is supranational, national governments do not have complete control in the sense that they do not have a veto over the taking of decisions.

Over the years decision-making in the Council has become more supranational in character. This has happened as a result of two factors. First, the governments of the member states have increasingly been prepared to use majority voting when it is available to them. The preference is to proceed by consensus if at all possible, but if no unanimous agreement exists and majority voting provisions apply the governments are more willing than they used to be to proceed to a vote. Second, the circumstances in which majority votes can be taken have been progressively expanded by the SEA, the TEU, and the Amsterdam Treaty. Majority voting is now available for most types of decisions, the main exceptions being for treaty amendments, accessions, some types of agreements with third countries, most pillar two and pillar three matters, and certain budgetary-related issues.

Organisational Changes in Governance

EU membership has had significant organisational implications for the structure and institutions of British governance. This has been because the structure and the institutions have had to adapt, or be adapted, so as to be able to undertake functions and obligations arising from EU membership and also so as to be able to maximise effectiveness within the EU system of governance.

This section examines the major organisational changes that have occurred. The examination looks first at the general structure of governance and then at the two main institutions of central government – the executive and Parliament.

The Structure of Governance

The most important structural feature of British governance has long been its centralisation. This centralisation has had both functional and territorial aspects. Functionally, it has taken the form of one of the two political arms of government, the executive, consistently dominating the other arm, the legislative. Territorially, it has taken the form of Westminster and Whitehall controlling most important decision-making, with only strictly limited powers being delegated to and exercised at subnational levels.

EU membership has served to strengthen the first of these forms of centralisation but has played a part, along with other factors, in helping to disturb the second form. That is to say, it has contributed on the one hand to executive dominance and on the other hand to the increasing territorialisation that is beginning to be a feature of British governance.

Regarding the contribution to executive dominance, much of this stems from the fact that whilst Parliament is not a direct participant in EU decision-making, the government most certainly is. Governmental representatives in the Council of Ministers negotiate deals and decisions with representatives of the governments of the other member states on a constantly ongoing basis; and they do it behind closed doors. As is shown below, Parliament can attempt to influence what ministers and national officials do in the Council, but it cannot control them.

Within the executive, 'Europe' is contributing to the increasingly 'hands-on' policy role of the Prime Minister. Prime Ministers used to be able largely to decide for themselves whether, to what extent, and in which spheres, they wished to be directly involved in policy activity, but EU membership is an important reason why this is no longer the case. The attendance of the Prime Minister at European Council meetings (EU summits) and at many bi-lateral meetings with other EU heads of government means that he or she is an important EU policy-making player and must, at a minimum, acquaint himself or herself with the issues that habitually appear on EU agendas at leaders' level: EMU, the functioning of the European economy, major policy reforms, key foreign policy issues, EU enlargement etc. To acquire the necessary information, advice, and support on EU issues the Prime Minister can naturally make use of ministers, but also has available the resources of his or her private office, the No. 10 Policy Unit, and the European Secretariat (which is discussed below and which, though formally responsible to the Cabinet as a whole, may be requested to brief the Prime Minister directly via the No. 10 Policy Unit).

Regarding the contribution to increasing territorialisation, a number of factors at EU level have helped to promote a developing awareness of the potentiality of British regionalism and localism, and have played a part in bringing about significant changes in the nature and functioning of subnational governance. The most important of the factors at EU level have been: the existence of the EU's Structural Funds – especially the European Regional Development Fund (ERDF) – which are directed at regions and localities with problems of various kinds and which draw regional and local representatives into their management; the importance that has been attached by the EU since the early 1990s, at rhetorical level at least, to the concept of subsidiarity – a concept that most European politicians have interpreted as meaning that decisions should be taken at the lowest level that is compatible with efficiency, but which the Conservative government preferred to interpret as meaning that wherever possible decisions should be taken at national level rather than at EU level; the extensive discussions and debates in EU circles in recent years about building 'a Europe of the Regions'; the creation by the TEU of a 'Committee of the

Regions' – a body that though having little real power has considerable symbolic importance; and the willingness of the European Commission to deal not only with national-level decision-makers, but also with regional and local level representatives when appropriate.

These factors have played an important part in helping to stimulate and promote a number of territorial-based changes in the structure of British governance in recent years. Prominent amongst these changes have been:

- The Conservative government's establishment in 1994 of integrated regional offices in England to improve the coordination and liaison of central government departments 'in the field'. Wilks (1996, p. 164) suggests the establishment of these offices was partly a consequence of the Commission demanding that ERDF grants be tied to identifiable regional development plans.

- The Labour government's passage of legislation on devolution for Scotland and Wales. It can hardly be doubted that this was partly a response to the increased support won by the Scottish National Party since the late 1980s, which in its turn appears to have been at least partly a consequence of the party softening the edges of its independence stance by emphasising that this would not mean isolation but rather an independent Scotland firmly and safely located within the EU.

- The Labour government's proposals for regional development agencies in England (which are not finalised at the time of writing). According to Bulmer and Burch (1998), these proposals have their origins in Labour local authorities seeking alliances with Brussels during the prolonged period of what they saw to be unsympathetic Conservative government.

- The increasing tendency of subnational levels of government to deal directly with 'Europe' – especially the Commission – rather than relying for information on, and channelling communications through, central government. This tendancy has been accompanied by, and has been partly caused by, the establishment and/or expansion of European offices or units of varying sorts in Scotland, Wales, Northern Ireland, and most large English local authorities. It has also seen subnational authorities coming together to pool resouces and coordinate activities on EU matters. .

The Executive

Much of the work of the central executive is taken up, either directly or indirectly, with EU business. This is inevitable given the range and importance of EU policy activity and the interpenetration of much of that activity with domestic policy activity.

The nature of the central executive's EU-related business varies enormously in scope and kind. Just about every level and part of the central executive is involved to at least some degree. The most visible involvement is the attendance of the Prime Minister and the Foreign Secretary at EU summits (which are held at least twice a year) and the attendance of ministers at meetings of the Council of Ministers. (The Council of Ministers meets in different formations, with Foreign, Economic and Finance, and Agriculture Ministers meeting most regularly, and the likes of Education and Health Ministers meeting only occasionally. In total there are around ninety Council meetings each year.) Much less visible is the attendance of government officials at numerous and almost constantly ongoing rounds of meetings, negotiations and consultations in Brussels with representatives of other EU member states and of EU institutions (especially the Commission). And hidden completely from view are a host of routine formulating/promoting/liaising/administering and other tasks undertaken by central government departments and agencies at home – tasks that range from preparing EU directives for incorporation into national law, through channelling and monitoring British applications for EU funding, to implementing, or overseeing the implementation of, many EU policies and laws.

The central executive thus needs to be organised so as to enable it to undertake its many EU responsibilities in a coordinated, efficient, and effective manner. To this end, a number of special arrangements and mechanisms have been established to assist those who are formally responsible for the executive's work – the Prime Minister, the Cabinet, and the departmental ministers. The most important of these special arrangements and mechanisms are as follows:

- There is a Cabinet committee on European issues – The Ministerial Sub-Committee on European Issues (E)DOP. Chaired by the Foreign Secretary, it does not meet regularly since most EU issues that touch on the work of more than one government department are sorted out by officials. E(DOP) deals mainly with particularly important, especially sensitive, and unusually intractable issues.

- The Cabinet Secretariat, which is based in the Cabinet Office, is made up of five secretariats, one of which is the European Secretariat. The main tasks of the European Secretariat are: to promote policy coordination, for example by ensuring that where an issue cuts across the work of several departments all have an opportunity to make a policy input; to promote policy consistency, both in specific policy spheres and, more broadly, on the government's overall policy aims; and to check that departments are following through on policy commitments and objectives.

  Within the European Secretariat there is a small legal unit. It deals with some of the EU issues that cut across Whitehall, and it also provides support to departmental legal units and officials.

  The European Secretariat has only limited resources: leaving aside the legal unit there is a total staff of around twenty-five, of whom ten or so are officials. The Secretariat is therefore necessarily restricted in the number of issues and activities in which it becomes involved.

- The Foreign Office has overall responsibility for promoting coordination and ensuring consistency in the British government's policy activities in the EU. Most of the day-to-day work on this is undertaken by two divisions: the European Union Department (Internal) – EUD(I) – deals with such matters as the internal market, regional policy, and social policy; the European Union Department (External) – EUD(E) – deals mainly with external trade, foreign policy, development policy, and enlargement issues.

- Most departments, including all of those with a high volume of EU-related business – such as the Treasury, the Department of Trade and Industry, and the Ministry of Agriculture – have internal European units of some kind. Their main tasks are to provide information, guidance, and specialist advice, and to ensure that EU obligations are being met.

- The 'Brussels end' of affairs is managed by the United Kingdom Permanent Representation to the European Union (UKREP), which acts as a sort of embassy to the EU. In this capacity it is the 'eyes and ears' of the government in Brussels. Amongst its specific tasks it channels 'EU information' to the government, it liaises with the Commission and other EU institutions on behalf of the government, and its officials are closely involved with the work of the Council of Ministers. Administratively UKREP falls under the wing of the Foreign Office, but its officials – of whom there are around forty – are, like European Secretariat officials, seconded from a number of 'relevant' national departments. (The role of UKREP, and indeed of some of the other arrangements and mechanisms that are outlined in this part of the chapter, are explained in more detail in Humphreys, 1997.)

- Committees and meetings of various sorts bring together key officials from different parts of the administration. The European Questions (Officials) Committee – EQ(O) – is the main committee. It is chaired by the head of the European Secretariat, all the main departments are represented on it, and its decisions are circulated throughout Whitehall. Its main task is to resolve conflicts between departments and to assist collective policy formulation. EQ(O)L is similar to EQ(O) but deals with legal questions. EQ(O)[*], which meets only infrequently, is composed of senior officials and has as its main purpose the resolution of outstanding policy differences between departments before they are submitted to ministers.

  Particularly important is the weekly meeting in London between the head of the European Secretariat, the head of UKREP (the Permanent Representative), and senior officials from relevant departments. The main purpose of the meeting is to coordinate the UK's position in respect of important issues that are scheduled to be considered or decided in EU forums in the near future.

- Supplementing these established committees and meetings are a host of less formal, and often *ad hoc*, committees and meetings – ranging in kind from hastily convened gatherings of officials from departments that have an interest in an issue that has suddenly blown up to casual and/or routine enquiries and exchanges of information between officials on the telephone.

There is undoubtedly some organisational overlapping in these arrangements and mechanisms, which does sometimes lead to tensions. So, for example, departments that are extensively involved in EU affairs have established their own European units, have developed a considerable experience and confidence in handling EU business, and in consequence are sometimes resentful of what they see to be Foreign Office and European Secretariat 'interference'. Problems of this kind have arisen particularly with the Treasury, whose EU policy role has grown rapidly in parallel with the EMU project and increasing macroeconomic coordination at the EU level.

Notwithstanding such difficulties, however, the system appears to work reasonably well in so far as most observers are agreed that the UK achieves tighter EU policy coordination than most other EU member states. Whether the system produces good policy is, of course, an altogether different matter, for that depends not just on the system, but also on the quality of the policy steer provided by the politicians.

Parliament

It is not possible for national parliaments to exercise much direct control over EU decision-making. This is because of the nature of EU decision-making processes, which are essentially based on the Commission drafting proposals and the Council or the Council and the European Parliament taking decisions on the basis of these proposals. Only a very small number of EU decisions require the explicit approval of national parliaments.

But if it is not possible for Parliament to directly control much EU decision-making, it still has important tasks to perform in influencing, scrutinising, and monitoring EU decision-making.

In the House of Commons, much revolves around the Select Committee on European Legislation. This is a 16-member all-party committee that normally meets weekly when the House is in session. It has four main roles: (1) to assess the political and legal significance of EU documents; (2) to act as a source of analysis and information on developments in the EU; (3) to keep under review institutional and procedural developments in the EU that may have implications for the UK; and (4) to monitor the government's discharge of its EU obligations.

The Committee's work is essentially document-based, although it can call ministers and civil servants before it when this is deemed to be necessary. Around 1200 documents are referred to the Committee each year, including all proposals for Council legislation, all budgetary documentation, and most documents that are published by an EU institution with a view to submission to another EU institution – which includes Commission reports, Council decisions, and European Parliament legislative amendments. Each of the documents referred to the Committee is accompanied by an explanatory memorandum from the lead Whitehall department that sets out, amongst other things, the likely impact on UK law, the financial implications, and the policy implications. The Committee's task is to decide which of the documents are important enough to merit further consideration because of their political or legal significance. Around 400 documents are so identified each year and the Committee reports on these – usually briefly and frequently quickly (the Committee often has to report back within a few days of receiving documentation). Of the 400, around 60 are deemed to require debate and are referred elsewhere for this purpose. In most cases the reference is to one of the Commons' two European Standing Committees: Standing Committee A covers agriculture, fisheries, environment, and transport, and Standing Committee B covers other subjects. Each Standing Committee has thirteen members, but any member of the House is entitled to attend and speak at their meetings. In about a dozen especially important cases the reference is to the floor of the House, though a debate is by no means guaranteed since the government may decide not to make time available.

An especially important aspect of the work of the Commons on EU documents is to attempt to influence what ministers say and do in the Council of Ministers in respect of proposed EU legislation. Under a 1990 resolution of the House, ministers are, except in special circumstances, constrained from agreeing to any legislative proposal in the Council until it has passed the Commons' scrutiny procedures – which means that either it has been given clearance by the select committee without reference for debate in one of the standing committees or on the floor of the House, or clearance has been given following debate. (For the full text of this resolution, see House of Commons, 1997b.) This constraint on ministers means that sometimes they have to ask the Council to postpone consideration of a proposal or they are obliged to enter a reserve to indicate that UK approval is subject to scrutiny clearance.

The House of Lords seeks to complement rather than to duplicate the work of the Commons. It does so by concentrating on producing detailed reports on a few issues rather than attempting to sift and scrutinise the hundreds of EU documents which, like the Commons, it receives annually.

The detailed work of the House is undertaken by the Select Committee on the European Communities which has twenty members. The Committee has six sub-committees, which are able to co-opt other Lords so as to spread the workload and draw on available and required subject expertise. The select committee produces around twenty reports a year.

Looking at the overall position at Wesminster, it has to be said, as Bulmer and Burch have observed (1998), that it has not adapted to EU membership as fully or as well as Whitehall. Whereas 'Europeanisation' has been firmly incorporated within the Whitehall system, Westminster still tends to treat EU issues as special and separate, even though EU laws now penetrate into just about every sphere of public policy. This tendency to section-off EU business is seen in the very existence of the select committees of the two Houses and of the Commons' two standing committees, and even more in the practice of the Commons' departmental select committees – on agriculture, energy, transport etc. – not to deal directly and automatically with EU legislation that covers their policy interests and responsibilities. A recognition that this situation is unsatisfactory has prompted the Commons' select committee to encourage more cross-referencing and liaising between its work and the work of the departmental committees.

Concluding Remarks: Prospects for British Influence in the EU

Although Conservative governments between 1979 and 1997 contributed positively to some EU policy developments, their general stance was increasingly seen by other EU governments as being unhelpful. Mrs Thatcher and Mr Major were quite willing for their governments to be seen as awkward, and even confrontational, but the fact is that a consequence of their approach was that Britain was increasingly marginalised in EU decision-making and policy development. As Helen Wallace, one of the foremost authorities on Britain and the EU, has written: 'By 1997 British policy was characterized by its lonely search for the defence of the "national interest" and by bitter arguments inside the Conservative Government and Party. In exasperation Britain's partners in the EU were forging plans to "deepen" integration by escaping from British vetoes' (Wallace, 1997).

Mr Blair came to power promising a policy of 'constructive engagement' with the EU. The Foreign Secretary, Robin Cook, stated 'We know that we can better shape the direction of Europe if Britain takes its rightful place in the driving seat of Europe, instead of heckling from the back seat' (Golinio, 1998, p. 12). These sentiments were not so unlike those of Mr Major who, on assuming office, declared his intention to place Britain 'at the heart of Europe'. Labour does, however, have a much better chance than did Major of realising its ambitions and exercising a strong influence in the EU. There are four main reasons for this.

First, the Labour Government is more favourably disposed towards the developing nature of the EU than was Mr Major's government. Crucially, whereas the Conservatives throughout their years in office never departed from a view of Europe that was markedly different from the broadly pro-integrationist view of most continental governments, Labour's views are more mainstream. The Conservatives consistently took the view that the European integration process should not extend much beyond the completion of the internal market, but Labour is more prepared to view European integration as a shared political and economic enterprise in which states engage in a wide range of joint policy activity for their common good. If the construction of this enterprise requires the further transfer, or pooling, of sovereignty then – within limits – Labour is prepared to accept this. National sovereignty is not such a touchstone as it was for Thatcher and Major.

Second, the parliamentary Labour Party does not contain the sort of divisions on Europe that have so troubled the parliamentary Conservative Party since the late 1980s. Certainly, as Baker and Seawright have shown (1998, p. 88), the Labour Party has some potential for eruptions and fissures over Europe – especially if dissatisfaction with economic and social policies becomes entangled with perceived EMU and EU restraints – but there is neither the width nor the depth of euroscepticism to suggest that serious trouble is likely. The dominant view towards the EU appears to be one of constructive pragmatism.

Third, apart from the special case of EMU, the pace of European integration has slowed in recent years, which means that the EU policy agenda is not so ambitious – and therefore not so potentially controversial or divisive. The relatively modest integrationist advances that were contained in the Amsterdam Treaty were symptomatic of the more restrained mood that has prevailed in most EU capitals since the heady pre-Maastricht period.

Fourth, the Franco-German 'axis', which for years did much to set the pace of European integration, has not been so strong since President Mitterrand left office in 1995. This provides opportunities for the British government: if not to create a German-French-British trialogue, at least to be a genuine first team player.

But Britain's ability to be a genuine first team player and exercise real leadership and influence in the EU may well, as Lionel Barber has observed (1998), require it to make a firm commitment to the euro before too long. An indication of one of the consequences of not joining the first wave of EMU has already been seen, with the exclusion of Britain from the so-called Euro XI Committee – which brings together Finance Ministers from single currency members to discuss matters of common interest. Assuming the euro becomes firmly established, the Euro XI Committee, or some body like it, is likely in the foreseeable future to be making decisions on key economic, monetary, and financial issues that profoundly affect Britain, whether it is in the euro or not.

Membership of the euro is thus likely to be at the centre of British political debate on Europe for the foreseeable future. Much of the debate will be focused around the question of whether Britain will become marginalised from the EU core and will become a second tier EU state if it remains outside the single currency. But other questions are also likely to feature prominently: Labour will focus mainly on whether membership of the euro can be justified on economic grounds; the Conservatives will make much of the loss of independence and sovereignty that membership entails; and underlying all considerations will be the question of whether a referendum in which the government advocates euro membership can be won.

References

Baker, D. and Seawright, D (1998) 'A "Rosy" Map of Europe? Labour Parliamentarians and European Integration', in Baker, D. and Seawright, D. (eds), *Britain For and Against Europe: British Politics and the Question of European Integration* (Oxford: Clarendon Press), pp. 57–87.

Barber, L. (1998) *Britain and the New European Agenda* (Paris: Notre Europe).

Buller, J. (1995) 'Britain as an awkward partner: Reassessing Britain's relations with the EU', *Politics*, 15(1), pp. 33–42.

Bulmer, S. and Burch, M. (1998) 'Organising for Europe: Whitehall, the British State and European Union', *Public Administration* 76(4), pp. 601–28.

George, S. (1995) 'A Reply to Buller', *Politics*, 15(1), pp. 43–7.

George, S. (1998) *An Awkward Partner: Britain in the European Community*, 3rd edn (Oxford: Oxford University Press).

Golinio, L. R. (1998) 'Britain's European policy under Tony Blair and the British debate on European Monetary Union', *British Politics Group Newsletter*, Spring, pp. 9–16.

House of Commons (1997a) *Parliamentary Debates 1997–98*, Vol. 299, 27 October, Cols 583–88.

House of Commons (1997b) *The European Scrutiny System in the House of Commons: A Short Guide for Members of Parliament by the Staff of the Select Committee on European Legislation*, London: House of Commons.

House of Commons Select Committee on European Legislation (1996) *Twenty-Seventh Report: The Scrutiny of European Legislation*, London: HMSO.

Humphreys, J. (1997) *Negotiating in the European Union* (London: Century).

Labour Party (1997) *Because Britain Deserves Better* (London: The Labour Party).

Ludlam, S. (1998) 'The Cauldron: Conservative Parliamentarians and European Integration', in Baker, D. and Seawright, D. (eds), *Britain For and Against Europe: British Politics and the Question of European Integration* (Oxford: Clarendon Press).

Nugent, N. (1996) 'Sovereignty and Britain's membership of the European Union', *Public Policy and Administration*, 11(2), pp. 3–18.

Nugent, N. (1999a) *The Government and Politics of the European Union*, 4th edn (Basingstoke: Macmillan).

Nugent, N. (1999b) 'Decision Making', in Cram, L. Dinan, D. and Nugent, N. (eds) *Developments in the European Union* (Basingstoke: Macmillan).

Reflection Group's Report (1995) Brussels: General Secretariat of the Council.

Thatcher, M. (1988) *Britain and Europe: the Bruges Speech* (London: Conservative Political Centre).

Wallace, W. (1997) 'At Odds with Europe', *Political Studies*, 45(4), pp. 677–88.

Wilks, S. (1996) 'Britain and Europe: Awkward partner or awkward state?', *Politics*, 16(3), pp. 159–65.

9

Issues of Governance in Scotland, Wales and Northern Ireland

ALLAN McCONNELL

Rose (1982, p. 1) suggests that 'The territorial dimension is inevitably important in any government larger than a postage stamp.' This is particularly so in the case of the United Kingdom. Different political, economic and social traditions in Scotland, Wales and Northern Ireland have led historically to calls for a much greater degree of territorial self-determination to replace the various forms of 'regional' administration that exist. Whilst the Conservatives baulked at the prospect of such major constitutional change during the 1979–97 period, the advent of a new Labour Government post-1997 has swiftly brought with it packages of reform. Only English regional assemblies are missing (the proposals for these have been shelved officially since September 1997) in a new constitutional settlement which involves a Scottish Parliament, a National Assembly for Wales and a Northern Ireland Assembly. This chapter focuses on each of these in turn, looking at the legacy of the Conservative era, the specific nature of these new democratic bodies and the prospects and problems for the future. It concludes by examining the wider implications for the Union. In particular the chapter looks at how British governments are now dealing with problems of territorial governance; the likely impact on the procedures of the Westminster Parliament; whether Britain can still be considered a unitary state; and the implications of this new system of governance for centre-periphery relations in the UK.

Scotland

Ever since the 1707 *Act of Union* dissolved an independent Scottish Parliament and incorporated the governance of Scotland within the new Parliament of Great Britain, Scotland had always enjoyed an element of independence from Westminster. The legal, educational and religious institutions of civil society remained largely intact (Kellas, 1984, pp. 1–19). Coupled with this, Scotland retained a strong measure of cultural, social and linguistic identity. One consequence of all this was the piecemeal development of arrangements within the British state which catered for – and in doing so helped reinforce – this relative Scottish autonomy. The chequered history and specific arrangements are beyond the scope of this chapter (see Keating and Midwinter, 1983; Kellas, 1984; Kellas 1991; Levy, 1995; McConnell and Pyper, 1994). In brief, however, arrangements evolved to include the administrative devolution of a wide range of functions to the Scottish Office; Scottish representation in Cabinet via the Secretary of State for Scotland; two Scottish Standing Committees for the passage of legislation specifically for Scotland; an investigatory Select Committee on Scottish Affairs and the 'talking shop' of the Scottish Grand Committee of all Scots MPs. Yet such accommodations to 'Scottishness' stopped short of a Scottish Parliament with legislative powers. The absence of such a body lay at the heart of numerous nationalist and devolutionary moves throughout the years. By the late 1970s, with Labour attempting to 'tartanise' itself (Geekie and Levy, 1989) in the face of the rapid growth in support for the Scottish National Party, it seemed as though a devolved Scottish Assembly was imminent. However, a bitterly-fought referendum campaign in 1979 resulted in a marginal 'No' vote (Balsom and McAllister, 1979; Bochel *et al.*, 1981; Kellas, 1984). Thus, the Thatcher Government came to power in 1979 with moves for devolution apparently at a dead-end.

The Slow Fuse: 18 Years of Conservative Rule in Scotland

In retrospect, it is clear that devolutionary sentiments were not dead. Supporters of devolution were merely reeling from the shock of the referendum result and were about to be galvanised by the activities of the Thatcher and Major Governments between 1979–97. UK economic policy became geared substantially towards the bulk of economic activity in London and South East England. One consequence of this was that the Conservative agenda of freeing-up market forces, reducing the role of the state and prioritising anti-inflationary fine-tuning policies, often had a detrimental impact on Scotland where there was a much heavier reliance on public spending and a much higher incidence of industrial activity (Standing Commission on the Scottish Economy, 1989; Lee, 1995). In addition, the Scottish Office began to appear as something of a colonial outpost. Ministers expounded a political philosophy and produced accompanying policies (such as the poll tax, NHS trusts, school boards and the removal of water services from local authority control) which lacked popular support in Scotland. As a consequence, and as revealed by general election results (see Table 9.1), the tide of Conservatism at Westminster was in stark contrast to Conservative support in Scotland. Indeed the Party held only one-third of parliamentary seats in Scotland in 1979 and this had been reduced to one-sixth by 1992. Thus, many key political actors began to prepare the ground for a Scottish Parliament. Particularly important was the Scottish Constitutional Convention – primarily an alliance of the Labour Party, Liberal Democrats, trades unions, local authorities, churches and various other organisations. The Conservatives refused to participate on the grounds that devolution would undermine the Union, whilst the Scottish National Party refused because it did not want to compromise its goal of full independence for Scotland. The Scottish Constitutional Convention (1990) duly produced a blueprint for a Scottish Parliament although it had a mixed reception among academic commentators (Kellas, 1992; Levy, 1992). Nevertheless, the document was indicative of a wider appetite for constitutional reform.

The unsympathetic response by the Conservatives was simply to tinker with the existing system. The principles of Scottish administration via the Scottish Office remained at the heart of governance in Scotland (see Levy, 1995) and marginal change came via John Major's Taking Stock exercise (Scottish Office, 1993). This sought to highlight the benefits of the Union and to improve its workings via *inter alia* extending the powers of the Scottish Grand Committee and enhancing the mechanisms through which Scottish Office ministers were held accountable at Westminster. Bradbury (1997, p. 81) neatly encapsulates the Conservatives' rationale for this: 'This line of thought formed the basis for a new

TABLE 9.1   *General Election Results 1979–97 (UK, Scotland, Wales)*

General Election	Party	UK		Scotland		Wales	
		% of Vote	Seats	% of Vote	Seats	% of Vote	Seats
1979	Cons.	43.9	339	31.4	22	32.2	11
	Lab.	36.9	269	41.6	44	48.6	22
	Lib.	13.8	11	9.0	3	10.6	1
	SNP	1.6	2	17.3	2	8.1	2
	Others	3.8	16	0.7	0	0.5	0
1983	Cons.	42.4	397	28.4	21	31.1	14
	Lab.	27.6	209	35.1	41	37.5	20
	Lib./SDP	25.4	23	24.5	8	23.2	2
	SNP/PC	1.5	4	11.8	2	7.8	2
	Others	3.1	17	0.3	0	0.4	0
1987	Cons.	42.2	376	24.0	10	29.5	8
	Lab.	30.8	229	42.4	50	45.1	24
	Lib./SDP	22.6	22	19.2	9	17.9	3
	SNP/PC	1.7	6	14.0	3	7.3	3
	Others	2.7	18	0.4	0	0.2	3
1992	Cons.	41.9	336	25.7	11	28.6	6
	Lab.	34.4	270	39.0	49	49.5	27
	LD	17.9	21	13.1	9	12.4	1
	SNP/PC	2.3	7	21.5	3	8.8	4
	Others	3.5	17	0.8	0	0.7	0
1997	Cons.	31.4	165	17.5	0	19.6	0
	Lab.	44.4	419	45.6	56	54.7	34
	LD	17.2	46	13.0	10	12.4	2
	SNP/PC	2.4	10	21.9	6	10.6	4
	Others	4.6	19	1.9	0	2.7	0

Note: Figures may not add up to 100 because of rounding.
Sources: Craig (1989, pp. 45–50); Denver (1992, p. 3); *The Times*, 3 May 1997;
    Financial Times, 3 May 1997; *The Herald*, 3 May 1997.

tilt towards unionism: to erode dissent by celebrating and promoting the distinctive union-state characteristics of the government of Scotland, and to think about how they might be extended within the existing constitutional settlement. If the Scots were reminded of the advantages that they enjoyed under the existing arrangements then it would be a powerful antidote to calls for constitutional change and might arrest the Conservative decline.'

The impact of the 1997 General Election, however, would put paid to such ideas.

New Labour: New Referendum

Labour's victory at the polls in May 1997 produced a result of seismic proportions in Scotland (see Table 9.1). For the Conservatives, the doomsday scenario of losing every single seat in Scotland had finally arrived. For Labour, with a massive 179 seat majority at Westminster and an unprecedented 56 seats (out of 72) in Scotland, there was now a clear run at implementing its proposals for constitutional change in Scotland. A White Paper was produced in July (Scottish Office, 1997) and a referendum was held on 11 September 1997 (see Mitchell et al 1998). Two questions were put to the Scottish electorate on the separate matters of (i) support for a Scottish Parliament in principle and (ii) support for a Scottish Parliament to have tax-varying powers. The turnout was a fairly modest 60.4 per cent although no region had a figure of less than 50 per cent and turnout may have been affected by a number of factors: for example, a general feeling that devolution was inevitable anyway, a recent general election and the suspension of campaigning following the death of Princess Diana. Turnout aside, and as illustrated in Table 9.2, voters displayed substantial support for Labour on the two key questions.

TABLE 9.2 *Referendum Result in Scotland, 11 September 1997*

Question on ballot paper	No. of votes	%
I agree that there should be a Scottish Parliament	1,775,045	74.3
I do not agree that there should be a Scottish Parliament	614,400	25.7
I agree that a Scottish Parliament should have tax-varying powers	1,512,889	63.5
I do not agree that a Scottish Parliament should have tax-varying powers	870,263	36.5

Note: *Turnout 60.4%*

Source: Adapted from Scottish Office: http://www.scottish- devolution.org.uk. referendum/result.htm.

The *Scotland Bill* was published subsequently on 17 December 1997. Labour's large Commons majority meant a smooth Parliamentary passage. This was aided by the fact that the Liberal Democrats and SNP were pragmatically supportive of the general principles of devolution because it appeared to move them closer to their goals of a federal UK and an independent Scotland respectively. Also, the Conservatives had little alternative but to face-up to the inevitability of devolution. Elections took place on 6 May 1999 and the Parliament was established at Edinburgh on 1 July 1999. It is a body with substantial legislative powers: unlike anything which Scotland has seen for many centuries. The main features of a Scottish Parliament are identified in Box 1.

Box 1:   Main Features of the Scottish Parliament

- *Constitution*: Scotland remains within the UK.

- *Elections*: The Scottish Parliament comprises 129 elected Members of the Scottish Parliament (MSPs). The electoral system combines two forms. Seventy three of the MPs are elected under the traditional first-past-the-post-system based on existing boundaries for Westminster elections (with the exception of Orkney and Shetland which become two constituencies). A further 56 members are elected under an additional member system of proportional representation, selected from party lists drawn up for each of the eight constituencies used in elections for the European Parliament.

- *Powers*: The Scottish Parliament has primary and secondary legislative powers for a wide range of policy areas. These include health, education and training, local government, economic development and transport, law and home affairs, environment, agriculture, sports and arts. Matters not devolved and remaining at Westminster include the constitution of the UK; defence and national security of the UK; stability of the UK's fiscal, economic and monetary system; common markets for goods and services within the UK; employment legislation; social security systems and most aspects of transport safety and regulation in the UK.

- *Finance*: Finances follow the pre-existing arrangement of the Barnett Formula based on population factors, where

---

Scotland receives a block of resources equivalent to 10.66 per cent of that for England. The Scottish Parliament is able to raise or lower the UK basic rate of income tax by a maximum of 3 per cent.

- *Parliamentary arrangements*: The Scottish Parliament nominates a First Minister. He/she heads a Scottish Executive and appoints ministers. The Scottish Parliament is responsible for drawing up and adopting its own Standing orders based on the recommendations of an all-party Consultative Steering Group.

- *Europe*: Representation in the EU decision-making process remains with the UK Parliament, although the Scottish Parliament plays an important (but not constitutionally separate) role via 'Concordat' agreements.

A New Scottish Parliament: Prospects and Problems

The governance of Scotland enters a new era with the advent of the Scottish Parliament. It allows the Scottish people a substantial degree of self-determination over their own affairs. Furthermore, the nature of the new more proportionally-based electoral system will always tend to deny any single party a majority of Members of the Scottish Parliament (MSPs), ushering in a new system of governance based on coalitions and power sharing. The results of the Scottish Parliamentary elections in May 1999 confirm this (see Table 9.3), with Labour obtaining only 56 of the available 129 seats and so needing to enter into coalition with the Liberal Democrats for a partnership government to be formed. There are certainly many challenges to face in this new era. Pyper (1999) for example, looks at the implications for Scottish Office civil servants and suggests for example that an increase in the demands for new policy initiatives (with there being fewer opportunities to draw upon Whitehall expertise) will be coupled with demands on the part of MSPs for much greater accountability. Notwithstanding immediate challenges, however, two simple and connected facts should be stressed. First, the Scottish Parliament remains constitutionally linked to Westminster. Second, the Scottish Parliament does not have sole legislative powers over all aspects of Scottish affairs. Given these facts, the potential exists for the new system to be undermined. The first major factor to consider is policy/legislative tensions between the two parliaments. In some areas, the Scottish Parliament does not quite have the autonomy that it might appear to have. In theory, it has limited income tax varying powers yet this may conflict with Westminster's right to be concerned with the UK's fiscal, economic and monetary system. It is not inconceivable that a UK Chancellor would wish to block a Scottish Parliament's attempt to vary income tax on the grounds that this would be detrimental to UK macro-economic policy. Notwithstanding this, Clause 28 of the *Scotland Act* states that the powers of the Scottish Parliament 'do...not affect the power of the Parliament of the United Kingdom to make laws for Scotland'. This clearly creates scope – albeit that it would be legally contested – for the UK Parliament to intervene on matters previously thought to be the responsibility of the Scottish Parliament. The White Paper hints at this when it states that 'There may be instances (e.g. international obligations which touch on devolved as well as reserved matters) where it will be more convenient for legislation to be passed by the UK Parliament' (Scottish Office, 1997, p. 12). Indeed, this international dimension highlights a specific problem with regard to the EU. Ministers in the Scottish Parliament have no constitutional right to speak and vote in the EU Council of Ministers and their only safeguards are a series of concordats (which are not legally-binding) between the Scottish Parliament and Whitehall Departments. Added to this, the UK ministerial team must adopt a common stance. This means, for example, that Scottish Ministers responsible for agriculture in Scotland are severely restricted because of the need to adopt a common ministerial line on UK agricultural matters.

A second matter of contention is likely to be Westminster's funding of a Scottish Parliament. The White Paper stated that block funding would be based on 'existing arrangements' (Scottish Office, 1997, p. 22) but the *Scotland Act* does not commit itself to anything as specific (or even vague!). These arrangements are based on the Barnett formula – originating in 1978 and named after the then Chief Secretary to the Treasury, Joel Barnett. In essence, the Barnett formula is a population-based formula which gives Scotland, Wales and Northern Ireland a specified share of planned spending increases or decreases in relation to comparable

TABLE 9.3 *Results of Elections to the Scottish Parliament 6 May 1999*

Party	Share of constituency votes %	Share of regional list votes%	Number of constituency MSPs	Number of regional list MSPS	Total number of MSPs Elected	Percentage of seats
Labour	38.8	33.6	53	3	56	43.4
SNP	28.7	27.3	7	28	35	27.1
Lib Democrat	14.2	12.4	12	5	17	13.2
Conservative	15.6	15.4	0	18	18	14.0
Green	0.0	3.6	0	1	1	0.8
Scottish Socialist	1.0	2.0	0	1	1	0.8
M for Falkirk West	0.8	1.2	1	0	1	0.8
Other	0.9	4.5	0	0	0	0.0
Totals	100.0	100.0	73	56	129	100.1

Turnout: 59%

Note: Figures for % of seats gained by each party does not add up to 100% because of rounding.
Source: Adapted from Curtis and Vidler (1999, pp. 7–8).

programmes in England (see Twigger, 1998; Kay, 1998).This produces a situation whereby Scotland commands more per-capita public spending than the UK as a whole. In 1995–96, expenditure in Scotland was 19 per cent above the UK average (Treasury Select Committee, 1997, para. 5). Many consider it misleading, however, to perceive this as a gross over-subsidy of Scotland. The figures cover only about three quarters of all public spending and they do not take into account the fact that there is a higher level of need in Scotland because of specific localised factors such as a sparse population, higher levels of poverty and higher morbidity rates. Indeed, the Scottish National Party (1997, p. 4) goes much further and uses Treasury figures to show that Scotland (particularly because of oil revenues) paid £27 billion *more* to Westminster between 1979–97 than it received in return. Yet regardless of these matters, the means of financing the Scottish Parliament is already under pressure. A report by the Treasury Select Committee (1997) examined the Barnett formula and argued for a needs assessment to be carried out. The Government's response (Treasury Select Committee, 1998) argued that there was no case for such a review at the present time, although it did not rule this out with appropriate consultation in the future. Thus, with the Scottish Parliament now in operation, it is not difficult to imagine a situation whereby the Barnett formula is again called into question by MPs south of the border who feel that Scotland is unfairly advantaged. It will be particularly vulnerable when the three-year public spending settlement initiated by the 1998 Comprehensive Spending Review is reviewed again in 2000–1.

The final major factor to consider is the possibility that the structures and limitations of a Scottish Parliament may lead to independence. Financial matters are a case in point. A report by the Labour-dominated Select Committee on Scottish Affairs (1997–98, para. 46) suggested that the perception of Scotland commanding an unjustifiably large amount of UK money is a 'dangerous' one which may create resentment which could encourage moves towards independence. There is more to the independence issue, however, than just this. Several opinion polls in recent years have provided evidence of a dramatic upsurge in support for the Scottish National Party with some predicting them to be the largest single party. These polls both shocked and puzzled the Labour hierarchy in Scotland (and London). Indeed, one analysis based on July 1998 voting intentions in a System Three poll, put the number of likely seats as Scottish National Party (56), Labour (46), Liberal Democrats (15), Conservative (12) (Dickson, 1998, p. 7). An ICM poll only a few months previously also found that 58 per cent of voters felt that there was more reason for voting SNP in Scottish elections than in Westminster elections (*Scotland on Sunday*, 3 May 1998, p. 11). The reasons for this are debatable and a combination of factors may be at work (assisted by the opportunity for split voting). These might include disenchantment with recent Labour 'sleaze' allegations in local government and a general suspicion of New Labour from more traditionally-minded Labour voters in Scotland. Indeed, there is a certain anti-establishment component of the Scottish psyche and it may be that because Labour is now the establishment – it will suffer because of the effects of this. Whatever the reasons, a constitutionally 'safe' Labour-Liberal Democrat is the outcome *this* time of the most recent elections to the Scottish Parliament, but clearly the potential exists for nationalist upsurges in the future. The Labour-Liberal Democrat coalition was put under severe strain almost immediately on the issue of tuition fees for students, and tensions like this create 'space' for Nationalists to argue that devolution is unable to fully address the needs of the Scottish people. The ultimate aim of the Scottish National Party is an independent Scotland. For better or worse, the arrival of a Scottish Parliament may in the longer-term stoke up the fires of independence.

Wales

After several centuries of sporadic conflicts and partial conquest by English forces, Wales became formally united with England via Acts of Union in 1536 and 1542. Unlike Scotland which had the experience of statehood behind it, a sense of Welsh political identity was much weaker. It was only in the latter part of the nineteenth century that widespread economic, social and political changes produced what Morgan (1981) describes as the rebirth of a nation. Despite this, and in comparison to Scotland and Ireland, Welsh nationality tended to be based more on language and culture as opposed to demands for self-rule. Thus, Birch (1989, p. 77) makes an overly simplistic but nevertheless broadly accurate statement when he suggests that from the Acts of Union onwards:

Wales...[was] governed as if the Welsh were part of England, save for
some slight administrative differences in the earlier part of this long
period...

Amidst all this, however, nationalist (although rarely separatist)
pressures did exist. As a concession to these in 1964, the Welsh
Office was established in Cardiff (Kellas, 1991). It never attained
the status or responsibilities of its Scottish counterpart (see Levy,
1995) but did bring an element of 'administrative devolution.'
Arrangements at Westminster (in many but not all respects similar
to those in Scotland) also existed via *inter alia* a Secretary of State
for Wales; special arrangements for the scrutiny of Bills exclusively
to Wales; a Select Committee on Welsh Affairs and a Welsh Grand
Committee. Demand for change in the 1970s tended to concentrate
more on the need for greater cultural recognition and linguistic
autonomy. Nevertheless, proposals for a Welsh assembly became
tied-in with devolution for Scotland, although only 20.3 per cent of
voters voted 'Yes' in the 1979 referendum – amounting to only 11.9
per cent of the entire Welsh electorate (see Balsom and McAllister,
1979).

1979–97: The Legacy of the Conservative Era in Wales

Under the Conservatives and in a similar vein to Scotland, the
freeing up of market forces and a consequent reduction in regional
aid had a profound effect on an economy with a heavy incidence of
industrial activity (particularly steel and coal) and employment in
the public sector. Unemployment rose substantially and average
earnings were persistently lower than in both Scotland and England
(Levy, 1995, pp. 205–6). If there was anything like a Conservative
'strategy' for Wales, it was to encourage inward investment in the
context of global economic forces seeking skilled workforces at low
cost. The focus for this became the Welsh Development Agency
which helped attract over 300 overseas companies in the 1980s and
early 1990s (Jones, 1997, p. 60). The Thatcher and Major governments enhanced the role of the Welsh Office in certain respects by
handing over administrative responsibility for areas such as agriculture, health service and education (secondary, further and higher).
In other respects, however, public accountability was questionable.
Practical responsibility lay with a proliferation of arms-length

quangos and there was a badly handled consultation process for structural reform in local government. Furthermore, four Welsh Secretaries (Walker, Hunt, Redwood, Hague) were English MPs who represented English constituencies. The only major concession to Welsh linguistic and cultural demands was the establishing in 1982, of the Welsh language TV channel (S4C).

Table 9.1 reveals the political repercussions of all this with regard to general election results. Over the years 1979–1992, the Conservative vote fell progressively. By 1992, the Party in power at Westminster commanded only 28.6 per cent of the vote in Wales and a mere six MPs. Yet despite this relative decline, nationalist and home rule demands in Wales fell far short of those in Scotland. Plaid Cymru failed to make any major inroads into Welsh consciousness (particularly in the Labour heartland of south Wales) and the Welsh economy lacked any major national resource which would allow it to stake a claim to self-sufficiency. Indeed, Wales generated revenue approximately 15 per cent less than was needed to sustain its level of public expenditure. Nevertheless, the Conservative era acted as a catalyst for devolution because it began to raise serious concerns regarding accountability, democracy and legitimacy in the governance of Wales. As a consequence, public opinion generally and Labour Party policy specifically (primarily after 1992) began to shift in favour of devolution and an elected assembly. The Conservatives, however, remained out of tune with this new mood. John Redwood (1995, p. 38), writing in his capacity as Secretary of State for Wales, castigated a Welsh Assembly as:

> responsible for the creation of a new breed of lobbyists, glib PR men and opinion-formers, creating nothing and responsible for nothing. The assembly would be a Trojan horse in the body politic . . . and eloquent testimony to Labour's stubborn belief in big government as the answer to every human problem.

New Labour: Proposals for a New Wales

The 1997 General Election produced a result as seismic as that for Scotland. The Conservative vote collapsed to just under 20 per cent and the Party was left with not a single MP in Wales. With Labour taking 34 of the available 40 Welsh seats and Plaid Cymru failing to build on the 4 seats that it already held, the pathway was clear for the victorious devolutionary forces. A White Paper *A Voice for Wales* (Welsh Office, 1997) was published in July and a referendum was held on 18 September 1997. McAllister (1998) in her study of the campaign perceived a lack of informed debate and a failure on the part of the Labour Party to convince a rather sceptical Welsh electorate. On a turnout of just over 50 per cent (which barely allowed devolutionists to claim some form of electoral legitimacy for the exercise in direct democracy), the 'Yes' vote for a Welsh Assembly scraped through by a mere 6,721 votes. The final result was 559,419 (50.3 per cent) in favour and 552,698 (49.7 per cent) against, with victory being clinched in the traditionally loyal Labour supporting valleys and the Welsh speaking nationalist areas in the west (MacLeod, 1997, p. 6).

The *Government of Wales Bill* was introduced in the Commons on 27 November 1997 and there was never any danger of the Bill falling. Labour dominated the Commons and the Conservatives bowed reluctantly to political realities. The Bill received Royal Assent on 31 July 1998 and elections took place on 6 May 1999. Surprised by strong support for Plaid Cymru, Labour fell three seats short of an overall majority (see Table 9.4) but decided to press ahead as a minority administration in the new Cardiff-based body. The Assembly shares many features with the Scottish Parliament although, as indicated in Box 2, it is in crucial respects a far weaker body.

The Welsh Assembly: Prospects and Problems

Sharing some similarities with Scotland, the advent of a National Assembly ushers in a new era for politics in Wales. The functions of the Welsh Office and responsibility for quangos – two areas previously criticised on grounds of democracy and accountability – are now brought under the control of an elected assembly. Much Westminster legislation is now capable of being 'fine-tuned' to cater for the needs of Wales. Furthermore, the dual electoral system gives voters the opportunity to vote (in effect) for more than one party if they so wish. In comparison to Scotland, however, nationalists have generally been considered as weak although the May 1999 results may be an early sign of previously untapped nationalist sympathies benefiting from the new electoral system. Such matters aside, there are liable to be a number of difficulties ahead.

Box 2:   Main Features of the National Assembly for Wales

- *Constitution*: Wales remains within the UK.

- *Elections*: The Welsh Assembly comprises 60 elected members. The election system combines two forms. Forty members are elected under the traditional first-past-the-post system, based on existing Westminster boundaries. A further 20 are elected under an additional member system of proportional representation, selected from party lists drawn up for each of five constituencies used for elections to the European Parliament.

- *Powers*: The Assembly takes over most of the powers held by the Secretary of State for Wales, including industrial and economic development, education and training, health, agriculture, local government, housing, social services, transport, planning and environment, arts and cultural heritage. Particular emphasis is placed on the ability of the Assembly to restructure or abolish quangos. In all policy areas, however, and unlike the Scottish Parliament, its powers are *strictly limited* to passing secondary legislation (formally called Assembly Orders). These are rules and regulations which fill in the details of a framework set by Acts of Parliament. Thus, primary legislation remains with the Westminster Parliament.

- *Finance*: Financial arrangements largely replicate the existing Barnett-based system whereby Wales receives a block of resources, based on population size, equivalent to 6.02 per cent of that for England. Unlike a Scottish Parliament, the Assembly *does not* have income tax varying powers.

- *Assembly Arrangements*: The Assembly elects an Assembly First Secretary. He/she heads an Executive Committee (normally drawn only from the majority party) which provides overall direction. Standing orders are decided by the Secretary of State for Wales acting on the recommendations of an Assembly Preparations Group appointed by him.

- *Europe*: Representation in the EU decision-making process remains the responsibility of the Westminster Parliament, although the Welsh Assembly is entitled to make its own judgements on relevant EU matters relating to Wales and communicate these to Whitehall.

The first factor is one of funding for the Assembly. As with the Scottish Parliament, funding for the vast bulk of the activities of the Welsh assembly is protected at the moment by the Barnett Formula. As previously indicated, however, this has come under pressure from many English MPs unsympathetic at having to finance the activities of non-English elected bodies. Wales, however, generates revenue which falls some 15 per cent short of that needed to sustain its level of expenditure. The Welsh Assembly does not have the ability to raise income tax and so some English MPs *may* be more sympathetic about financial matters when compared with Scotland. But the practicalities of the matter are that the Welsh situation is linked with that of Scotland, and so the next round of the Comprehensive Spending Review in 2000–01 is liable to see funding for the Welsh Assembly come under pressure.

The second factor is likely tensions between the Welsh Assembly and the Westminster Parliament. In essence, the reforms attempt to weld together two principles which – in combination – are a breeding ground for conflict. On the one hand, as the former Secretary of State for Wales Ron Davies (1997: col. 671) stated at Second Reading of the Bill: 'The United Kingdom Parliament is sovereign. The provisions ... do not challenge that sovereignty in any way – nor could they'. On the other hand, he argued that 'The Welsh Office and the quangos will come under the control of a democratically elected body. Far from introducing another tier of government, the creation of the assembly will democratise an existing, powerful tier' (Davies, 1997: col. 675). This holds the potential for conflict because democratic aspirations are raised but there is the absence of primary legislative powers to accompany them. This simple fact means that in broad terms, the Welsh Assembly essentially implements or fleshes out central legislation. Certainly, it can give a Welsh 'flavour' to this, but the Assembly can only operate *intra vires* (in the same manner as local government). For example, the Welsh Assembly is responsible for forestry policy in Wales but it does not have the power to create a separate Forestry Commission for Wales because the (UK) Forestry Commission retains a strategic role for Great Britain as a whole. The Assembly is responsible for local government yet it could not (for example) introduce a local income tax because this would require primary legislation. It is also responsible for further and higher education but could not (if it desired) keep the maintenance grant for students. Certainly, Clause 31 of the

TABLE 9.4 *Results of Elections to the Welsh Assembly 6 May 1999*

Party	Share of constituency votes %	Share of regional list votes %	Number of constituency seats won	Number of regional list seats won	Total number of seats won	Percentage of seats
Labour	37.6	35.5	27	1	28	47.7
Liberal Democract	13.5	12.5	3	3	6	10.0
Plaid Cymru	28.4	30.6	9	8	17	28.3
Conservative	15.8	16.5	1	8	9	15.0
Others	4.7	4.9	0	0	0	0.0
Totals	100.0	100.0	40	20	60	100.0

Turnout: 46%

Source: Adapted from Morgan (1999, pp. 4–7).

Act allows for the Welsh Assembly to be consulted on Westminster legislation, but there is no guarantee that the views of the Assembly will be taken on board. Furthermore, the Whitehall Secretaries of State only consult 'as appears . . . to be appropriate'. Wales also has no separate voice in UK representations within the EU. There *are* a series of concordats between the Assembly and Whitehall departments for ensuring 'Welsh' input, but these are not legally binding and the overriding consideration is that ministers and civil servants adopt a common UK line. The Welsh Assembly also lacks tax-varying powers, thus operating on a system of representation without taxation.

Finally, there is the likely longer-term impact of this new-found 'democracy' in Wales. Certainly, there are many Conservatives and anti-devolutionist Labour MPs such as Llew Smith (Blaenau and Gwent) and Alan Williams (Swansea West) who perceive conflict as a predictable outcome for an assembly with only marginal support in a referendum (indeed, only about one quarter of the entire Welsh electorate supported it) and holding little power of any real substance in comparison to Westminster. Given the general constitutional trend towards power sharing, however, the likelihood of reversing the policy of devolution for Wales is unlikely, even although Westminster still retains the right to do so. More likely is the scenario portrayed by Conservative MP Oliver Letwin (1997: cols 748–9):

> It creates a poodle, and, moreover, a poodle that can be kicked . . . [and] will react by becoming very vicious. It will try to obtain the maximum mileage by running up and down and yapping, and by trying to bite the heels of those who attempt to control it.

One does not have to be a Conservative to support this view. There is a strong possibility that the disparity between the powers of the Scottish Parliament and those of the Welsh Assembly will become an increasingly important issue. Some pro-devolutionists are likely to argue that many of the difficulties could be resolved by empowering the Assembly with primary legislative powers. Among the Labour hierarchy (many of whom were sceptical of Welsh devolution in the first place) this might not have seemed *too* difficult to concede, given the relatively marginal role of Plaid Cymru and the historical lack of a strong nationalist movement desirous of an independent Wales. The strong showing of Plaid Cymru in the May 1999 elections, however, will have made many Labour figures think again and so the problems of a disparity are liable to remain.

Northern Ireland

Northern Ireland is a special case. The development of administrative arrangements pales beside other factors of much greater significance. The history of Ireland is a highly sensitive one, where political violence (on many sides) and religious affiliation has played a much more important role than in Scotland and Wales. English conquest of a poor nation was formalised in the *Act of Union* 1801 which brought Ireland into the United Kingdom, but as Boyce (1996, p. 1) comments:

> the difference between what England could consent, and Ireland be contented to receive, was the essence of the Irish Question in British politics.

The north-eastern corner of the island had become colonised largely by Protestant settlers from Scotland and England who saw themselves as 'British' (deeply resented by the remaining Catholic minority), whilst the south remained predominantly Catholic. The abortive uprising of 1916, followed by the IRA led insurrection in 1919–21 culminated in the *Government of Ireland Act* 1920 and the partition of Ireland – creating the Republic of Ireland in the south and Northern Ireland in the six north-eastern counties. Having opted out of the republic, the latter remained in the UK with its own devolved parliament at Stormont and its own administration. Nevertheless, what 'Ireland was contented to receive' was intensely problematic, with the predominantly Catholic south still laying claim to the north (enshrined in articles 2 and 3 of its constitution) and a whole series of discriminatory practices being carried out against the Catholic minority in the north. Simmering unrest degenerated into virtual civil war in the late 1960s and early 1970s, as a consequence of which the Stormont Parliament was suspended in 1972 and direct rule imposed from Westminster. A failed power-sharing agreement of 1973 collapsed in 1974 and direct rule was resumed. For the remainder of the 1970s, regular atrocities by both

Republicans and Loyalists were contained only by the massive security forces of the British state. The Troubles seemed insuperable and the main objectives of British government policy were now set (Coxall and Robins, 1998, p. 100). These were: creating a framework within which a viable settlement could emerge and developing a security policy in order to contain the violence instigated by both Republican and Loyalist forces.

1979–97: Northern Ireland under the Conservatives

For most of the Conservative era, the focus of official government policy was to marginalise terrorism and the advocates of terrorism – particularly Sinn Féin and the IRA. The murders of Conservative MP Airey Neave and Lord Mountbatten in 1979 stiffened Mrs Thatcher's resolve in this regard. Relations with Dublin also suffered over her handling of the 1981 republican hunger strike at the Maze prison. In this context, the first major attempt to develop a settlement was in 1982 when a new assembly was established on the initiative of Northern Ireland Secretary James Prior. It was a 78 member elected body which, on the basis of 'rolling devolution', would gradually take over powers from the Northern Ireland Office. However, it effectively collapsed almost as soon as the elections were held. Unionists were sceptical that it might in fact 'roll' them out of the UK, whilst the prospect of an internal settlement was too much for the Social Democratic and Labour Party (SDLP) and Sinn Féin who refused to take up their seats (Boyce, 1996).

In the context of improved Anglo-Irish relations, the Anglo-Irish Agreement of 1985 provided 'unequivocal acceptance that the problem was a joint one' (Arthur and Jeffery, 1988, p. 16). It put forward a number of aims (Lyons, 1990, pp. 220–1) but three are particularly important. First, it stated that any change to the constitutional status of Northern Ireland could only happen with the consent of the majority of the people of Northern Ireland. Second, it laid out the broad framework for regular meetings of a north-south Intergovernmental Conference dealing with political, security, legal and cross-border co-operation matters. Third, it provided for a longer-term aim of devolution in a way that would secure widespread acceptance among the community. Although rejected by Sinn Féin and the Provisional IRA as simply affirming the status quo (Mrs Thatcher had no wish to cultivate their support anyway), the nationalist SDLP welcomed it as a constructive way of representing all-Ireland interests. Ultimately, however, the agreement alienated those crucial to its success because Unionists felt betrayed by the admission (however cryptically) that a constitutional change in the status of Northern Ireland might be possible, and by the consultative role of Dublin in Northern Ireland affairs. In the meantime, terrorist attacks continued within Northern Ireland and on the British mainland.

Throughout the Conservative era, electoral politics in Northern Ireland was dominated by the Troubles. As Table 9.5 indicates, the combined vote for Unionist parties fell gradually from 59.0 per cent in 1979 to 50.4 per cent in 1992. This was particularly worrying for Unionists because the 1991 Census revealed the Catholic population of Northern Ireland to be above 40 per cent and maybe even as high as 42 per cent. At the same time, votes for the nationalist SDLP increased gradually, although Sinn Féin support fell steadily from 13.4 per cent in 1983 to 7.4 per cent in 1992. Added to this, the loss of Gerry Adams' seat in 1992 meant a blow to Sinn Féin's electoral legitimacy. One should be wary of over-generalising about the impact of this. Nevertheless, it seems reasonable to suggest that whilst Unionists became more fearful that they would become weaker and marginalised by the British Government, republican terrorists and their political supporters wavered between rebuilding electoral legitimacy and a policy of bombing and sectarian attacks in order to force the British Government to take heed of their views.

It is against this background that there was a fundamental change in policy under Prime Minister John Major and Irish Taoiseach Albert Reynolds:

> The common purpose of the British and Irish governments became the search for an agreement which would enable the *inclusion* of those formerly designated the enemies of democracy. (Aughey, 1997, p. 241)

The agreement was the Downing Street Declaration of December 1993. It was a complex and ambiguous document, which attempted to square the political circle by raising the prospect of a united Ireland whilst at the same time recognising that any agreement needed the consent of the majority of the people in Northern

Ireland. With more self-confidence on the part of nationalist politicians (particularly because of the rising Catholic birth-rate in the North), growing international pressure and an astute handling by the Major Government, the IRA eventually called a cease-fire in August 1995 and the Loyalist paramilitaries followed shortly afterwards. The search for a working peace solution was taken further in February 1995 with the publication of two framework documents dealing with: proposals for devolution involving *inter alia* a 90-member assembly and Anglo-Irish relations. Shortly afterwards, the British Government entered into exploratory dialogue with Sinn Féin and the smaller loyalist parties. However, this faltered over the decommissioning of arms and so a new Twin Track initiative was established. The first component was the appointing of US Senator George Mitchell to chair an international enquiry into the decommissioning of illegal arms. The second component was a parallel phase of talks, aimed at preparing the ground for all-party negotiations. The Mitchell Commission reported in January 1996 and recommended that decommissioning take place *while* all-party negotiations were taking place, rather than before, or after. The Commission also recommended that parties should be committed to six key principles of democracy and non-violence. Two weeks later, however, the IRA bombed London Docklands and brought about an end to the 17-month cease-fire. It argued that John Major had squandered the opportunity for peace by stating that he wanted the decommissioning of weapons *prior* to talks. Subsequently, in May 1996, with London and Dublin committed to inclusive negotiations, 110 representatives were elected in Forum elections – a vehicle which would allow successful parties to enter automatically into multi-party talks (backed by electoral legitimacy). Ultimately, however, Sinn Féin's absence (refusing to countenance a restoration of the cease-fire) and the thorny matter of decommissioning resulted in little real progress being made. Nevertheless, the Conservative era ended with a British Government prepared to talk with advocates of terrorism, rather than marginalise them.

New Labour and the Search for Peace

The advent of the Blair Government (in conjunction with the election of a Fianna Fáil government in the Dáil and Bertie Ahern as Taoiseach) saw rapid development towards the most realistic hope

TABLE 9.5 *General Election Results 1979–97 in Northern Ireland*

Party	1979 % of vote	1979 Seats	1983 % of vote	1983 Seats	1987 % of vote	1987 Seats	1992 % of vote	1992 Seats	1997 % of vote	1997 Seats
DUP	10.2	5	20.0	3	11.7	3	13.1	3	13.6	2
UUP	36.6	11	34.0	11	37.8	9	34.8	9	32.7	10
Others	12.2	6	3.1	1	5.3	1	2.5	1	4.2	1
(Total Unionist)	(59.0)	(22)	(57.1)	(15)	(54.8)	(13)	(50.4)	(13)	(50.5)	(13)
APNI	11.9	12	8.0	0	10.0	0	8.7	0	8.0	0
SDLP	18.2	9	17.9	1	21.1	3	23.5	4	24.1	3
SF	–		13.4	0	11.4	1	10.0	0	16.1	2
Others	16.5	21	0.6	0	2.7	0	7.4	0	1.3	0

Note: Democratic Unionist Party (DUP), Ulster Unionist Party (UUP), Alliance Party of Northern Ireland (APNI), Social Democratic and Labour Party (SDLP), Sinn Fein (SF).

Source: Craig (1989, pp. 44–9); Collins (1992, p. 27); O'Leary and Evans (1997, p. 675).

of a peace settlement since the imposition of direct rule. At an early stage, in July 1997, the IRA declared another cease-fire and seemed prepared to throw itself (via Sinn Féin) behind engagement in the democratic process. After the demise of John Major (whom Sinn Féin had also grown to distrust – accusing him of effectively dumping the Mitchell Report because of his precondition of decommissioning prior to talks), the conditions for this seemed more favourable. Tony Blair had the simple advantage of not being Mr Major. He also made a shrewd appointment in Mo Mowlam as Northern Ireland Secretary, an amiable and feisty woman without any baggage of excessive sympathy to nationalism or loyalism. Additionally, Blair in effect reciprocated the cease-fire and invited Sinn Féin President Gerry Adams and his colleagues to Downing Street for talks – an act of little practical but enormous symbolic significance. All-party talks resumed in June 1997 and Sinn Féin joined the talks on 9 September. UUP leader David Trimble, managed to keep his party committed to the talks – despite considerable pressure from hard-line Unionists to withdraw. Unlike the Sunningdale Agreement in 1973, therefore, almost all the main parties were present. The only absentees were Ian Paisley's Democratic Unionist Party (DUP), the independent unionist Robert McCartney and various paramilitary groups on both sides. As discussions progressed, a deadline of 10 April 1998 was set in order to give the talks a degree of urgency and a historic agreement emerged on that day – known colloquially as the Good Friday Agreement or the Belfast Agreement (HM Government, 1998). The main elements of the Agreement are outlined in Box 3.

Referendums followed on 22 May 1998. In Northern Ireland, a high turnout of 81.1 per cent produced 71.1 per cent in favour of the Good Friday Agreement and 28.9 per cent against (Gay, 1998, p. 73). In the Republic, a lower turnout of 56.3 per cent nevertheless produced a massive 94.4 per cent voted in favour of constitutional change (*The Irish Times*, 1998). Elections to the new Northern Ireland Assembly took place one month later on 25 June 1998. The results are given in Table 9.6 and indicate that parties supporting the Good Friday Agreement took 80 seats – assisted by the vagaries of the electoral system – and opponents gained 28. David Trimble, as leader of the largest party the Ulster Unionist Party, was voted in as First Minister. The Assembly's first meeting in shadow form was held in July 1998 .

Box 3: *Main Features of the Good Friday Agreement*

- *Constitution*: Northern Ireland to remain part of the UK. Nevertheless, the status of Northern Ireland is a matter for the majority of the people of Northern Ireland and it is also for the people of the island of Ireland as a whole to exercise their right to self-determination. A referendum to be held in the Irish Republic on amending Articles 2 and 3 of its constitution in order to renounce the territorial claim to Northern Ireland.

- *Strand One*: A 108-member assembly, elected by Single Transferable Vote, based on existing Westminster constituencies. It will have full primary legislative and executive authority over those policy areas within the remit of the six Northern Ireland Government Departments i.e. health, education, environment, economic development, agriculture and finance. Safeguards will be built-in to ensure *inter alia* that key-decisions are taken with cross-community support (in effect, to ensure that Unionists cannot dominate Nationalists).

- *Strand Two*: A North-South Ministerial Council, acting as a forum for Ministers from Belfast and Dublin to promote joint all-Ireland policies. Possible areas may include agriculture (animal and plant health); education (teacher qualifications and exchanges); social security (entitlements of cross-border workers and fraud control) and health (accident and emergency services). All Council decisions must be agreed between the two sides.

- *Strand Three*: A British-Irish Council (also known as Council of the Isles). Membership will comprise representatives of the British and Irish Governments as well as from the Northern Ireland Assembly, Scottish Parliament and Welsh Assembly. It will meet in a variety of formats to exchange information, discuss, consult and (if possible) co-operate on matters of mutual interest.

- *Decommissioning*: All participants reaffirm their commitment to the complete disarmament of all paramilitary organisations.

- *Prisoners*: An accelerated programme of release for paramilitary prisoners. All those qualifying should be released within two years after the commencement of a review process.

TABLE 9.6   *Election Results 25 July 1998 for the Northern Ireland*
Assembly (by first preferences and seats)

Parties supporting Belfast Agreement			*Parties against Belfast Agreement*		
Party	*% vote*	*Seats*	*Party*	*% vote*	*Seats*
PUP	1.9	2	DUP	18.5	20
WC	1.9	2	UKUP	4.6	5
Alliance	5.6	6	Indep	2.8	3
Sinn Féin	16.7	18			
SDLP	22.2	24			
UUP	25.9	28			
Totals	74.2	80		25.9	28

Notes: [1] Social Democratic and Labour Party (SDLP), Ulster Unionist Party (UUP),
Progressive Unionist Party (PUP), Women's Coalition (WC), Democratic
Unionist Party (DUP), United Kingdom Unionist Party (UKUP).
[2] Figures do not add up to 100% because of rounding.
Source: Adapted from Winetrobe (1998, p. 12).

Northern Ireland: Prospects and Problems

Prospects for a lasting peace are as good as they have been since the late 1960s, although it would foolish to be too optimistic in a situation which is liable to change overnight and where there are many exceptionally difficult issues still to resolve. Certainly, on a broad level, however, a coalition of forces has emerged with commitments to non-violence and the constitutional settlement embodied in the Good Friday Agreement. The New Labour Government, for its part, has attempted to cultivate a climate which entrenches this even further. Among other things, it has undertaken several initiatives to inject cash – notably a £315 million investment package covering innovation, tourism, employment, skills and enterprise. It has set up a review of the criminal justice system and the controversial no-jury system of handling terrorist trials. It has withdrawn military foot patrols from the streets of Belfast. It has pressed ahead swiftly with the programme to release almost every terrorist inmate within the agreed two-year timescale. Also, in the wake of the Omagh bombing in August 1998 (with the Real IRA claiming responsibility for the death of 29 people in the worst single atrocity in the history of the Troubles), the Government capitalised on public revulsion and recalled Parliament to introduce the *Criminal Justice (Terrorism and Conspiracy) Act* 1998. Among other things, this made it illegal to be a member or supporter of an organisation advocating terrorist activity.

Sinn Féin also remains committed to the settlement (at least on the surface) and seems reasonably confident about its growing support. A special conference in May 1998 voted overwhelmingly to support the Good Friday Agreement. Latterly, in the Assembly elections, it increased its vote by 2.7 per cent across the eighteen constituencies and secured 45 per cent of the nationalist vote. In the wake of the Omagh bombing, Gerry Adams went further than ever before and described paramilitary violence as 'over, done with and gone'. Sinn Féin members also made home visits to members of the Real IRA and its political wing, the 32-County Sovereignty Committee, giving them an ultimatum to cease violence. A cease-fire duly followed. These matters aside, it is nevertheless now more difficult (but not impossible) for Sinn Féin to extract itself from the settlement – even if it wanted to. The two-year programme of accelerated release for political prisoners has received substantial popular support among republicans. To see this through, Sinn Féin needs to adhere to the Mitchell principles of non-violence. Irrespective of this, however, and as Bruce (1998) comments:

> Crucial to the taming of republicanism is the referendum vote in the Irish Republic. The IRA gains its legitimacy from the claim to embody the will of the Irish people. Well, the Irish people have spoken and they unanimously said Yes to the Good Friday accord.

At the present time, Unionists – by and large – also remain committed to the new settlement although the path has been less smooth than that of the Republicans. A poor showing by the Ulster Unionists of only 21.3 per cent in the Assembly elections (down 3 per cent on their previous worst performance in the Forum elections) was confirmation for many in the DUP, UK Unionist Party and the Orange Order generally that the Good Friday Agreement was flawed in its ability to defend Northern Ireland Unionist interests within the UK. However, an attempt in 1998 by the Orange Order to (in effect) bring down Ulster Unionist Leader David Trimble over its insistence on parading at Drumcree, was ultimately defeated. Attacks on the RUC and the murder of three young boys in Ballymoney turned the tide against those seeking to destabilise the major players in the peace process. Thus, Trimble survived and remains as First Minister. His party's comparatively poor performance in terms of the popular vote nevertheless resulted in 28 seats – the largest number of any party in the Assembly – as a consequence of securing a high number of transfers under the Single Transferable Vote system. Also, the DUP and UK Unionist members may be opposed to the agreement but (for the moment at least) they have taken their seats. Meanwhile the Loyalist Volunteer Force, Ulster Defence Association and Ulster Volunteer Force have called cease-fires. This has helped secure prisoner releases which in turn helps encourage some form of (tacit) support for the Assembly from many individuals previously sympathetic to terrorist activity but now seizing the opportunity to be reunited with a relative, friend or colleague. This matter aside, as long as the Republican paramilitaries do not breach their 'ceasefire', any major terrorist atrocities on the part of Loyalists would isolate them even further.

Prospects for the future, therefore, seem in *some* respects to be as bright as they have been for a generation. Nevertheless, it is in many respects a highly fragile settlement and a number of forces may knock it down. In the short term, the thorny matter of decommissioning has still to be realised in practice and many consider it be insoluble. Common agreement on broad principles cannot hide the fact that for the paramilitaries, this is a symbolic and practical emasculating of their only real power. At a seminar on the future of Northern Ireland in August 1998, a representative of the Loyalist paramilitaries stated 'If I ordered decommissioning at breakfast I would be dead by teatime'. There was instant agreement from his counterpart in Sinn Féin (Cochrane, p. 1998). Thus, Unionist support (at times reluctant) for the Assembly has been put under enormous pressure. Sinn Féin has so far refused to consider the prospect of the IRA handing in any weapons at all until it had taken up its two seats on the Executive, yet David Trimble as First Minister refuses to let Sinn Féin take its two seats in government precisely *because* it has failed to decommission. Added to this is an increase in punishment beatings on both sides (but particularly Republican) and arguments over whether these constitute a breach of cease-fire agreements. Northern Ireland Secretary Mo Mowlam declared in August 1999 (with some reserve and to the chagrin of Unionists) that these did not constitute a breach of the IRA ceasefire. In an attempt to break the decommissioning deadlock, therefore, the services of Senator George Mitchell were called upon once again in order to chair a review of the implementation of the Good Friday Agreement.

In the longer term, should the Assembly proper get off the ground, it seems likely that there will be a host of disputes over matters such as funding for the Assembly, standing orders and its areas of legislative competence. One factor which must not be forgotten is that Unionists and Nationalists ultimately want different things. For example, at a fringe meeting at the Labour Party conference in September 1998, Gerry Adams took the opportunity to reiterate that Sinn Féin saw the new agreement merely as a *transitional* one on the road to a united Ireland. Thus, disputes over the powers and funding of the various bodies involved in the new constitutional settlement will be a manifestation of underlying long-term attempts to stretch it in two different directions.

Conclusion: Analysing the New System of UK Territorial Governance

The differing contexts of, and the arrangements for a Scottish Parliament and National Assemblies for Wales and Northern Ireland are immensely complex. Nevertheless, if we are to say anything meaningful about these new systems of territorial governance in the United Kingdom, we must be prepared to impose a sense of analytical order. In this regard, it seems useful to address four key matters: each telling us something about the new systems of governance. These are:

1. How do we understand the strategy which the British state is now using to deal with problems of territorial governance?
2. How is the Westminster Parliament adapting to the fact that many aspects of its former business is now be carried out by devolved assemblies?
3. Can the UK still be described as a unitary state?
4. How do we understand the new nature of centre–periphery relations in the UK?

The first factor is to comprehend the strategy which the British state is now deploying to deal with problems of territorial governance.

Prior to May 1997, the Conservative era was characterised by what Nairn (1998) portrays scathingly as 'glacial immobilism'. The basic response to the problems and disputes emerging in Scotland, Wales and Northern Ireland, was the constitutional *status quo* – accompanied by a few tinkerings here and there to cater for 'national circumstances'. Thus, territorial interests were marginalised: whether it be to pour scorn on calls for a Scottish Parliament and a Welsh Assembly, or refusing to enter into dialogue with advocates of terrorism in Ireland. The only exceptions to this were in Northern Ireland. In this regard, the Conservatives produced several limited power-sharing proposals. Also, under John Major's final term of office, significant talks took place at ministerial level with Sinn Féin (the first since 1921). Now, however, the tide has well and truly turned against 'immobilism' and has started to build on *some* of the initiative displayed by the Major Administration. Territorial interests have been *integrated formally* into a constitutional settlement based loosely on what Lijphart (1996) describes as 'power sharing' or 'consociational democracy'.

Second, there is the matter of how the Westminster Parliament is adapting to this new era of devolution. The way in which it dealt previously with Scottish, Welsh and Northern Ireland business is now in many respects no longer appropriate. In July 1998, the Select Committee on Procedure began an investigation into the consequences of devolution for Westminster and reported in May 1999, promising a more detailed review in due course. In essence, it recognised that mechanisms for accountability and control would be installed *within* the new Parliament/Assemblies as an integral part of their new standing orders. A consequence of this, therefore, is a slimming down of much Westminster business and its transference to the new devolved bodies, coupled with a recognition of the need for co-ordination between Westminster and the devolved administrations. Recommendations include:

- The encouragement of links between House of Commons Committees and their equivalents in each of the three devolved bodies. This is particularly important with regard to European legislation where the UK Parliament remains the main body for scrutinising EU legislation.
- Ministers in the House should not answer oral and written questions on matters for which they are no longer responsible.

Thus, the time allocated to Scottish Questions should be reduced but there should be no hasty change with regard to Wales and Northern Ireland.

• A suspension of the Grand Committees.

• The terms of reference of the Select Committees for Scottish, Welsh and Northern Ireland Affairs should be confined to scrutiny of the remaining responsibilities of the appropriate Secretary of State. These terms of reference should also include liaison with the devolved legislatures.

(Select Committee on Procedure, 1999)

There is also likely an ongoing debate on the so-called West Lothian Question (now also applicable to Northern Ireland). This refers to the situation whereby Scottish and Northern Ireland MPs are/will be able to vote at Westminster on 'reserved' legislation affecting only England, yet MPs representing English constituencies cannot do likewise for the same policy areas devolved to the Scottish Parliament and Northern Ireland Assembly. Some see this as an horrific example of the absurdity of devolution. Others see it as a minor constitutional anomaly (occurring previously during the reign of the Stormont Parliament and also in other multi-level systems throughout the world) which is a small price to pay for a UK-wide enhancement of democracy and accountability.

The third factor is how we understand the nature of the new 'Union' of the United Kingdom. Until the 1960s, the UK was labelled traditionally as a unitary state. All power flowed from a sovereign Parliament at Westminster in a homogeneous society where national, regional, social and religious identities were considered relatively unimportant. The subsequent coming to the surface of territorially-based national identities and debates in the late 1960 and 1970s (particularly in Scotland and Northern Ireland), led Rose (1982) in his major study of territorial governance to describe the UK as a multinational state. Rokkan and Urwin (1982) adopt a slightly different focus and describe it as a union state, where considerable regional autonomy is preserved through the perpetuation of many pre-union rights and institutional infrastructures. Mitchell (1996) concurs with this, stressing that it is a flexible union state which has failed (historically) to incorporate proper democratic accountability within it. So, what of the new post-1997 territorial settlement? Certainly, we can view it as simply a further development in the union state: building-in (to varying degrees) territorial structures and powers which are both pluralistic and democratic. Perhaps there is a danger, however, in forgetting that the Scottish Parliament, National Assembly for Wales and the Northern Ireland Assembly, are attached by a constitutional 'string' to Westminster. All relevant legislation could in fact be rescinded by Parliament if it so desired. Even the statement in Clause 1 of the *Northern Act* recognising the sovereignty of the people of Northern Ireland over its place within the United Kingdom (there was no equivalent for the Scottish and Welsh legislation) could – paradoxically – be reversed by an Act of the Westminster Parliament. We can call it what we like: unitary state, multinational state, union state or whatever. But we should not forget that ultimate sovereignty still remains at Westminster and hence the new system cannot be categorised as 'federal'. The Thatcher era was witness to Westminster enacting a host of legislation which would in other circumstances have been unthinkable: from the abolition of the democratically-elected Greater London Council and six Metropolitan County Councils, to the introduction of a *de facto* tax on the right to vote via the poll tax. Under a different set of historical circumstances (where a Westminster government perceives the *nation*s of Scotland, Wales and Northern Ireland as a threat on a similar scale as the *locality* was considered to be in the 1980s) Westminster could in theory use its constitutional right to turn again.

The final and perhaps most complex matter is how we understand the new nature of centre-periphery relations. A multitude of perspectives have hitherto been put forward in an attempt to conceptualise the relationship (however vaguely defined) between centre and periphery in the United Kingdom. Some of these emphasise stability whilst others emphasise contradiction. Stability is stressed by centrist and New Labour-sympathising constitutional reform bodies such as Charter 88 and Demos. In essence, the United Kingdom is seen as a partnership which is enriched by distinct national traditions, culture and identities. Devolution is said to preserve these in a meaningful sense within a democratic constitutional settlement which removes separatist threats and so strengthens the Union.

By contrast, those stressing contradiction have a long line of political and historical research to call upon. A rich tradition emphasises (in a variety of different ways) a clash between the authority of the centre and forces seeking to remove themselves – in whole or in part – from this authority. For example, Hechter (1975) sees Scotland, Wales and Northern Ireland as disadvantaged internal colonies which in time are liable to assert their own culture and seek independence. Nairn (1977) sees the uneven development of capitalism as producing peripheral elites who will seek to cultivate a populist opposition to centralised development. Rhodes (1988) sees policies towards Scotland, Wales and Northern Ireland as helping maintain the dominance of the centre but doing so in a contradictory way by creating structures of sub-central government which politicise the often recalcitrant 'territories' even further. The views of the SNP, Plaid Cymru and Sinn Féin could all – in their own individual ways – find some merit in these perspectives. For each, the new Assemblies/Parliament are likely to produce a host of disputes over matters such as funding and policy autonomy. Thus, the feeling within this broad camp is that the new structures have started a nationalist 'bandwagon' which will continue to roll, once the inadequacies of the new settlements are evident for all to see. This, it is argued, will be assisted by the trend towards subsidiarity within the European Union, where the idea is that decision-making is taken at the lowest possible level.

In conclusion, perhaps it is possible to perceive an element of truth in both views. On the one hand, those holding a critical view of governance by Westminster and particularly the bitter experiences of the 1979–97 Conservative era and its 'glacial immobilism', will be heartened by many aspects of the reforms. They bring with them a partial withering away of hegemonic Westminster power over Scotland, Wales and Northern Ireland, and usher in a more pluralistic era of proportional voting systems, power sharing and subsidiarity. On the other hand, there are very real problems to face. In Scotland and Wales, there is a likelihood that serious disputes will occur over funding and spheres of responsibility. These will be rooted in a host of conflicts between the demands of the newly created democratically elected bodies seeking to cater for 'national' interests and aspirations, and the demands of the Westminster Parliament seeking not to make concessions which will undermine the Union. The Welsh Assembly may be particularly awkward if it seeks to make a strong case regarding its absence of primary legislative powers when compared to Scotland and Northern Ireland. The Northern Ireland

Assembly itself will also face a particularly testing time. Disputes over decommissioning may prevent it functioning at all. Even if this is resolved, longer-term disagreements are liable to occur over Assembly powers, procedures and funding. Ultimately, these would be manifestations of fundamental and bitterly fought differences between Unionists and Republicans – many of whom have been prepared previously to sanction political violence.

Overall, therefore, the Conservative era stored-up contradictions which ultimately provided the final impetus for devolution. Sharing some similarity with this, the New Labour era stores-up contradictions which will put devolution itself under substantial pressure. Those lining up behind the Union will proclaim the legitimacy of the new settlement whilst others will attempt to capitalise and proclaim counter 'national' legitimacies. Whatever the outcome, one thing is certain – issues of territorial governance in the UK can never be the same again.

References

Arthur, P. and Jeffrey, K. (1988) *Northern Ireland Since 1968* (Oxford: Basil Blackwell).

Aughey, A. (1989) *Under Siege: Ulster Unionism and the Anglo-Irish Agreement* (London: Hurst & Company).

Aughey, A. (1997) 'Northern Ireland' in Dunleavy, P., Gamble, A., Holliday, I. and Peele, G. *Developments in British Politics 5* (Basingstoke: Macmillan).

Balsom, D. and McAllister, I. (1979) 'The Scottish and Welsh Devolution Referenda of 1979: Constitutional Change and Popular Choice', *Parliamentary Affairs*, 32, pp. 394–409.

Birch, A.H. (1989) *Nationalism and National Integration* (London: Unwin Hyman).

Bochel, J., Denver, D. and McCartney, A (eds) (1981) *The Referendum Experience: Scotland 1979* (Aberdeen: Aberdeen University Press).

Boyce, D.G. (1996) *The Irish Question and British Politics 1868–1996*, 2nd edn (Basingstoke: Macmillan)

Brown, A., McCrone, D. and Paterson, L. (1996) *Politics and Society in Scotland* (Basingstoke: Macmillan).

Bradbury, J. (1997) 'Conservative Governments, Scotland and Wales: A Perspective on Territorial Management' in Bradbury, J. and Mawson, J. (eds), *British Regionalism and Devolution* (London: Jessica Kingsley).

Bruce, S. (1998) 'Taming of Republicanism', *The Herald*, 11 August.

Cochrane, A. (1998) 'Taking Out the Hard Men of Ulster', *The Scotsman*, 18 August.

Collins, N. (1992) 'The General Election in Northern Ireland', *Politics Review*, 2(2), pp. 26–29.

Compton, P.A. (1998) 'Why There May Not be a Catholic Majority', *Parliamentary Brief*, 5(6), May/June, 52–53.

Coxall, B. and Robins, L. (1998) *British Politics Since the War* (Basingstoke: Macmillan).

Craig, F.W.S. (1989) *British Electoral Facts 1832–1987*, 5th edn (Aldershot: Gower).

Curtis, S. and Vidler, G. (1999) *Scottish Parliament Election Results 6 May 1999*, Scottish Parliament Research Paper 99/1 (http://www.scottish.parliament.uk/whats_happening/research/rp991–00.htm)

Denver, D. (1992) 'The 1992 General Election: In Defence of Psephology', *Talking Politics*, 5(1), pp. 2–6.

Dickson, M. (1998) 'No Let up in Labour's Pain', *The Herald*, 6 July, p. 7.

Gay, O. (1998) *The Northern Ireland Bill: Some Legislative and Operational Aspects of the Assembly* Research Paper 98/77 (London: House of Commons Library).

Geekie, J. and Levy, R. (1989) 'Devolution and the Tartanisation of the Labour Party', *Parliamentary Affairs*, 42(3), pp. 399–411.

Griffiths, D. (1996) *Thatcherism and Territorial Politics: A Welsh Case Study* (Aldershot: Avebury).

Hechter, M. (1975) *Internal Colonialism: The Celtic Fringe in British National Development 1536–1966* (London: Routledge & Kegan Paul).

HM Government (1998) *The Belfast Agreement: An Agreement Reached at the Multi-Party Talks on Northern Ireland*, Cm 3883 (London: HMSO).

Holtham, G. and Barrett, E. (1996) 'The Head and the Heart: Devolution and Wales' in Tindale, S. (ed.) *The State and the Nations: The Politics of Devolution* (London: Institute for Public Policy Research).

Irish Times (1998) 'The Path to Peace' (http://www.irish-times.com./irish-times/special/peace/counts.results.cfm).

Jones, B. (1997) 'Welsh Politics and Changing British and European Contexts' in Bradbury, J. and Mawson, J. (eds) *British Regionalism and Devolution* (London: Jessica Kingsley).

Kay, N. (1998) 'The Scottish Parliament and the Barnett Formula', *Quarterly Economic Commentary*, 24 (1) pp. 32–48.

Keating, M. and Midwinter, A. (1983) *The Government of Scotland* (Edinburgh: Mainstream).

Kellas, J.G. (1984) *The Scottish Political System*, 3rd edn (Cambridge: Cambridge University Press).

Kellas, J.G. (1991) 'The Scottish and Welsh Offices as Territorial Managers', *Regional Politics and Policy*, 1(1), pp. 87–100.

Kellas, J.G. (1992) 'The Scottish Constitutional Convention', in Paterson, L. and McCrone, D. (eds) *The Scottish Government Yearbook 1992* (Edinburgh: Unit for the Study of Government in Scotland).

Lee, C.H. (1995) *Scotland and the United Kingdom: The Economy and the Union in the Twentieth Century* (Manchester: Manchester University Press).

Levy, R. (1992) 'The Scottish Constitutional Convention, Nationalism and the Union', *Government and Opposition*, 27(2), pp. 222–34.

Levy, R. (1995) 'Governing Scotland, Wales and Northern Ireland', in Pyper, R. and Robins, L. (eds) *Governing the UK in the 1990s* (Basingstoke: Macmillan).

Lijphart, A. (1996) 'The "Framework" Proposal for Northern Ireland and the Theory of Power-Sharing' *Government and Opposition*, 31(3), pp. 267–274.

Lyons, F. (1990) 'Beyond Political Statement: New Thinking on Northern Ireland' in Savage, S.P. and Robins, L. (eds) *Public Policy Under Thatcher* (Basingstoke: Macmillan).

McAllister, L. (1998) 'The Welsh Devolution Referendum: Definitely, Maybe?', *Parliamentary Affairs*, 51(2), pp. 149–65.

MacLeod, C. (1997) 'Adrift on a Wave of Apathy', *The Herald*, 20 September, p. 6.

McConnell, A. (1992) 'Scotland After the General Election: The Constitution in Flux?', *Talking Politics*, 5(1), pp. 15–17.

McConnell, A. (1997) 'The Doomsday Scenario: 1997 General Election in Scotland', *Talking Politics*, 10(1), pp. 9–13.

McConnell, A. and Pyper, R. (1994) 'The Revived Select Committee on Scottish Affairs: A Case Study of Parliamentary Contradictions' *Strathclyde Papers on Government and Politics*, 98 (Glasgow: University of Strathclyde).

Mitchell, J. (1996) *Strategies for Self-Government: The Campaigns for a Scottish Parliament* (Edinburgh: Polygon)

Mitchell, J., Denver, D., Pattie, C. and Bochel, H. (1998) 'The Devolution Referendum in Scotland' *Parliamentary Affairs*, 51(2), pp. 166–81.

Morgan, K.O. (1981) *Rebirth of a Nation: Wales 1880–1980* (Cardiff: University of Wales Press).

Morgan, B. (1999) *Welsh Assembly Elections: 6 May 1999*, House of Commons Research Paper 99/51 (http://www.parliament.uk/commons/lib/research/rp99/rp99–051.pdf).

Nairn, T. (1977) *The Break-up of Britain* (London: New Left Books).

Nairn, T. (1998) *Memorandum of Evidence Submitted to the Select Committee on Scottish Affairs 16 June 1998* (http://www.parliament.the-stationery-office.co.uk/pa/cm199798/cmselect/cmscotaf/460/8062408.htm).

Northern Ireland Office (1998) *The Search For a Political Settlement in Northern Ireland* (http://www.nio.gov.uk/polcnts.htm).

O'Leary, B. and Evans, G. (1997) 'Northern Ireland', *Parliamentary Affairs*, 50(4), pp. 672–680.

Pyper, R. (1999) 'The Civil Service: A Neglected Dimension of Devolution', *Public Money and Management*, April–June, pp. 1–5.

Redwood, J. (1995) 'Welsh Devolution: A Talking Shop Neither Wales Nor Britain Needs', *Parliamentary Brief*, June, pp. 38–9.

Rhodes, R.A.W. (1988) *Beyond Westminster and Whitehall* (London: Routledge).

Rokkan, S. and Urwin, D. (1982) 'Introduction: Centres and Peripheries in Western Europe' in Rokkan, S. and Urwin, D. (eds) *The Politics of Territorial Identity – Studies in European Regionalism* (London: Sage).

Rose, R. (1982) *Understanding the United Kingdom: The Territorial Dimension in Government* (London: Longman).

Scotland on Sunday (1998) 'The ICM Research Scotland on Sunday Poll', *Scotland on Sunday*, 3 May, p. 11

Scottish Constitutional Convention (1990) *Towards Scotland's Parliament* (Edinburgh: COSLA).

Scottish National Party (1997) *Yes We Can – The Manifesto of the Scottish National Party for the 1997 General Election* (Edinburgh: Scottish National Party).

Scottish Office (1993) *Scotland in the Union – A Partnership for Good*, Cm 2225 (Edinburgh: HMSO).

Scottish Office (1997) *Scotland's Parliament*, Cm 3658 (Edinburgh: HMSO).

Select Committee on Scottish Affairs (1997–98) *The Operation of Multi-Layer Democracy*, HC460–I (London: HMSO).

Select Committee on Procedure (1998–99) *The Procedural Consequences of Devolution*, HC 185 (London: HMSO)

Standing Commission on the Scottish Economy (1989) *First Report* (Glasgow: Standing Commission on the Scottish Economy).

Treasury Select Committee (1997) *The Barnett Formula: Second Report of the Treasury Select Committee*, HC341 (London: HMSO).

Treasury Select Committee (1998) *The Barnett Formula: The Government's Response to the Committee's Second Report of Session 1997–98*, HC 619 (London: HMSO).

Twigger, R. (1998) *The Barnett Formula*, Research Paper 98/8 (London: House of Commons Library)

Welsh Office (1997a) *A Voice for Wales*, Cm 3718 (London: HMSO).

Welsh Office (1997b) *An Economic Strategy for Wales: A Welsh Office Consultation Document* (http://www.welsh-ofce.gov.uk/aesfw(e).html).

Winetrobe, B. (1998) *The Northern Ireland Bill: Implementing the Belfast Agreement* Research Paper 98/76 (London: House of Commons Library).

10

New Labour, New Local Governance?

DAVID WILSON

The 1997 Labour Party manifesto asserted that 'local decision-making should be less constrained by central government, and also more accountable to local people'. While there was no Local Government Bill *per se* in the Labour government's Queen's Speech, intended to cover the first eighteen months of its period in office, there were, as Table 10.1 shows, promises of action in a number of areas directly related to local government (e.g. devolution, education, housing, elected mayors). At one level, therefore, change was clearly on the agenda. At the same time, however, the erosion of local authorities as direct service providers did not seem likely to be suddenly or dramatically reversed – not least because of the manifesto's view of their role (p. 34):

> we see no reason why a service should be delivered directly (by local councils) if other more efficient means are available.

Change, then, was in the air at the end of the 1990s, but not an uncritical return to the era of elected local authorities as near monopolistic service providers. Indeed Tony Blair warned in March 1998:

> The government will not hesitate to intervene directly to secure improvements where services fall below acceptable standards. And if necessary, it will look to other authorities and agencies to take on duties where an

256

authority is manifestly incapable of providing an effective service and unwilling to take the action necessary to improve its performance.

This chapter, which focuses on the nature of contemporary local government, is in two distinct parts. The first part examines the changing role and functions of local government at the end of the 1990s and discusses the advent of local governance. The second part focuses specifically on the single most contentious area, central –

TABLE 10.1   *The Blair Government – Proposed Legislation Affecting Local and Regional Government*

Referendums (Scotland and Wales) Referendums on devolving powers to a Scottish Parliament and Welsh Assembly	**Regional Development Agencies** Regional development agencies to coordinate economic development in England, working with organisations such as regional bodies representing local authorities
Education Raise education standards, including setting local education authorities targets for improvements; put parents on education committees and subject LEAs to inspection by the Office of Standards and Effectiveness and the Audit Commission	**National Lottery (amendment)** Establish fund from proceeds of midweek lottery to support innovative education and health projects
Education (reduction in class sizes) Cut class sizes to 30 or less for all five, six and seven-year-olds, funded by phasing out the assisted places scheme	**Local Authority (capital receipts)** Phased release of capital receipts from the sale of council houses to build and renovate social housing
Crime and Disorder Establish local crime prevention partnerships; take action against anti-social neighbours	**Data Protection** Tighten data protection rules to give greater protection to the individual; will include some manual records
Greater London Authority (referendum) Vote for a London-wide authority and a directly-elected mayor	**Freedom of Information** White Paper due as first step towards fulfilling pledge to more open government

Source: *Local Government Chronicle*, 16 May 1997.

local relations, and discusses what impact the transition to a Labour government is having upon relationships. A concluding section reflects upon Labour's commitment to enhance the democratic dimensions of local governance.

The Changing Role and Functions of Local Government

The Advent of Governance

In its February 1998 consultative paper, *Modernising Local Government* (Department of the Environment, Transport and the Regions, 1998) the Labour government emphasised its belief in democratic local government (p. 1) 'We do so because democratically elected local government is vital in ensuring people have the quality of life that they deserve. Local government matters'. But elected local government is now but one part of a complex mosaic of bodies operating locally. It is part of what has become known as 'local governance'. Whereas local *government* is concerned with the formal institutions of government at the local level, local *governance* focuses upon the wider processes through which public policy is effected in localities.

Governance refers to the development and implementation of public policy through a broader range of public and private agencies than those traditionally associated with elected local government. Partnerships, networks and contracts have thereby become integral parts of the local political scene.

Under the Thatcher and Major governments elected local authorities were seen as 'enabling' in the *limited* sense of agencies which made arrangements for the provision of those services which the market could not or was not prepared to provide. The Labour government, however, has adopted a more *expansive* interpretation of 'enabling', largely reflecting the view expressed by Clarke and Stewart (1988, p. 1): 'the role of an enabling council is to use all the means at its disposal to meet the needs of those who live within the area'. Negotiation with the private sector to stimulate economic activity, empowerment of local communities, imaginative use of regulatory powers, partnerships with other public bodies and private sector organisations are all means to this end. In other words, the Blair government appears to have adopted a much more positive interpretation of enabling than the minimalist one which dominated the 1979–97 era.

A fragmented pattern of service delivery at local level has become a reality. But, as Goldsmith (1997, p. 7) emphasises, the idea of governance implies more than simply a variety of local institutions providing services:

> It places an emphasis on vertical co-operation between institutions and tiers or levels of government, and on horizontal co-operation between public, private and voluntary sectors at the local level . . . Governance raises other particular problems: of openness and transparency; of accessibility to citizens; and of public accountability for actions.

But how new is governance? Contrary to much of the prevailing wisdom, Stanyer (1996, p. 1) argues that it has a long pedigree. Following an overview of the last 200 years he concludes:

> Local public functions have always been carried out by local quangos, field administration, local trusts, local co-operatives and local firms and these have been noticeable elements in society, economy and the political system since industrialisation began . . . The use of organisational forms which are not local government narrowly defined has always been a feature of the British system of government.

While important lessons can undoubtedly be drawn from the past, the context is very different today. This inevitably makes the drawing of parallels rather problematical. What is clear though is that the central position of elected local authorities is under challenge as they find themselves 'sharing the local turf' (Davies, 1996, p. 1) with a whole range of bodies also exercising governmental powers at the local level. Diversity characterises the contemporary world of local governance.

Structural Change: Democratic Deficit?

Following the reorganisations of local government in London in the 1960s, in the rest of the country in the 1970s and in metropolitan England in the 1980s (see Wilson and Game, 1998, ch. 4), there was further country-wide structural reform during the 1990s. The most convincing explanation for this, Leach suggests (1995, p. 50):

centres on the political ambition of one individual. It was part of the vision of a contender for the leadership of the Conservative Party, who became instead Secretary of State for the Environment.

This minister was Michael Heseltine and it was his enthusiasm that drove the reform process forward even when other members of the government (and, indeed, his own successors at the DoE) seemed lukewarm.

The Conservative government had wanted to see a substantial increase in the number of unitary authorities as a result of the work of the commission which it had established under Sir John Banham. At one point it looked as though almost 100 new unitary authorities embracing more than two-thirds of the population of the English non-metropolitan counties would emerge but, faced with a public sceptical about the likely benefits of such fundamental change, the commission adapted many of its draft recommendations to 'hybrid' solutions: the occasional unitary authority in otherwise unchanged two-tier counties.

The reform saga was tortuous. Few people regarded the upheaval and turmoil as worthwhile. In the end a total of 46 new unitary authorities emerged, covering about a quarter of the population of non-metropolitan England and beginning their lives variously from 1995 to 1998 (Wilson, 1996). In Scotland, as in Wales, there was no commission to oversee the reform process. Here the respective Secretaries of State effectively determined the outcomes. In April 1996, 22 new Welsh unitary authorities replaced the existing 45 councils and in Scotland 32 single-tier authorities replaced the existing 65 authorities. The reduction in the number of British local authorities during the 1990s is highlighted in Table 10.2. There was no change in Northern Ireland where the 26 district councils remained, albeit with substantially less functions than their counterparts in mainland Britain.

While in the mid-1990s elected local government in England, Scotland and Wales was streamlined there was a gradual deterioration in terms of its 'closeness to the people' to such an extent that some saw local democracy as being seriously threatened. In the early 1970s there were 1425 principal local authorities in England and Wales. In 1974 this was cut back to 456, a reduction of 68 per cent with an accompanying reduction in the number of elected councillors. In Scotland, the mid-1970s saw 65 councils replace

TABLE 10.2   *The Reduction of British Local Authorities in the 1990s*

Year	Shire Districts	Shire Counties	New Unitaries	London Boro/Met Authorities	Scottish	Welsh	Total
1994	296	39	0	69	65	45	514
1995	294	38	1	69	65	45	512
1996	274	35	14	69	32	22	446
1997	260	35	27	69	32	22	445
1998	238	34	46	69	32	22	441
	−58	−5	+46	–	−33	−23	−73

TABLE 10.3   *Britain's Large-Scale Local Government*

	Inhabitants per elected member	Population per council
France	116	1 580
Iceland	194	1 330
Germany	250	4 925
Italy	397	7 130
Norway	515	9 000
Spain	597	4 930
Sweden	667	30 040
Belgium	783	16 960
Denmark	1 084	18 760
Portugal	1 125	32 300
UK	2 605	118 400

Note: To enable realistic comparison with other countries' local and communal councillors, these Council of Europe figures illustrate only councillors of principal authorities, i.e. *not* the approximately 80 000 members of parish, town and community councils, which are not universal and are mostly very small with very limited service responsibilities.

Source: Council of Europe (1996) *Local and Regional Authorities in Europe*, No. 56.

430 authorities. The mid-1990s witnessed further reductions, as we saw earlier, with 22 new unitary authorities replacing the existing 45 councils in Wales and 32 replacing 65 in Scotland. Councillor numbers were reduced in line with the above. As Table 10.3 shows, compared with much of Europe, Britain has significantly bigger local authorities and far more inhabitants per

elected member. To what extent does this represent a 'democratic deficit'?

The numbers of local authorities and elected councillors have declined markedly over the past two decades, but given the advent of a fragmented pattern of local governance in which councillors have a less direct operational role it could be argued that it is not unreasonable for there to be fewer councillors. Is it not a more pressing priority to search for new forms of accountability for those non-elected bodies which are delivering services at local level rather than simply lamenting the demise of an often idealised directly-elected element? Are more councillors necessarily the answer if, once in office, they have relatively little influence on policy initiation or implementation? Traditionalists such as Jones and Stewart argue strongly that local government is enhanced as local democracy by the closeness of council members to those they represent (1993, p. 15):

> A greater number of members embeds local government into the grass roots. They make local government more responsive to the local community and understanding of its wishes and needs.

In a similar vein, traditionalists see the rise of non-elected bodies, such as Training and Enterprise Councils (TECs), District Health Authorities (DHAs), Health Trusts, and Housing Actions Trusts (HATs), as sinister, largely because they are not directly elected. Certainly, local authorities currently remain the only agencies subject to local electoral control but, as Stoker notes (1995, pp. 10–11), 'the forms of direct participation offered through some of the new agencies of local governance and the capacity of these agencies to work together to tackle a range of social and economic needs in localities might be seen as a gain for local democracy and government'. Local democracy must be seen as more than occasional trips to the ballot box by a minority of the electorate. Only 29 per cent of the electorate voted in the 1998 local elections; in a by-election in December 1998 for a Tamworth Borough Council ward the turnout was a paltry 6 per cent. Alternative modes of accountability should not be dismissed out of hand, particularly given revelations of corruption in a not inconsiderable number of largely one-party local authorities in the late 1990s. Too idealistic a view of elected local government is simply naive.

Internal Management: Local Experimentation

Interest in the internal management of local authorities is reviving, largely because of the Labour Party's 1997 election manifesto commitment to 'encourage democratic innovations in local government, including pilots of the idea of elected mayors with executive powers in cities'. Indeed, in May 1998 a referendum was held on the establishment of a strategic authority for London, headed by a separately elected mayor. Only 34 per cent of the electorate in London voted, but they were overwhelmingly in favour of the directly-elected mayor model.

Proposals for internal management reform ran parallel with Michael Heseltine's enthusiasm for structural reform. In July 1991 he produced a consultation paper entitled *The Internal Management of Local Authorities in England* (Department of the Environment, 1991) which put forward a range of options, most of which involved replacing the committee system – which Heseltine believed to be inefficient – with some form of either separate appointed or elected executive. The consultation paper was not enthusiastically received by councillors who were predictably unimpressed by the democratic implications of the emphasis on streamlining the decision-making process. The Conservative government's next move was to set up a joint working party of DoE nominees and representatives of the local authority associations, which produced a report entitled *Community Leadership and Representation: Unlocking the Potential* (Department of the Environment, 1993). This argued that councils should at least consider the merits of more radical and experimental forms of internal management, something which the Blair government was keen to pursue. What are the advantages and disadvantages of such executive models of local political leadership?

Stoker and Wolman (1991), drawing on USA experience, argue that such mayors in the UK could provide a focal point and driving force for a more dynamic and influential local government. The system produces a high profile figure with whom the public can identify and hold to account – but in such contexts scandals over, for example, the letting of contracts and the use of public funds are not uncommon. Directly-elected political executives, individual or collective, could lead to a far more elitist local government system, with relatively few councillors having any really decisive policy-making significance. The representative nature of local government could thereby suffer; fewer decision-takers with less detailed local knowledge could result in more streamlined but less sensitive community government. Local government might raise its public profile but in doing so become less representative of grassroots need, unless the scrutiny role of the full council were to be considerably strengthened.

The tremendous diversity of local authorities means that it is not desirable to have a single 'standardised package' which can be taken off the shelf and applied to every authority. Internal management patterns need to relate to the particular circumstances and culture of each individual authority. In this context the Blair government came up with three possible models in its July 1998 White Paper, *Modern Local Government: In Touch with the People.* Central to the White Paper was the splitting of the executive and scrutiny functions.

Table 10.4 summarises the three models of executive leadership outlined in the White Paper. Each local authority will be expected to make a response to central government on the basis of one of the three models. If a local council is perceived to be dragging its feet the government will use reserve powers 'to require the council to hold a referendum asking the local electorate to support one of the approved models'. In other words, if the carrot fails to deliver a satisfactory response the government will be unafraid to use the stick and force local authorities to modernise.

TABLE 10.4   *New Models of Political Management*

Option	Model
1	*A directly-elected mayor with a cabinet.* The mayor will be directly elected by the whole electorate and will appoint a cabinet from among the councillors
2	*A cabinet with a leader.* The leader will be elected by the council, and the cabinet will be made up of councillors either appointed by the leader or elected by the council.
3	*A directly-elected mayor with a council manager.* The mayor will be directly elected by local people, with a full-time manager appointed by the council to whom both strategic policy and day-to-day decision-making would be delegated.

Source: *Modern Local Government: In Touch with the People* (July 1998).

Changing Patterns of Service Provision

In the context of local governance John Stewart laments what he calls the rise of a 'new magistracy' (1995, p. 62), non-elected, largely central government-appointed personnel controlling an increasing proportion of service provision at local level. Such nominees now greatly exceed the number of elected local councillors (some 75 000 'quangocrats' compared with about 23 000 elected members). The bodies on which such nominees sit form an increasingly important part of governance at the local level. Davies (1996, p. 1) outlines the major steps in the growth of government by appointment:

- Local authority representatives removed from District Health Authorities.
- Appointed boards set up to run newly created Health Service Trusts.
- Training and Enterprise Councils (TECs) created to exercise training and development functions at local level, many of which were once exercised by local authorities.
- Self-appointing boards of governors took over responsibility from local authorities for polytechnics, further education colleges and sixth form colleges.
- Under the Conservatives, schools encouraged to opt out of local authority control and become grant-maintained, financed by new nationally-appointed funding councils.
- Housing Action Trusts and Urban Development Corporations appointed to take over local authority responsibility in selected localities.
- The establishment of new police authorities, substantially weakening the link with elected local government.

In Autumn 1997 the Cabinet Office published a consultation paper on quangos, *Opening Up Quangos: A Consultation Paper*, covering issues of accountability, appointments and openness. Responses to this were to be fed into the 'Better Government' initiatives to be announced in 1998. Among the proposals put forward by the Labour government in the discussion paper were:

- quangos should be reviewed every five years, to see if their functions are still required;

- quangos should produce annual reports;
- they should hold meetings in public, such as an annual open meeting, and release summary reports of meetings and press releases;
- membership of the quango boards to be published on the Internet;
- efficiency reports on the larger quangos to be published.

Despite the greatly increased service delivery role of such non-elected quangos, it is a mistake to underestimate the continued importance of elected local authorities as service providers. Indeed, according to Midwinter (1995, p. 131) 'despite the welter of rhetoric, the image of radical reform, the language of new public management, the glitz of marketing and public relations, the central role of a local authority remains – municipal provision of services'. As noted earlier, partnerships with the non-elected, private and voluntary sectors have become increasingly prevalent, one of the best examples being the provision of community care. Nevertheless, while there is less *direct* provision by local government, service provision remains a major role, albeit not necessarily through direct employment and in-house management. Its combined current and capital expenditure in 1996/97 was well over £80 billion, or more than a quarter of all government spending. Providing services locally is still big business. The categorisation in Table 10.5 indicates the range of services for which local authorities are responsible.

The Labour government's first budget allowed local councils to spend just £900 million on social housing in the first two years of the government's period in office. Since capital receipts from council house sales totalled around £5 billion, this represented a cautious start to the regeneration of social housing. Given the government's plan to allocate spending to improve housing based on a formula weighted two-thirds according to relative housing need and one-third to receipts set aside from council house sales, Birmingham City Council will be the biggest beneficiary with £21.8 million in 1998/99.

Another significant area of change is the dismantling of Compulsory Competitive Tendering (CCT). Of all the changes introduced by the 1979–97 Conservative Governments, probably the most fundamental and far-reaching were those associated with CCT. Legislation forced local authorities to put specified services out to

TABLE 10.5 *A Categorisation of Local Services*

1. Need Services – e.g. education, personal social services. Services provided for all, regardless of means, and which therefore contribute to the redistribution of resources within the community. Need services account for well over half the total net expenditure on all local government services.
2. Protective Services – e.g. fire and rescue, and most obviously, the police, until the creation of the new independent police authorities in April 1995. Services provide for the security of people, to national guidelines. Access to them cannot be restricted, and use by one person does not affect availability to others.
3. Amenity Services – e.g. highways, street cleansing, planning, parks and open spaces, environmental health, refuse disposal, consumer protection, economic development. Services provided largely to locally-determined standards to meet the needs of each local community.
4. Facility Services – e.g. housing, libraries, museums and art galleries, recreational centres, refuse collection, cemeteries and crematoria. Services for people to draw upon if they wish, sometimes in competition with private sector provision.

Source: Adapted from Hollis *et al.*, 1990.

competitive tender on terms and timescales established by the centre. The 1997 Labour Party manifesto promised an end to the blanket compulsion: 'Councils should not be forced to put their services out to tender – but [they] will be required to obtain *best value*' (author's emphasis). The aim was for CCT to disappear as quickly as possible and the November 1998 Queen's Speech announced a Local Government Bill which set out to replace CCT with best value and abolish crude universal capping, all by April 2000. The 'Twelve Principles of Best Value' set out by the Government are presented in Table 10.6. While competition is set to continue to be an 'important management tool' it will be insufficient on its own to demonstrate best value.

Local authorities are only one part of a complex mosaic of agencies operating at the local level, but they remain a uniquely, pivotal, multi-functional, directly-elected part of the mosaic, not easily sidelined even by a relatively hostile central government. Their role has changed but that must not be allowed to obscure their continuing importance. Where, though, inside local authorities does power and influence reside?

TABLE 10.6   *The Twelve Principles of Best Value*

1	Councils will owe a duty of best value to local people, both as taxpayers and service customers. Performance plans should support local accountability.		performance indicators to support competition between councils.
2	Best value is about effectiveness and quality, not just economy and efficiency. Target-setting should underpin the new regime.	8	National and local targets should be built on performance information.
3	The best value duty should apply to a wider range of services than CCT.	9	Auditors should confirm the integrity and comparability of performance information.
4	There is no presumption that services must be privatised or delivered directly. What matters is what works.	10	Auditors will report publicly on whether best value has been achieved and contribute to plans for remedial action.
5	Competition will continue as an important management tool but will not in itself demonstrate best value.	11	There should be provision for DETR intervention, on Audit Commission advice, to tackle failing councils.
6	Central government will continue to set the basic framework for service provision.	12	The form of intervention, including requirements to expose services to competition and accept external management support, should be appropriate to the nature of the failure.
7	Local targets should have regard to national targets and		

Source: *Local Government Chronicle*, 6 June 1997.

Who makes policy?

Traditionally, a number of models are used to describe the distribution of power and influence inside local authorities. The *formal* model, with its legal-institutional emphasis, argues that theory and practice equate, namely that elected councillors make policy while appointed officers advise them and carry it out. At the other extreme, the *technocratic* model views officers, with their specialised technical and professional knowledge, as the dominant force in local politics. Both these models simplify reality and have obvious shortcomings, hence the development of a further perspective – the *corporate* or joint elite model – which argues that policy-making is dominated by a small group of senior councillors *and* officers. This model sees backbench councillors and junior officers as only marginally involved. The merits of this model are proclaimed widely. For example, Blowers (1980, pp. 10–11) observes:

> The power to make policy and take decisions is concentrated among a few leading officials and politicians. The interaction of these decision-makers and the transmission of ideas and hopes and fears among them, reveals how power is exercised and to what purpose.

This model helpfully distinguishes between senior councillors and officers and their more junior colleagues, but it ignores other elements (e.g. pressure groups, intra-party influences, interdepartmental rivalries) which need to be incorporated into any genuinely realistic model of decision-making inside local authorities (see Stoker and Wilson, 1986). But while the centrality of the joint officer-councillor elite is not questioned, their exclusive dominance is. Local authorities are *political* institutions; they incorporate a whole range of elements that impinge upon policy-making, depending on an authority's traditions, culture, leadership, political balance and so on. Policy making is not solely the preserve of leading councillors and officers. It is far more ambiguous and messy than any single model can portray.

Centrally important in the culture of the vast majority of contemporary local authorities is the role of *political parties*. Over four-fifths of British local authorities have either all or a great majority of councillors elected under the labels of national or nationalist political parties. In the more rural areas, however, party systems are largely absent; indeed, in some 68 authorities (in 1996/97) over 20 per cent of seats were held by Independents (see Wilson and Game, 1998, Exhibit 14.1). As Table 10.7 illustrates, in 1997/98 the Labour Party was particularly strong locally. The Liberal Democrats were in an unambiguous second place, ahead of the Conservatives who had lost nearly 95 per cent of the councils they controlled in 1979. The widespread party politicisation of local government received a further boost with the recent reorganisation and the spread of geographically larger unitary authorities.

Despite all the potential disadvantages associated with 'one party states' there is much to be said for conflicting views being marshalled and articulated openly by consciously accountable party

TABLE 10.7   *Party Control of Local Authorities, 1997/98*

Type of control	Number	%
Conservative	23	5
Labour	205	47
Liberal Democrat	50	11
Nationalist Parties	4	1
Independent	25	6
No overall control	134	30
Total	441	100

politicians, rather than by self-styled 'non-political representatives' whose motives and policy objectives could be left publicly unspecified. With the exception of the relatively few non-partisan authorities the party political dimension is an essential ingredient of the policy-making mix.

In a similar vein, local pressure groups can be an important influence in shaping policy. For example, Marinetto (1997, p. 27) argued that in Camden the dominant 'elite axis' of senior officers and elected members has been 'increasingly undermined by the assertiveness of members and interest groups'. Indeed, most studies of local communities point to an extensive local group universe. Newton, in a study of Birmingham City Council in the 1960s, entitled his chapter on local pressure groups 'The Politics of the Four Thousand', reflecting the fact that he had identified no fewer than 4264 voluntary organisations in the city (Newton, 1996).

Most early studies emphasised that pressure-group influence was largely related to local party control, so radical-left groups were marginalised in Conservative-controlled authorities, and radical-right groups were equally impotent in Labour-controlled authorities. But the significance of local pressure groups has grown partly because of the way in which many groups now collaborate with local authorities in the provision of services. Local authorities are increasingly prepared to provide grants to, or establish service level agreements with, local groups in exchange for help with the provision of community services. Such contracts between local authorities and groups are a constraining influence on local group activity since few groups deem it prudent to bite the hand that feeds them.

In today's fragmented world of local governance, elected local authorities are no longer the automatic hub of the local political system. Groups are increasingly finding sponsorship and support from non-elected agencies (e.g. TECs) as well as from Europe. At the same time, legislative changes have increased the dependence of local authorities on the voluntary sector to implement their programmes and deliver services (e.g. Community Care). In a similar vein, some measures incorporated in recent environmental legislation require councils to look to the voluntary sector for help and technical assistance. As with everything else in local government, patterns vary from authority to authority, but pressure groups have undoubtedly become integral parts of the world of local governance. Even the apparently least political of groups can be drawn into the political process, if only intermittently. Thus a local gardening association resisting a proposal to build a road over its land becomes temporarily a pressure group. At local level many groups are precisely such single-purpose groups which rise and fall with specific issues, e.g. local planning matters. *Ad hoc* and transient as many such groups might be, their significance, on occasions, can be considerable.

Central–Local Government Relations

Central government was quick to signal a new commitment to dialogue and consultation with local government. As Hilary Armstrong, the new Labour government's first Minister for Local Government promised in a speech in June 1997:

> We are not just a new Government, we are a new type of Government. Our decisions will not be handed down from on high ... We do not have a monopoly of wisdom and ideas. We want to hear your ideas and we want you to tell us what you think of ours.

In the same speech the new Minister called for an end to old style consultation arrangements between central and local government:

> Let us sweep away the formal, ritualistic gatherings of ministers and local government leaders which I think we all agree have become rather pointless affairs. We would like to replace these sessions with more coherent and constructive contacts on main service issues and finance.

A few months later, in November 1997, Deputy Prime Minister John Prescott and Local Government Association chairman Sir Jeremy Beecham signed a Concordat setting out the terms of the working relationship between central and local government. The framework document outlined six major principles, including a promise to give local government greater authority and financial freedom – within the constraints of national economic policy – and enshrined the commitment to 'best value' in service provision. It also recognised the 'independent democratic legitimacy of local government'. One crucial paragraph in the accompanying 12 point schedule emphasised:

> Where the Government considers that a local authority (or a local authority service) is falling below an acceptable standard it will work with the authority concerned to secure improvements. The Government reserves its right to exercise any powers under statute to intervene in cases of service failure and will discuss with the LGA its policy for the use of those powers including how best to facilitate a supportive role for the LGA. (See *Municipal Journal*, 7 November 1997)

The retention of such powers by central government – particularly the special improvement teams or 'hit squads' to address serious failings in education and social services standards – caused a good deal of concern amongst local authorities because of the perceived failure to honour the spirit of the 1997 Concordat which promised a 'supportive role for the Local Government Association' in such instances. Likewise, there is a concern that local government has been marginalised in key consultation exercises such as the Royal Commission on long-term care, and that the 'partnership' spirit has been breached in instances such as the government's surprise announcement of details of education action zones in 1998 (see Lowndes, 1998). Similar fears were expressed in January 1999 when the LGA launched a campaign to 'keep education democratic' following reports that the government was about to privatise failing schools and local education authorities (see *Local Government Chronicle*, 8 January 1999).

The Formal Framework

There are a number of formal elements shaping the relationship between central government departments and local authorities. *Legislation* is the most direct instrument of control and one that has been used with great frequency in recent years. The Conservative governments from 1979 to 1997 produced over 210 Acts of Parliament affecting local government, at least a third of them in major and far-reaching ways. *Statutory instruments* provide a means whereby ministers can 'flesh out' their own primary legislation and thereby strengthen, if they choose, their controls over local authorities' actions and activities; currently there are some 3000 statutory instruments issued each year. In addition to statutory instruments, government departments issue *circulars* to local authorities containing 'advice' and 'guidance' on how they should exercise their various responsibilities. Such circulars are often seen as vehicles for central direction, but not all circulars are directive, and some are the product of genuine negotiation with relevant local government professional bodies and contain useful practical advice for local authorities.

The period since 1979 has seen an explosion in the number of disputes between central government and local authorities being settled in the courts. In 1974 leave for what is known as *judicial review* was sought 160 times. By 1995 this had increased to 4 400. This figure reflects the deteriorating informal networks. As old understandings collapsed under the impact of politicisation, the courts stepped in to regulate the relationship.

Default powers, namely central government taking over a local authority's service provision in a specific policy area, have become increasingly topical, especially in the fields of education and social services. In 1995, the Education Secretary, Gillian Shepherd, appointed an 'Education Association' – or 'government hit squad', as the media labelled it – to run Hackney Downs Comprehensive School in East London following a critical report from the Office for Standards in Education (OFSTED). In a similar vein, the Blair government, emphasising its 'zero tolerance' of poor standards, quickly issued a hit list of some eighteen allegedly failing schools that would receive similar visitations.

In October 1997 the Labour government served notice on councils which offered sub-standard social services. Attacking one of them, Cambridgeshire County Council, Paul Boateng, junior health minister observed, 'Those who persistently fail the vulnerable have no place in public life or the public service. The Secretary of State will be ready to use his powers to intervene in the running of social services in the county, should this be necessary'. The threat of 'hit squads', already a reality for failing education authorities, loomed large for social service departments. Government-appointed *inspectors*, like those of OFSTED referred to above, are a further means of central supervision of local authority services.

It is important to recognise that *finance* remains a major vehicle through which central government can attempt to control local authorities, first through regulating the amount of money which can be spent locally, and, secondly, by scrutinising the way in which money is actually spent. The Local Government Bill in November 1998, set out to end crude universal capping but it also introduced reserve powers to limit excessive council tax increases. Indeed, during its second reading debate in the Commons (January 1999) the Conservatives attacked the Bill for handing ministers 27 new powers to control councils. Conservative environment spokesman Bernard Jenkin claimed that the Bill represented 'a further lurch towards the nationalisation of local councils. Even the best-run councils will live in fear of the Secretary of State exercising his new and wide-ranging discretionary powers'. Jenkin argued that the 27 new powers encompassed the ability to constrain budgets and the ability to take over the running of services. He also claimed crude and universal capping was to be replaced 'by capping that is secretive and retrospective'. Government ministers attempted to calm fears about the powerful intervention powers created by the Bill, which passed its second reading by a 164 majority. The centre's financial powers nevertheless remain a major bone of contention.

Working Relationships

While formal frameworks are clearly important, actual working relationships are frequently very different from those portrayed on organisation charts. In practice the picture is far from straightforward. Relationships vary over time, from authority to authority and from one service area to another. The uniqueness of local political systems, with their distinctive political outlooks, policy agendas, histories and traditions, means that universally applicable generalisations about 'central–local relations' are elusive. Complexity is compounded because 'the centre' is not a monolith either. Each of the major departments of state has its own traditions and culture and its preferred operating style: some departments are laissez-faire in their approach, intervening as little as possible; some are more regulatory; and some have a promotional outlook.

The reality, then, is very complex. Not only is there a multiplicity of local authorities, a diversity of central government departments and policy arenas, and a constantly changing party political dimension to consider. Realistic analysis must also take account of the many other appointed and representative intermediate agencies that go to make up 'sub-central government'. The decentralised offices of central government departments, local authority associations, pressure groups, professional associations, political parties, and voluntary sector organisations all require recognition. Linked to this are the territorially decentralised departments in Edinburgh and Cardiff (the Scottish Office and the Welsh Office) and the emergent devolved assemblies with their new array of powers. Complexity is the order of the day.

In England the Department of the Environment, Transport and the Regions (DETR) is the centre of extensive formal and informal communications networks within Whitehall relating to local government matters. Numerous other central government departments also have interests in local government which are handled through formal and informal civil service meetings, various *ad hoc* groups and committees. Rhodes, however, reminds us (1997, p. 137) that the creation of special purpose bodies and the bypassing of elected local government has fragmented service delivery systems and multiplied networks. More actors, notably from the private and voluntary sectors, are now involved. In this context central government 'can set the boundaries to network actions. It still funds the services. But it has also increased its dependence on multifarious networks'.

From April 1997 an umbrella Local Government Association (LGA) became the new representative voice of English local authorities, established to bring together a hitherto fragmented collection of smaller bodies with the aim of obtaining greater power and influence for local authorities. It soon became involved in government consultations on no less than fifty policy areas such as democratic renewal, capping, best value, and developing an integrated transport policy.

Integrated Regional Offices

In 1993 the Conservative Government announced a new single budget and new integrated regional offices (IROs) for England to take effect from April 1994. Environment Secretary John Gummer

claimed that these innovations would make government programmes and departments 'more responsive to local needs and
acceptable to local people'. He also declared that 'this signals an
important shift from the centre to the localities'. In practice, however, these have been perceived as central government regional
outposts rather than local offices in their own right. The 'integrated'
dimension is not helped by the fact that not all government departments are incorporated into the IROs. They cover only the regional
offices of the DETR, Trade and Industry, Education and Employment, all of which already had regional structures of sorts. Health is
not included, nor is the Department of National Heritage with its
focus on broadcasting, tourism and sport.

While the IROs have provided *some* integration at regional level,
local authorities in England still have to deal with a wide range of
government bodies and agencies, often with very different boundaries. The Labour government's Regional Development Agencies
(RDAs), became operational from April 1999 and, potentially,
provide a vehicle for greater decentralisation but the relationship
of RDAs with elected local authorities has yet to be worked out in
detail.

The Hunt Report: 1996

A major report on central–local relations in 1996 from an all-party
House of Lords select committee chaired by Lord Hunt, called for a
radical overhaul of central–local relations so that local government
'does not wither away through sheer neglect'. The committee
warned:

> There is a risk of a continued attrition of powers and responsibilities
> away from local government until nothing is left. We hope this report will
> help to alert the public to this danger, and lead to a more constructive
> partnership and the rebuilding of trust. (House of Lords, 1996)

The Conservative government issued a White Paper in response
to Hunt which was positive about the need for change in some
places but rather less so in others. For example, it refused Hunt's
recommendations to sign The European Charter of Local Self-
Government, or to return business rates to local control, but it
was prepared to support elected mayors and cabinets in some

councils, and it did promise new guidelines for central–local relations in England and Wales. The Hunt Report provided a challenging agenda for the incoming Labour government which promised to give its backing to Lord Hunt's Local Government (Experimental Arrangements) Bill, published in November 1997, which sought to give councils the freedom to experiment with new management structures – from elected mayors to cabinet-style executives. This Bill was widely perceived as the first step in introducing the necessary permanent powers to underpin a revived local democracy, but was 'talked out' by the Conservatives in March 1998 thereby necessitating the Labour government bringing in its own legislation to facilitate executive government at local level. The ensuing White Paper, *Modern Local Government: In Touch with the People* (July 1998) emphasised the need for modernisation, strong executive leadership and more meaningful public participation.

Beyond the English Dimension

When examining central–local government relations it is important to look beyond the rather narrow focus of Whitehall (English)–local authority relations to the considerably more complex and fragmented, but also more lifelike, world of sub-central governance. Perhaps most significant are the distinctive patterns of central-local relations which operate in Scotland, Wales and Northern Ireland.

Much of the literature ignores this distinctiveness and generalises from the English model. Change is happening in Scotland and Wales with the establishment from May 1999 of a 126-member Scottish legislative and tax-raising Parliament and a 60-member Welsh Assembly/Senedd with rather less powers, both elected by proportional representation. This brings a measure of home rule to Scotland and Wales for the first time since the Acts of Union in 1707 and 1535. The 'centre' for local authorities in Scotland and Wales is either Edinburgh or Cardiff, not London.

It is not really surprising that the Scottish Office, longer established and representing a country with its own distinctive legal and civil institutions, tends to be more pro-active in its relations with London than its Welsh counterpart. Both the Scottish and Welsh Offices are in the cross-pressured position of being at the same time agents of 'the centre' and advocates of the interests of particular territories. Ultimately, though, they are closer to and more part of

Whitehall than they are part of Scotland or Wales. In short, central–local relations in Scotland and Wales are distinctive more for how decisions are made than for the nature of the decisions themselves (see Midwinter, 1995, pp. 21–2).

The 26 district councils in Northern Ireland have relatively few executive functions: refuse collection and disposal and the provision of recreation and community services being their chief item of expenditure. It follows that the extent of regular interaction between central government – in this case the Northern Ireland Office in Belfast – and local authorities is less than in the rest of the UK. Major services – education, libraries, housing, health and social services – are run by appointed boards. As Connolly (1986, p. 15) has observed, the 'factor of size, combined with the lack of local powers and the tradition of looking to Stormont, means that there is a tendency for the centre to be the dominant influence'. Despite occasional concessions, taking Scotland, Wales and Northern Ireland together there can be no doubt where, in a unitary system of government, the source of power resides. The extent to which devolution will change this remains an open question.

In recent years central–local government relations have become high profile and contentious partly because, as Cochrane (1993) points out, the Conservative government met numerous obstacles in its attempts to exert control:

> Every change from above seems to have been met by adjustments else-where in the system first to take account of and then to evade the intended consequences of the central legislation. If the relationship between central and local government is a hierarchical one, it is certainly a complex hierarchy. It looks rather more like a constant process of negotiation in which the ground rules are not always clear and may be changed by the centre with often unpredictable consequences.

According to Rhodes (1988), the phrase 'policy mess' rather than 'centralisation' best characterised the post-1979 Conservative years. In others words, centralisation was an unintended by-product of a range of policy initiatives with other primary objectives. It needs to be recognised, however, that the 1979–97 era witnessed a clearly interventionist strategy in a wide range of areas (e.g. finance, compulsory competitive tendering, education, housing). Intervention became a reality even if control proved rather more elusive. The aim was to weaken and bypass elected local authorities and empower consumers.

As noted earlier, the 1997 Labour Party manifesto declared that local decision-making should be less constrained by central government and more accountable to local people. In June 1997 Hilary Armstrong, Labour Local Government Minister promised: 'We want to reinvigorate local government, to rekindle and reignite the energy that is so patently there to provide energetic local solutions to local problems'. Time will tell whether a new horizon is really set to emerge, but whatever happens the complexity of contemporary local governance means that it is no longer acceptable to see central–local relations purely in terms of central government and local authorities. Networks, alliances and partnerships between elected and non-elected bodies, voluntary organisations and private business operate at local level, albeit within a framework set down by the centre.

Conclusion

The Blair government soon began to implement its commitment to decentralise government and increase democratic participation. The most obvious examples were the Scottish, Welsh and Greater London referendums. More subtly the government allowed local authorities to come up with their own pilot schemes for 'best value' to replace Compulsory Competitive Tendering. Local authorities were also widely consulted about regional development agencies and elected regional chambers. In June 1997 the Labour Government signed the European Charter of Local Self-Government which commits signatory member states to guarantee 'the right and ability of local authorities to regulate and manage a substantial share of public affairs under their own responsibility'. Signing this Charter, one of the recommendations of the Hunt Report, was widely seen as an important symbolic gesture by the Blair government in the context of its commitment to improve central–local relations and enhance local democracy.

Speaking in February 1998 Hilary Armstrong observed: 'My aim is that authorities will be so respected by their local people that no central government will be able to come in again and undermine them like the last one did'. In this context she announced:

What we are saying is we do not believe reform isn't necessary. Reform is necessary. Reform is critical... We want local government to be secure in the hearts and minds of local people, and nobody, but nobody, could say that is the case now. (*Local Government Chronicle*, 6 February 1998)

Tony Blair used the language of 'rewards' for local authorities prepared to embrace a new policy agenda, particularly in the context of developing modern organisational structures and more effective participatory democracy. 'Where councils embrace this agenda of change and show that they can adapt to play a part in modernising their locality, then they will find their status and powers enhanced'. At the same time, he emphasised, 'If you are unwilling or unable to work to the modern agenda then the government will have to look to other partners to take on your role' (Blair, 1998, pp. 20, 22). Sticks and carrots seem to be the order of the day, a theme emphasised in the Local Government Bill which passed its second reading in the House of Commons in January 1999. While this bill proposed to replace CCT with best value and abolish crude universal capping by April 2000 it also introduced new external audit and inspection arrangements and gave ministers extensive powers of intervention. By the end of 1999 the 'modernise or perish' message to local authorities was clear and unambiguous. Change had to become the order of the day.

References

Blair, T. (1998) *Leading the Way: A New Vision for Local Government* (London: Institute for Public Policy Research).

Blowers, A. (1980) *The Limits of Power* (Oxford: Pergamon).

Cabinet Office (1997) *Opening up quangos: a consultation paper* (London: Cabinet Office).

Clarke, M. and Stewart, J. (1988) *The Enabling Council* (Luton: Local Government Management Board).

Cochrane, A. (1993) *Whatever Happened to Local Government?* (Buckingham: Open University Press).

Connolly, M. (1986) 'Central–Local Government relations in Northern Ireland', *Local Government Studies*, September/October.

Davies, H. (1996) 'Quangos and Local Government: a changing world', *Local Government Studies*, 22(2), pp. 1–7 Special Issue on Quangos.

Department of the Environment (1991) *The Internal Management of Local Authorities in England* (London: HMSO).

Department of the Environment (1993) *Community Leadership and Representation: Unlocking the Potential* (London: HMSO).

Department of the Environment, Transport and the Regions (1998) *Modernising Local Government: Local Democracy and Community Leadership* (London: DETR).

Goldsmith, M. (1997) 'Changing Patterns of Local Government', *ECPR News*, 9(1) pp. 6–7.

Hollis, G. Foster, C., Harle, R., Jackman, R., Travers, T., Foster, G., Thompson, G., Ambler, M., Gilder, P. and Sussex, P. (1990) *Alternatives to the Community Charge* (York, Joseph Rowntree Foundation Coopers Lybrand Deloitte).

House of Lords (1996) *Select Committee on Relations Between Central and Local Government, Vols I–III*, (London: HMSO).

Jones, G. and Stewart, J. (1993) 'When the numbers don't add up to democracy', *Local Government Chronicle*, 8 January, p. 15.

Labour Party (1997) *New Labour – Because Britain Deserves Better* (London: Labour Party Publications).

Leach, S. (1995) 'The Strange Case of the Local Government Review' in J. Stewart and G. Stoker (eds) *Local Government in the 1990s*, pp. 49–68, (Basingstoke: Macmillan).

Lowndes, V. (1998) *The Future of Central/Local Relations: Rebuilding Trust?* (London: Local Government Management Board).

Marinetto, M. (1997) 'The Political Dynamics of Camden: 1964–94', *Local Government Studies*, 23(2) pp 26–41.

Midwinter, A. (1995) *Local Government in Scotland: Reform or Decline?* (Basingstoke: Macmillan).

Newton, K. (1976) *Second City Politics* (Oxford: Oxford University Press).

Rhodes, R.A.W. (1988) *Beyond Westminster and Whitehall* (London: Allen & Unwin).

Rhodes, R. A. W. (1997) Review of *Legality and Locality; The Role of Law in Central–Local Government Relations* by Loughlin, M. in *Local Government Studies*, 23(2) pp. 135–37.

Stanyer, J. (1996) 'Local Governance in Historical Context: The Evidence of Two Centuries of Change' ESRC Local Governance Programme, Summary of Research Results.

Stewart, J (1995) 'Appointed Boards and Local Government', in Ridley, F.F. and Wilson, D. (eds), *The Quango Debate*, pp. 48–63 (Oxford: Oxford University Press).

Stoker, G. (1995) 'The Struggle to Reform Local Government 1970–1995', PAC Annual Conference, September.

Stoker, G. and Wilson, D. (1986) 'Intra-organisational politics in local authorities', *Public Administration*, 64(3), pp. 285–302.

Stoker, G. and Wolman, H. (1991) *A Different Way of Doing Business – The Example of the US Mayor* (Luton: Local Government Management Board).

Wilson, D. (1996) 'Structural solutions for local government: An exercise in chasing shadows?', *Parliamentary Affairs*, 49(3), July, pp. 441–54.

Wilson, D. and Game, C. (1998) *Local Government in the United Kingdom*, 2nd edn (Basingstoke: Macmillan).

11

A 'Hollow State'?

CLIVE GRAY

Introduction

The state in the United Kingdom has undergone a large number of changes over the last twenty years. The intended aims of the new Labour administration imply that these changes have yet to finish. The intention of this chapter is to analyse these changes and their implications for the administration of the United Kingdom. To do this the chapter firstly discusses the idea that the recent changes to the British system of government and administration have created a 'hollow state'. Secondly, it discusses the evidence that exists to support this view. Thirdly, it will outline how the intentions of the new Labour government will support or hinder the 'hollowing out' of the state. Lastly, it will consider whether the idea of the 'hollow state' captures the essential essence of the alterations that have been taking place or whether it is simply a metaphor that has only restricted significance for understanding these changes.

The Changing State

Even at the most superficial level the British state has been massively transformed over the last twenty years. Privatisation has seen the transfer to the private sector of previous state monopolies; the European Union has had an increasing impact on the content and direction of state policy; quangos have become major spenders of public money; the central organisations of the state – government departments – have been increasingly transformed into executive agencies, operating in a different fashion from previous forms of public management; local government and the National Health Service (NHS) have seen major changes in their financing, management and formal structures; and there has been a growing trend towards multi-organisational forms of policy implementation.

These changes have had far reaching implications not only for the management and delivery of public services but also for the intellectual environment within which they operate. Increasingly questions are being raised about the accountability of public sector organisations, how they are, and should be, controlled, and the extent to which the public can exercise a meaningful role within them. Indeed, the very idea of the state itself as a major actor in the management and administration of the United Kingdom has been called into question by these changes.

Rhodes (1994, p. 138) has argued that the changes that have been affecting the British state have contributed to a 'hollowing out' of the state: a loss of capacity by the central administrative machinery to control and manage the public sector. This erosion of central capabilities is seen to arise from a number of interrelated trends that serve to set limits to an effective managerial role for the state over an increasingly fragmented public sector.

The idea that the state is becoming increasingly weaker in its capacities and capabilities has been emphasised by a number of commentators (see Burch, Holiday and Wood, 1994; Moran, 1994; Loughlin and Scott, 1997). All argue that the trends that they identify have far-reaching implications for the future of the state, not least in transforming it into a new sort of state that is markedly different from that which has existed for much of the period since 1945.

The major trends that are seen to be responsible for this transformation and 'hollowing out' of the state are:

- the move from direct service provision to 'enabling' and 'regulating';
- the increasing use of quasi-governmental and private organisations to deliver public services;
- the increasingly important role of the European Union in influencing British governments and their policies;

- the restructuring of state organisations at all levels;
- the increasing emphasis that has been placed on the New Public Management (NPM); and
- the growth of both horizontally and vertically organised forms of 'governance'.

Each of these changes has its own specific implications for the role of the state in Britain and these need to be addressed in the context of the evidence that exists to support the claim that 'hollowing out' is a real trend.

The Transformation of the State

At the outset of this consideration it is important to bear in mind that it is not argued that the state has actually arrived at a position of 'hollowness', rather that the impact of the changes taking place has been to lead to a remaking of the purposes and processes of the state. This process of transformation is not actually finished as yet but, instead, is an on-going one. This raises the question of what impact the trends that have been identified have actually had in this transformative process.

The first point to consider is the move from direct service provision to 'enabling' and 'regulating'. The picture presented here is one where the state has changed from a direct concern with the day-to-day delivery of goods and services to citizens to simply overseeing this provision by creating the right climate for a multiplicity of service providers to undertake delivery to customers and consumers.

This view implies two things: that the state is being withdrawn from the accepted post-war role that it had adopted, and that the view adopted by the state towards the individual members of society is changing.

Certainly there has been a retreat by the state from the direct provision of services. This is partly as a consequence of legislation enforcing Compulsory Competitive Tendering in local government and the NHS, and partly through the selling off to the private sector of previously state-owned companies, particularly gas, water and electricity. A consequence of this movement away from direct provision has been the creation of a new range of regulatory mechanisms to oversee the providers of services (Table 11.1).

TABLE 11.1   *New Regulatory Mechanisms*

Regulator	Area of regulation
OFTEL	Telecommunications
OFWAT	Water Services
OFLOT	The National Lottery
OFSTED	Educational Standards
OFGAS	Gas Supply
OFFER	Electricity Regulation
OPRAF	Rail Franchising
ORR	Rail Regulation

In some ways this movement is the twentieth-century version of the nineteenth-century idea of the 'minimal state': a state that oversees the processes of service provision and which protects the individual by establishing a framework of rules and guidelines within which service providers operate. This *regulatory* state is buttressed by both a *contract* state and an *enabling* state which are variants of the same nineteenth-century neo-liberal ideas of the 'minimal' state.

Of particular significance in this move is the change in the view of the individual within society that is adopted by the state. The post-war welfare state consensus treated individuals as citizens who had democratic rights and democratic responsibilities towards the other members of society. The newer regulatory view sees individuals as consumers and customers with economic rights rather than democratic ones. (What the responsibilities of these customers and consumers are is largely unclear – if they exist at all.)

This changed view has implications for the accountability of state organisations, and for the role that they are expected to play within society. In the case of the former, accountability is defined by economic models rather than political ones and, in the case of the latter, the state must be seen as being a secondary actor when compared with the primary ones of the private sector.

In effect the argument is that 'enabling' and 'regulating' lead to a weakened role for the state, with control and accountability being loosened and relocated with non-state (normally private sector) actors. The consequence of this is that the capacity of the central state to exercise effective control is weakened to a considerable extent.

The increasing use of quasi-governmental and private sector organisations to deliver public goods and services is a matter of degree. The use of such organisations has a long tradition in the British system of government, dating back at least to the eighteenth century (Greenleaf, 1987). What has been significant is the massive expansion in the amount of public money that is actually controlled by these organisations.

When the Conservative Party came to power in 1979 their intention was to sweep away the 'corporate state' that they believed had become entrenched over the previous 30–40 years. The strategy to achieve this end involved the abolition of various quangos and forms of bureaucratic red tape, moves which were argued to be essential for the aim of creating a successful and competitive economy. The reality, however, took another form.

The long-standing Conservative dissatisfaction with the public sector meant that existing state organisations came under increasing pressure to justify their continued existence. The fact that these organisations did not fit the criteria of efficiency, economy and effectiveness that the Conservatives supported led to attempts to find new ways of providing goods and services that did meet such criteria.

The solution adopted was the creation of a new set of organisations which would operate in a different fashion from the 'old' public sector and which were more in line with an image of an effective, efficient and economic private sector standing in stark contradistinction to the public sector. Effectively the public sector was placed in a no-win position: the model with which it was being compared was based on an ideal-type private sector that the actual private sector, let alone the public sector, could not live up to. By aiming at fulfilling the model the public sector would have to cease to be the public sector and become, instead, a private sector clone.

The practical solution to this problem lay in an expansion of the quasi-governmental sector and in making an increased use of private and voluntary sector organisations to actually deliver goods and services for the public sector. In some cases this involved the creation of new organisations that were designed to operate on private sector lines, such as the urban development corporations. In others it involved creating the opportunity through contracting out for existing private and voluntary organisations to play a larger role in the provision of public goods and services than they had done previously.

As with the move towards regulation, enabling and contracting out the consequence of making increased use of quasi-governmental and private organisations was that the central state lost control of the management and administration of goods and services. The result of this was a diminished chance for the state to plan and coordinate service delivery effectively.

The increasing significance of the European Union for British government and administration is obvious. Apart from becoming a growing source of legislation it has also affected the way in which public goods and services are organised and managed. Perhaps the clearest example of this came with the privatisation of the water industry in the 1980s. During this process a new regulatory mechanism needed to be developed to oversee the provision of water services. As a consequence of European-level rules the original ideas of the Conservative government had to be changed to establish an independent agency (the National Rivers Authority) to undertake this role (Maloney and Richardson, 1995).

British central government thus finds itself in a position where not only policy but also details of administration and management have been removed from it. Of course this does *not* mean that *every* area of decision has been removed from the centre of British government, only that in *some* areas, as outlined in the various treaties governing the EU (such as the Maastricht Treaty), the principle of parliamentary sovereignty has been done away with.

Clearly this spells a weakened role for national governments, not only in the United Kingdom but also throughout the member states of the European Union. When allied with the European principle of subsidiarity (where functions should be carried out at the lowest tier of government with the competence to undertake them), and the increased roles that have been assigned to the Committee of the Regions in influencing European legislation, the central state throughout the European Union is finding itself under increasing pressure.

In this case the role of increasing European Union involvement in the internal affairs of the state imply not so much a 'hollowing-out' of the state as an effective bypassing of it altogether in some areas of policy and administration. The extension of Qualified Majority Voting in the Council of Ministers extends this possibility of being bypassed. Thus, the loss of control of the central state that is a key theme of the 'hollow state' thesis is present here – even if for rather different reasons than the thesis implies.

The restructuring of state organisations within the British system of government and administration has a long-standing tradition. Over the last twenty years all of the major elements of the previously existing system – central government departments, local government, the NHS, and the privatised industries – have undergone organisational reform of one sort or another.

In the case of central government the reviews of central administration which took place from the Rayner scrutinies to the Ibbs Report saw change as being essential. The end result saw the creation of the new executive agencies as the prime mechanism for the delivery of central goods and services. These agencies effectively removed the older implementation role of central departments by hiving service delivery off to free-standing organisations. Ministers were no longer responsible for the role played by these agencies in implementing government policy but were meant to concentrate on policy formulation instead. As a consequence of this the old idea of there being a meaningful distinction to draw between policy and administration was given new life.

For local government the system of two-tier governance enshrined in the reorganisations of local government in 1974 and 1975 in England, Wales and Scotland was increasingly questioned as to its effectiveness, not only in terms of service delivery but also of accountability. The solutions that were arrived at to remedy the perceived inefficiencies varied across the components of the British state. In Scotland and Wales, for example, new single-tier organisations were created by government ministers. In England a peripatetic Local Government Commission examined each county area in turn, recommending the creation of a new local government system that combined both single and two-tier structures that increasingly resembled the position before the 1974 reorganisation. The reform of local government in Northern Ireland had been a specific response to the endemic conflict that existed.

Alongside these structural changes local government was also confronted by a series of reforms of its financing, ending with the creation of a modified version of the old rating system that had existed before these reforms took place. At the same time pressure was exerted to change local government into an example of the 'enabling state', with a weakened potential for effective control by local authorities.

In the case of the NHS the fragmentation of the older system by the introduction of NHS Trusts and the creation of fund-holding General Practitioner practices were the major reforms designed to create a quasi-market for health services by creating a distinction between 'purchasers' and 'providers'. It was assumed that the use of market-like mechanisms to manage demand and supply would create a better distribution of resources within the NHS and would increasingly replace state direction with economic management.

The privatisation of the nationalised industries was the final major area of organisational change, where assets previously publically owned were sold to a combination of private individuals and companies.

Alongside these structural changes, however, there have also been moves towards the creation of multi-organisational structures for the delivery of public services which, it is argued, mark the beginnings of a change from 'government' to 'governance'. Instead of policy implementation and control being the preserve of isolated organisational units (e.g. local authorities or health authorities) there has been the development of linkages *between* organisations. A classic example of this would be the Care in the Community programme which brings together local and health authorities, private and voluntary organisations to provide a package of 'care' for some of the most vulnerable members of society. While local authorities have been given the lead role in managing this process they cannot carry it out successfully without the input of a range of partners.

A similar picture has also developed in a range of other policy areas from economic development to the arts. By creating a network of organisational actors to deliver state services the potential of any *one* actor to control the process is severely limited.

The sum effect of all of these changes was to create a far more fragmented state machinery. Lines of accountability and control became increasingly blurred, particularly when the role of quasi-governmental, private and voluntary organisations was included. The possibility for achieving any sort of meaningful control over the disparate range of organisations that had been created became increasingly remote, not only for central government but also for individual local government and NHS organisations as well.

Underpinning many of these changes was the emphasis placed on a new form of management for the public sector. The NPM was meant to be a development of older models of public administration and management influenced by the lessons that could be learned from the private sector (Hood, 1991). In practice the private sector models that it seemed to derive from were curiously dated ones but, more importantly, they failed to recognise that there *are* differences between the two sectors.

At its crudest the NPM is concerned with 'letting managers manage': creating clear objectives and managing from the top downwards. The standards managers are meant to work towards are those associated with the private sector, particularly in terms of economic efficiency in resource usage. The effect of this is to reorient public managers towards measures of success that escape from older qualitative concerns, for example equity and accountability, and replace them with quantitative measures of, for example, economic effectiveness. This clearly ties in with the idea that the perception of the individual receiving priority is that of the consumer or customer, rather than that of the citizen.

It might be assumed that the NPM implies a greater control being exercised over the public sector by central figures within the governmental machinery. If this were true then the idea that the state is being 'hollowed out' would be misleading, if not wrong. However, the use of the NPM extends beyond simple management techniques and incorporates as well the fragmentation of the state and an emphasis on competition within the public sector (Hood, 1991). New styles of management as a result are part and parcel of the process of 'hollowing out' the state, not least by allowing managerial control to be exercised independently of central actors.

The impact of the NPM is, at present, unclear although there is some evidence from local government to imply that its impact will increase as time goes by and older managers who were socialised in previous patterns of management retire or are replaced (Pratchett and Wingfield, 1996).

In total the trends identified by the 'hollowing out' thesis work together: they each have a distinct contribution to make to decreasing the ability of the centre to effectively control and manage the public sector. There is some evidence to suggest that this process of 'hollowing out' the state is a reality: the question to turn to now is what the Labour Party intends to do about this situation.

New Labour and Old Problems

The election of the new Labour government in 1997 offered the prospect of an administration that had promised to revitalise the systems of government and administration bequeathed to it after eighteen years of Conservative rule. The extent to which this new administration confronted the factors that seemed to be leading to a 'hollowing out' of the state is thus an indication of how serious it is about reforming the machinery and practices of the state. This is particularly important given that shortly before the 1997 general election the then Shadow Minister for the Public Services stated that

> some would like me to announce a reversal of all recent changes in the public service ... that, of course, is not an option. (Foster, 1996, p. 261)

In terms of the movement towards a 'regulating' or 'enabling' state it would appear that some slowing and even reversal of this trend is evident. In the case of the NHS, for example, the promise to end the 'purchaser/provider' split implies an enhanced role for the state in managing scarce resources. Instead of allowing a quasi-market to determine the allocation of resources for health care, new methods of state-directed planning and allocation will be necessary. Likewise, the relaxation of the requirements of Compulsory Competitive Tendering will allow more scope for the exercise of political, rather than economic, judgement in the awarding of contracts in both the NHS and local government.

The role of the citizen was argued as altering from the view of them as consumers and customers to one where they were 'stakeholders' in society (Hutton, 1995): active participants in the allocation of resources in a more politically-aware way. Whether this move, however, was ever entrenched as a principle or whether it was simply a piece of rhetoric is open to question, particularly since the idea has become increasingly neglected in recent debates.

The increasing use of quasi-governmental and private sector organisations to deliver public goods and services does not, as yet, appear to be changing. The emphasis on ideas of 'partnership' with the private sector, allowing it an enhanced role in the delivery of public policies, is still strong. None of the major new quasi-governmental organisations created by the Conservatives have been threatened with abolition indeed new regulatory-type organisations have been introduced, as for example, in the arts. Rather their leadership is changing to entrench Labour supporting actors, rather than Conservative supporting ones, at their head. The use of patronage in controlling quasi-governmental organisations is a long-standing tradition and is ritually abused by opposition parties (Stott, 1995). Changing the system, however, to reduce the opportunities for such politically-loaded patronage to take place does not seem to be on the agenda.

To this extent at least the situation appears to be largely unchanged as a result of the Labour Party's election victory: central control of the policies and resources which have drifted away from the centre remains as problematic as ever. Patronage allows the chance for some arm's-length control but this is not the same as taking power back to the centre.

The new Labour government has been quite explicit in stating its intention to be a 'good' European, as evidenced by the almost immediate ending of the opt-out from the Social Chapter that had been negotiated by the Conservatives. The determination to integrate the United Kingdom more closely with the mainstream of opinion within the European Union, of course, implies that the increasingly significant role of the Union for British policy and practice is unlikely to change.

In addition, the creation of elected assemblies for Scotland and Wales gives a new impetus to the principle of subsidiarity within Britain. By creating new political forums that are independent of the central state, the government is opening up the prospect of a further diminution of central control by establishing organisations with the competence to undertake tasks for themselves that were previously the reserve of the centre. Decentralisation could conceivably be the mechanism by which the central state manages to undercut its own position and status, particularly if the English regions start to follow in making demands for increased autonomy from the centre.

The role and status of state organisations has received only limited attention as yet, being largely restricted to the cases of the NHS and the creation of a new governmental system for London headed by an elected Mayor. At present neither of these have actually been changed but discussion documents, White Papers and establishing legislation have been produced. For the rest of government, however, there has been little real movement in changing the trends that were in place under the Conservatives, particularly in the case of the new multi-organisational clusters that have developed. Thus the fragmentation and loss of central control that was implicit in these trends remains in place.

Lastly, the impact of the NPM has not yet been fully addressed. The depoliticised form of management style that is embodied in the NPM remains in place as the dominant pattern in management thought *for* the public sector. (Again, the question of whether this management thought is accepted *in* the public sector is another matter). As long as this managerial style remains in place the older political version of management that was associated with the public sector remains at risk. The consequence of this is that the potential for the centre to exercise effective control over public life remains weak.

The general picture provided by this brief summary of the early period in office of the new Labour administration implies that the process and trend towards a 'hollowing out' of the state remains in place. The two areas where some slowing or reversal of this trend appears to be occuring are in the move towards a 'regulating' or 'contracting' state, and in the restructuring of the organisations of the state. In both cases, however, much more would need to be done to show that the centre is assuming a stronger role.

In practice it is probable that a much longer period of time will be needed to determine whether the Labour government is either capable of, or even interested in, reversing the trends which have developed over the eighteen years of Conservative rule from 1979 to 1997. The extent to which the re-establishment of a strong system of government and administration throughout the United Kingdom is possible will be a major area of concern in future years. At present it is simply too soon to say.

How Hollow is the 'Hollow State'?

The assumption so far in this chapter has been that there is some truth in the argument that the changes that have taken place to the British state over recent years *have* led towards a 'hollowing out' of the structure. The extent to which this expression actually captures what has been taking place is, however, open to debate. While some evidence exists to support the claim that this 'hollowing out' is occurring, a deeper analysis is required before it can be accepted at face value.

The term 'the hollow state' can be used either descriptively, to identify a real process leading to a loss of central capability on behalf of the state, or it can be used metaphorically, to identify an image of what the state is changing into. In the case of the former there are reasons to doubt whether the 'centre' is actually 'losing' control; in the case of the latter, alternative images can be presented that are equally persuasive in their analysis of what is occurring – even if they do not have such a catchy name attached to them.

Hogwood (1997, p. 714) has argued that the very title 'the hollow state' is confused: is the lack of control that is involved on behalf of the *state* or of *ministers*? It has been argued that ministers have actually been taking powers for themselves to a far greater extent than at any time since the distant past (Foster and Plowden, 1996, p. 244). If such is the case then how has the *state* lost a capacity to govern?

In this respect the reorganisation of the machinery of the state becomes significant. The separation of policy from implementation implicit in many of the changes that have taken place in the public sector, not only through the creation of free-standing executive agencies but also through the increasing reliance on arm's-length quangos, creates a differentiation between a politicised, policy-oriented, core and a technical, managerially-oriented, periphery in terms of the state. If this is what is actually occurring then it could be argued that what is happening is a reappraisal of the core competencies with which the state is involved.

To this extent the concept of a 'hollow' state works at the descriptive level. By concentrating on matters of policy rather than on the administration and management of the practicalities of these policies the state is divesting itself of secondary responsibilities, with a concomitant reduction in the need for a large bureaucratic machinery. The perceived loss of control over issues of implementation thus becomes a necessary consequence of the decision to separate policy from its administration and management.

The fact that any such division between policy and administration is a nonsense (Greenwood and Wilson, 1989, pp. 3–4) implies that governments, of whichever political persuasion, are doomed to create further problems than they resolve by pursuing this path. In essence governments cannot 'hollow out' the state by attempting to

separate the twin components of policy and implementation, implying that the metaphor involved is weakened. If this aspect of the
'hollow state' argument is untenable in practice this, in turn, implies
that whatever is occurring is not simply concerned with the loosening
of central control but is, instead, a much more complex phenomenon.

Making a distinction between the descriptive and the metaphorical dimensions of the 'hollow state' argument indicates that great
care needs to be taken in dealing with this label. At the descriptive
level it is obvious that the changes that have taken place in the
machinery of the state are large scale and far reaching. Whether
these changes carry the implication of a loss of control on the behalf
of the state is, however, another matter.

To answer this depends to a large degree on how the term 'the
state' is being defined. A descriptive definition would have to
include both elected politicians and appointed bureaucrats. In this
case the changes that have been taking place *do not* imply a loss of
central capacity to control policy. Elected politicians, following
Foster and Plowden (1996), have attained a new grasp on policy
(as illustrated by the appointment of Jack Cunningham as the
Cabinet's policy 'enforcer' and his replacement by Mo Mowlam):
appointed bureaucrats have had their capacity to control policy
implementation enhanced by the creation of free-standing executive
agencies and quangos, and by the development of multi-organisational 'partnerships' for the delivery of goods and services. Confu-
sions may arise where these two roles overlap, as a result of the
practical impossibility of separating policy from implementation,
creating new political conflicts (as in the case of Michael Howard
and Derek Lewis over Prison Service policy), but this does not mean
that there has been a *loss* of control.

An alternative definition of the state could entail a concentration
on the functional role that it plays within society. In this case
attention would focus, not on the people involved, but rather, on
what they do. Thus, attention moves to questions of political sovereignty and the exercise of political power within the British political
system. The changes that have been taking place in these respects
leave the question of central capacity open. The increasing influence
of the European Union is a simple reflection of the truth that
absolute British sovereignty vanished on the occasion of joining
the forerunner of the European Union (the European Economic
Community) in 1973. This necessarily limits the capacity of British

governments to act independently in areas where Europe takes precedence. Apart from these areas, however, the central state has not seen any real diminution of its ability to wield both effective power and influence.

The case of sub-national government is a clear example of how the centre has become increasingly intrusive into the affairs of public organisations (see, *inter alia*, Gray, 1994). The Conservative governments of 1979–97 may have begun this trend, particularly in the field of finance, but the new Labour government has also made it clear that it intends to take a much more 'hands-on' approach than might have been anticipated by many observers in the past. A number of warning shots across the bows of local authorities regarding the management of their assets and the quality of the services that they provide – particularly in the field of education – imply a determination on behalf of central political actors to manage this area of state activity in a potentially more intrusive manner than has been seen for many years.

From this more functional perspective, therefore, the idea that the centre has been losing control over the activities of state organisations is open to question. The diminution in power and authority that has arisen as a consequence of the increasing effectiveness of Europe as an alternative source of political leadership has, perhaps, been balanced by a stronger determination of central governments to exercise effective control over matters of policy than was previously the case.

Problems, therefore, exist with the 'hollow state' idea. The complexities of what is occurring to the state make a simple assessment of the overall picture hard to make. This being the case questions remain of how the multiple changes that have been occurring can be understood, and what their significance actually is for British government, management and administration into the new millennium.

The Changing British State

Jordan (1994, p. 2) has argued that

> British public administration is made up by governments as they go along. It is characterised precisely by features that might be least expected: uncertainty, inconsistency, disorder.

The lack of any coherent strategy for the development of the British state in recent years is no exception to this claim. While certain themes and trends are apparent in the multiplicity of changes that have taken place over recent years this does not mean that they have been applied with any rigour, or, indeed, that they have not, at times, acted in a contradictory manner, creating further problems and unintended consequences for governments to cope with.

Making sense of these changes requires a movement away from descriptive or metaphorical labels towards a theoretically informed position that is capable not only of making sense but also of providing a capability for *explaining* change. The many reforms that the British state has undergone in recent years (and is still in the process of going through – witness the debates about elected assemblies for Northern Ireland, Scotland, Wales and Greater London) have not occurred by chance. Governments seek to manipulate the machinery, the content and the direction of the state for political reasons. The ideological content of these changes is a response to both external and internal stimuli that encourage the already existing reforming tendencies of any government.

The sheer scope of the changes that have taken place in the recent past is evidence of a belief inside governments that multiple reforms are necessary to confront the impact of the new pressures that are generated by these stimuli. Many of the trends that are contained within the 'hollow state' thesis are tied together by a belief that new managerial forms are required both to overcome perceived weaknesses in older forms of management and administration and to create the conditions for the exercise of new forms of authoritative control over the provision of public goods and services.

This tendency has led towards the creation of not so much a 'hollow' as a 'managerial' state where new sets of relationships between 'state and citizen . . . public and private . . . providers and recipients . . . and "management" and "politics" ' are being created (Clarke and Newman, 1997, p. ix). In this respect control has not been 'lost' by the state, it has, instead, been relocated to new arenas of power. These new arenas are commonly at one remove from the direct patterns of accountability and control that were to be found in previous state forms, and may be overseen by non-elected organisations and actors (such as in quangos), or by combinations of state, quasi-state and private organisations in new forms of 'governance'.

The consequence of these changes has been that the state itself has been altered into new forms that allow for the management and administration of public goods and services to take place in new ways. A prime example of this is to be found in the way that public policies have increasingly been dealt with in a commodified form, where new approaches are necessary to fulfill the requirements of government (Gray, 1995).

Changes such as these have more wide-ranging implications than are to be found in the basic 'hollow state' thesis, implying as they do a host of changing relationships between the parts of the system that go beyond the simple question of central capacity. How far the Labour government will go in following through the changes to the British state that were set in train by the preceding Conservative governments remains to be seen. What cannot be questioned, however, is that the process of change has yet to come to an end.

References

Burch, M. Holliday, I. and Wood, B. (1994) 'The Transformation of the State', *Talking Politics*, 7(2), pp. 108–10.

Clarke, J. and J. Newman (1997) *The Managerial State* (London: Sage).

Foster, C. and F. Plowden (1996) *The State under Stress* (Buckingham: Open University Press).

Foster, D. (1996) 'Labour and Public Sector Reform', *Parliamentary Affairs*, 49, pp. 256–61.

Gray, C. (1994) *Government Beyond the Centre* (Basingstoke: Macmillan).

Gray, C. (1995) 'The Commodification of Cultural Policy' in Britain, pp. 307–15 in J. Lovenduski and J. Stanyer (eds), *Contemporary Political Studies, 1995* (Belfast: Political Studies Association).

Greenleaf, W. (1987) *A Much Governed Nation* (London: Methuen).

Greenwood, J. and Wilson, D. (1989) *Public Administration in Britain Today* (London: Allen and Unwin).

Hogwood, B. (1997) 'The Machinery of Government, 1979–97', *Political Studies*, 45, pp. 704–15.

Hood, C. (1991) 'A Public Management for all Seasons?', *Public Administration*, 69, pp. 3–19.

Hutton, W. (1995) *The State We're In* (London: Cape).

Jordan, G. (1994) *The British Administrative System* (London: Routledge).

Loughlin, M. and Scott, C. (1997) 'The Regulatory State', in Dunleavy, P. Gamble, A. Holliday, I. and Peele, G. (eds), *Developments in British Politics 5* (Basingstoke: Macmillan), pp. 205–19.

Maloney, W. and Richardson, J. (1995) *Managing Policy Change in Britain* (Edinburgh: Edinburgh University Press).

Moran, M. (1994) 'Reshaping the British State', *Talking Politics*, 7(3), pp. 174–7.

Pratchett, L. and Wingfield, M. (1996) 'Petty Bureaucracy and Woolly-minded Liberalism', *Public Administration*, 74, pp. 639–56.

Rhodes, R. (1994) 'The Hollowing Out of the State', *Political Quarterly*, 65, pp. 138–51.

Stott, T. (1995) 'Snouts in the Trough', pp. 145–62 in Ridley, F. and Wilson, D. (eds), *The Quango Debate* (Oxford: Oxford University Press).

Conclusion: Governance by Reformers

ROBERT PYPER and LYNTON ROBINS

This book has portrayed the United Kingdom's system of government as it engages with and is subjected to a series of very significant reforms and changes. At every level of the system, structures, processes or policies (in some spheres, all of these) are being reworked, reformulated and reordered. It might be argued that the reform dynamic has become a much more conspicuous feature of the United Kingdom polity than at any previous stage in our modern political history. The great reforming Liberal governments of 1905–15 primarily pursued piecemeal change in the realm of social policy. It was only relatively belatedly that they embarked on broader constitutional reform with respect to the House of Lords and Ireland, and it could be argued that in these cases the reforms were, at least in part, the consequences of short-term crises (respectively, the rejection of the 'People's Budget' and the Liberals' enforced reliance on the Irish Nationalist Party in the Commons). Despite their radicalism in the fields of social and industrial policy, Attlee's Labour governments between 1945 and 1951 were remarkably conservative in other spheres, including the constitution. As we note in more detail below, the Conservative governments of Margaret Thatcher and John Major in the period 1979–97 also pursued reform in certain clearly defined spheres, while eschewing change in others. Some of the more significant reforms, including the privatisation programme, were only fully embraced in the second term of the Thatcher administration.

The reform agenda which characterises the UK polity in the new millennium appears to be much more comprehensive in scale and scope. To some extent, this can be attributed to the background of the reformers themselves.

Party Reformers to Reforming Government

As Richard Kelly noted in Chapter 6, the Labour Party which entered government in 1997 was, if not entirely 'new', a much altered political machine. Uniquely in modern political history, the reins of government were taken up by a group of politicians who had successfully carried out a series of significant reforms within their own party. There was no precedent for this. The reforming governments cited above (Liberal, Labour and Conservative) did not emerge from periods of intensive internal change carried out in their opposition years. Furthermore, the policies on which they were elected were, in the main, based upon long-established party principles and ideals. The most recent Labour governments, formed in 1964 and 1974, were based around a party machine that was fundamentally unaltered by the preceding period of opposition, and in the key policies of these governments observers could discern significant degrees of continuity with the party's recent past. However, in certain important respects, the Labour Party of 1997 bore little relationship to the party which had ceded power in 1979.

Following a period of severe internal strife after 1979, which culminated in the massive electoral defeat of 1983, a rolling programme of internal reform began to take shape within the Labour Party, and this was gradually implemented (albeit with the occasional hiatus) under the leaderships of Neil Kinnock, John Smith and Tony Blair. The reforms, which came to be referred to as 'modernisation', encompassed the party's policy-making machinery, finances, relationship with the trade unions, constitution, relationship with its members, and policies (for details, see Gould, 1998; Kelly, 1999; Mandelson and Liddle, 1996; and Rentoul, 1996). Labour was elected in 1997 on a manifesto which combined specific policy objectives with commitments to constitutional reform while explicitly linking the party's programme for government with the preceding internal party changes: 'We have modernised the Labour Party and we will modernise Britain' (Labour Party, 1997, p. 5).

In the chapters of this book the early fruits of the Blair government's reform programme have been set out, and most of these need not be reiterated in detail here. In some spheres, major changes were delivered as priorities within a relatively short period, while in others a piecemeal approach was adopted.

Devolution for Scotland, Wales and, in a different context, Northern Ireland was enacted with remarkable speed (given the complexities and implications of this major constitutional change) in the manner set out by Allan McConnell in Chapter 9. Reordering the relationship between the Treasury and the Bank of England took place in the immediate wake of Labour's 1997 election victory. Only five days into the new administration, the Chancellor of the Exchequer, Gordon Brown, announced that the first stage of a Treasury reorganisation would involve reversing the arrangements for managing interest rate policy which had existed since 1946. The Bank of England was to be given operational control over interest rates, with immediate effect. In practice, the decision gave the Bank of England a significant degree of independence from the Treasury. Under the new system, the Chancellor of the Exchequer would establish a target for inflation, and the Bank would then have operational control over the setting of interest rates to achieve this. The management of this key decision would be handled by a new monetary policy committee within the Bank (comprised of the governor, two deputy governors, the Bank officials responsible for monetary policy and market operations, and four outsiders appointed by the Chancellor), which would meet monthly to set interest rates.

Further reforms were to follow in the realm of public finance. The Blair government accepted the outgoing administration's overall public expenditure commitments for the forthcoming two years, while reserving the right to shift cash around within the agreed total in order to prioritise certain programmes, including health and education. However, the new government also made it clear that its longer-term expenditure plans would be moulded by the outcome of a Comprehensive Spending Review (CSR) which would cover every department and expenditure programme over three-year cycles and result in fixed total expenditure plans. The results of this CSR were announced in July 1998 and prioritised increased spending over the medium term in several key policy areas, including health, education and transport. This was to be financed though scheduled spending cuts in other areas including defence, coupled with the imposition of strict efficiency targets on all government departments (HM Government, 1998).

The *Modernising Government* White Paper, published in the spring of 1999 (Prime Minister, 1999) encapsulated the Labour government's approach to the new public management. This document set out the government's plans for further improvements in managerial efficiency, enhanced service quality, greater use of technology in the delivery of public services ('information age government') and a more strategic and coordinated approach to policy-making and service delivery ('joined-up government').

The relatively speedy progress made in the spheres of devolution, management of public finance and expenditure, and public management more broadly, was not matched in all policy areas. Legislation on 'open government' was delayed, despite Labour's long-standing commitment to produce a Freedom of Information Act (based on extensive work already done in opposition). This whole policy seemed to come under question when dates for publication of a White Paper were repeatedly postponed and stories emerged regarding the failure of the first Minister for the Civil Service, David Clark, to have the policy prioritised within a Cabinet committee chaired by Lord Irvine (Draper, 1997, pp. 51, 167–8). Clark's removal in Blair's first government reshuffle, and his replacement by John Cunningham in a much more prestigious role did not herald any immediate move to implement the commitment to freedom of information. Similarly, the fundamental reform of welfare policy, which was signalled by the appointment of Frank Field to work alongside Harriet Harman at the Department of Social Security, ran into a series of problems which culminated in the departure of both of these ministers from the government, the appointment of Alistair Darling as Secretary of State for Social Security and the emergence of a much more piecemeal approach to welfare reform, beginning with pensions policy.

As we saw in Chapters 4 and 5, the Labour Party's manifesto commitments regarding the modernisation of Parliament (Labour Party, 1997, pp. 32–3) were taken forward through a series of reports examining the structures and processes of the House of Commons, legislation on ending the rights of hereditary peers to sit and vote in the House of Lords and the establishment of a Royal Commission on the future system of appointment of life peers. The Jenkins Commission on electoral reform, appointed by the government in December 1997, produced its report within a year. The fundamental proposal emanating from the report was the replacement of the plurality, 'first-past-the post' system by the two-tier alternative vote system. The government was committed to a referendum on electoral reform, although the precise timing of this was unclear.

There was no fundamental structural reordering of the relationship between the United Kingdom and the European Union. The Labour government did not take the country into the new European monetary system symbolised by the merging of several currencies into the euro in January 1999. Nonetheless, it would be fair to say that the tone of the relationship changed under Labour, with concerted efforts being made to avoid the confrontational approach which had characterised many aspects of the Conservative government's policy towards Europe. There were clear signs that the Blair government would seek to work within the EU agenda in broad terms, even to the point of merging sterling with the euro at some future stage (although, for domestic political reasons, this was not explicitly stated). In other non-domestic policy spheres, the watchword seemed to be continuity rather than fundamental change. There was some rhetoric about an 'ethical foreign policy' but, in time, as the pressures of *realpolitik* took hold, the government sought to play down the significance of this concept. The relationship with the United States seemed closer than ever in many respects, and this was confirmed by the United Kingdom's active support for military action against Iraq in 1998 following Saddam Hussein's persistent flouting of United Nations resolutions regarding weapons inspections, and the crucial role played by the US–UK axis within NATO when offensive action was mounted against Serbia during the Kosovo crisis in 1999.

To summarise, therefore, it is possible to say that, despite elements of unevenness, and areas where progress seems to be uncertain, changes can be discerned in several key spheres. Among these we can note substantive policy changes, attempts to create a new political culture (including, for example, moves towards cross-party collaboration with senior Liberal Democrats taking seats on a consultative Cabinet committee), and reform of the governing framework (involving a combination of institutional and constitutional change).

Perspective: Towards a Fuller Concept of Governance?

What are we to make of all this? Is it possible to make some sense of these developments in an analytical context, and what does it all mean for governance?

As we have seen in the course of this book, the concept of governance is multi-faceted. A key contributor to the developing debate about the meaning and usage of governance has argued that

> governance signifies a change in the meaning of government, referring to a *new* process of governing; or a *changed* condition of ordered rule; or the *new* method by which society is governed. (Rhodes, 1997, p. 46)

Beyond this, while synthesising and analysing the work of others, Rhodes identifies 'at least six' distinct usages of governance, as 'the minimal state'; 'corporate governance'; 'the new public management'; 'good governance'; a 'socio-cybernetic system'; and 'self-organising networks' (1997, pp. 46–7). Most of these potential usages are self-explanatory, but the last two require further comment.

Rhodes draws upon the work of Kooiman (1993) and Rosenau (1992) when describing the parts played by a multiplicity of active participants in specific policy areas ('system' referred to above). These participants may have social, political or legal bases, straddle the public, private and voluntary sectors, and ultimately they may produce policy outcomes which extend far beyond the initial intentions of central government. 'Self-organising networks' are complex sets of interdependent organisations, drawn from the public and the private sectors, charged with the function of providing services. Increasingly, these networks become closely integrated, resistant to 'steering' by government, and capable of developing their own policy agendas.

In simple terms, these systems and networks imply that governance is 'a broader term than government with services provided by any permutation of government and the private and voluntary sectors' (Rhodes, 1997, p. 51). To a considerable extent, this particular facet of governance has been steadily developing in the United Kingdom since the 1970s at the latest.

During the 1980s and early 1990s it became possible to discern the beginnings of a more general shift away from traditional forms of government, and towards the wider and looser concept of governance. In the United Kingdom, however, the approach of the Thatcher governments was rather limited and impoverished. The focus was narrow. Certain elements of governance were stressed, while others were ignored. In particular, there was a concerted drive towards the advent of a minimal state, with rolling programmes of privatisation and continuous attempts to cut the scale and scope of the public sector. The final outcome fell far short of the Thatcherite dream, and, in any case, the predisposition of these governments to interfere and intervene inevitably gave an ironic edge to the rhetoric about 'small' government. Nonetheless, there was a clear association in the Thatcherite project between the move towards governance and the attack on the public sector. An additional feature of this period was the increasing emphasis given to managerialism, later styled the new public management. In its myriad forms, the new public management embraced, *inter alia*, the transfer of a range of private sector management systems and techniques to the public sector, the advent of new structures for the delivery of public services, and the introduction of quasi-(or pseudo-?) markets, contractualism and consumerism. For the Thatcher governments, governance equalled the minimal state plus the new public management.

During the Major government, between 1992 and 1997, this approach continued, but another feature of governance became increasingly prominent. As a direct consequence of a series of scandals arising from allegations of 'sleaze', the moral and ethical dimensions of corporate governance loomed ever larger, leading to the establishment of the Nolan Committee and the Parliamentary Commissioner for Standards (Baggott, 1995; Berrington, 1995; Oliver 1997; Woodhouse, 1998).

Under the Blair government, it is possible to discern the emergence of a fuller, more comprehensive concept of governance. During the late 1980s and early 1990s, the Labour Party's gradual acceptance of many of the key features of the Thatcherite polity, including elements of privatisation, meant that the fundamental aspects of the minimal state dimension of governance would continue to be embraced by the party in government. The new public management dimension of governance was generally deemed to be unproblematic, indeed viewed as positively attractive, by many of the new occupants of ministerial offices in Whitehall. The continuing problem of ethics and 'sleaze', epitomised by the circumstances surrounding the departure of Peter Mandelson and Geoffrey Robinson from the government in December 1998, ensured that the imperatives of corporate governance would remain a lodestar for the Blair government. It is important to note in passing that a continuing interest in and concern for morals and ethics in government does not imply that all problems in these spheres are necessarily handled skilfully and effectively.

The organisational and sectoral complexities which are inherent to Rhodes's 'systems' and 'networks', would appear to sit reasonably comfortably with the Blair government's strategies for the creation and delivery of public policy, the developing discourse surrounding 'the Third Way', and the increasing emphasis being given to the concept of 'multi-layer democracy'. The latter was discussed within the introductory chapter to this volume, and was taken to refer to the increasing complexity of modern government and the questionable long-term utility of concepts such as the unitary state and federalism. Multi-layer democracy places particular emphasis on the complex policy-making, implementation and accountability relationships between a variety of state and societal actors at the levels of supra-national activity (including the EU), central government, devolved government, local government and 'quasi-government'.

However, above all of this, what distinguishes the governing style of the United Kingdom in the new millennium from the trends and approaches of the previous two decades, and justifies the deployment of the term governance, is the clear commitment to rolling programmes of reform. Rhodes's (1997) deployment of the term 'good governance', as a key component of governance *per se*, draws upon the ideas of Leftwich (1994) to emphasis the importance of using reforms in order to distribute and disperse power within a state which derives its legitimacy and authority from a democratic mandate. In the Thatcher and Major years, reform was largely limited to aspects of the economic and financial polity (perhaps the main exception to this being the significant reform of the civil service brought about through the Next Steps programme). There was a considerable debate about the centralisation of power, the apparent failure to recognise sub-national, regional and local diversity, and, ultimately, serious questions about the legitimacy of the mandates achieved by these governments. One does not have to subscribe in full to these types of critique of the Conservative governments, or indeed to accept fully the case for thoroughgoing institutional and constitutional reform, in order to appreciate the fact that after 1997 the reform process in the United Kingdom developed significantly, and was specifically designed to address the perceived deficiencies cited above. As we pointed out at an earlier stage, this process of reform encompassed policies, the political culture and the governing framework. It had a developing momentum, and amounted to a rolling programme. In this sense, one vital building block of the governance concept, largely missing throughout the 1980s and 1990s, looms large in the new millennium.

References

Baggott, R. (1995) 'Putting the squeeze on sleaze? The Nolan Committee and standards in Public Life', *Talking Politics*, 8(1).

Berrington, H. (1995) 'Political ethics: The Nolan Report', *Government and Opposition*, 30(4).

Draper, D. (1997) *Blair's Hundred Days* (London: Faber and Faber).

Gould, P. (1998) *The Unfinished Revolution* (London: London Books).

HM Government (1998) *Modern Public Services Reform for Britain. Investing in Reform*, Cm. 4011.

Kelly, R. (ed.) (1999) *Changing Party Policy in Britain. An Introduction* (Oxford: Blackwell).

Kooiman, J. (1993) 'Social-Political Governance: Introduction', in Kooiman, J. (ed.) *Modern Governance* (London: Sage).

Labour Party (1997) *Because Britain Deserves Better* (London: Labour Party).

Leftwich, A. (1994) 'Governance, the State and the politics of development', *Development and Change*, 25, pp. 363–86.

Mandelson, P. and Liddle, R. (1996) *The Blair Revolution. Can New Labour Deliver?* (London: Faber & Faber).

Oliver, D. (1997) 'Regulating the conduct of MPs. The British experience of combating corruption', *Political Studies*, 45(3).

Prime Minister (1999) *Modernising Government*, Cm. 4310.

Rentoul, J. (1996) *Tony Blair* (London: Warner Books, revised edn).

Rhodes, R. A. W. (1997) *Understanding Governance. Policy Networks, Governance, Reflexivity and Accountability* (Buckingham: Open University Press).

Rosenau, J. N. (1992) 'Governance, Order and Change in World Politics', in Rosenau, J. N. and Czempiel, E.-O. (eds), *Governance Without Government: Order and Change in World Politics* (Cambridge: Cambridge University Press).

Woodhouse, D. (1998) 'The Parliamentary Commissioner for Standards: Lessons from the "Cash for Questions" Inquiry', *Parliamentary Affairs*, 51(1).

Index